Books by Laura Bradbury

Grape Series
My Grape Year
My Grape Québec
My Grape Paris
My Grape Wedding
My Grape Escape
My Grape Village
My Grape Cellar

The cookbook based on the Grape Series memoirs that readers have been asking for!

Bisous & Brioche: Classic French Recipes and Family Favorites from a Life in France
by Laura Bradbury and Rebecca Wellman
Bisous & Brioche

The Winemaker's Trilogy
A Vineyard for Two
Love in the Vineyards

my grape year

my grape year

LAURA BRADBURY

Published by Grape Books

Print Edition

Paperback ISBN: 978-0-9921583-7-8
eBook ISBN: 978-0-9921583-6-1

Visit: www.laurabradbury.com

To Franck, for the *coup de foudre* of a lifetime.

Also, for our daughters Charlotte, Camille, and Clémentine.
Believe in fairy tales, because you are proof they exist.

"Non, rien de rien. Non, je ne regrette rien."
—EDITH PIAF "Non, Je Ne Regrette Rien"

chapter one

RULES FOR 1990–91
OUTBOUND EXCHANGE STUDENTS—THE FOUR "D"s

1. No Drinking
2. No Drugs
3. No Driving
4. No Dating

By signing this contract, I hereby accept my role as Ursus Youth Ambassador for the 1990–91 exchange year abroad and agree to abide by all four of the "Rules for Exchange Students."

The other outbound exchange students around me were scribbling their signatures on the forms.

No Drinking. I knew I was heading to Europe, Switzerland, if everything went according to plan, and even though I was drawn by the history and beauty and exoticism, I was also hoping to be able to enjoy a nice glass of beer or wine from time to time. I was seventeen and would be graduating from high school in three short months, so I hoped they wouldn't take this rule too seriously in what my grandmother always referred to as "the old country."

No Drugs. I seriously doubted that marijuana was as ubiquitous in Europe as it was on Vancouver Island, Canada, where it self-seeded in many people's back gardens. And since I had no intention of ever trying any other type of drug, this rule wasn't an issue.

No Driving. It would be weird to no longer be able to drive nor enjoy the independence that came with that. Still, like many

Canadians, I knew how to drive only an automatic and didn't like traffic very much, so I could live with this rule.

No Dating. This rule bothered me the most. It had just been explained to us that as Ursus Youth Ambassadors we would have to be available and open to all people we encountered during our year abroad. Having an exclusive romantic relationship would interfere with that goal. Also, the Ursus Club hosting us would be responsible for our welfare during our year in its country, and that would be far simpler to ensure when we students remained single. I could see the logic of it all, but my romantic life during my high school years had been seriously disappointing, if not to say practically nonexistent. My heart longed for romance and love.

Still, I felt as if the whole world was out there waiting for me, and I needed to take the step to meet it. If that meant signing this contract, then I would do whatever it took.

I picked up my pen and signed my name.

The men's polyester pants were off-gassing in the stuffy hotel room. The scorched smell of synthetic fabric tickled my nostrils. March was generally a cool month in Victoria, so the hotel staff hosting the annual Ursus District Convention hadn't anticipated the heat wave. The Rotary and Lions Clubs, similar community service organizations, had recently begun to welcome female members, which I was sure had lessened the polyester quotient. Ursus, though, stubbornly remained a men-only group, aside from their female International Youth Exchange Ambassadors like me.

A makeshift fan had been unearthed and stuck in the corner of the room, but sweat trickled inside my navy wool blazer, which had already been festooned with at least forty pins. Pins were the currency of the incoming and outgoing exchange students and were traded with the fervor of stocks on Wall Street.

The interview was almost over, thank God. If they liked me, I would get the final confirmation that I would be spending the 1990–1991 academic year as an exchange student in what I hoped would be my first choice of host country, Switzerland. There was only one available spot in Switzerland, and it was contested hotly every year. Belgium, my second choice, was better than nothing. Germany was my third choice, but I knew I definitely didn't want to end up in Germany. I'd never found blond men attractive, and I vastly preferred wine to beer. It was a crime that Italy, France, and Spain weren't options. I could completely envision myself at some Spanish or Italian bar, dancing on the tables after a night fueled by sangria or Prosecco—though I'd apparently signed away my rights to drink either of these.

"I see Switzerland was your first choice, Laura," the head of the committee observed.

Was? Not is?

Every one of the ten or so men around the table had a copy of my application in front of him. "Can you explain your reasons for that?"

I had answered this question so many times in previous interviews that I could do it in my sleep. "One of my main motivations for going on a year abroad is to learn a foreign language," I said. "Switzerland has not one but *three* official languages—French, German, and Italian. I would love to be exposed to more than one language during my year as an Ursus Youth Ambassador." Actually, I was hell-bent on a year abroad because I sensed this huge, marvelous world waiting for me beyond the mossy shores of my island home, and I vibrated with the need to meet it.

The Ursunian who was chairing the interview cleared his throat. "That is an excellent answer, Miss Bradbury. However, we just received the news that the Switzerland spot was nabbed by another district." The men exchanged shocked looks at this breach of fair play.

What? What about my fantasies of racing up and down the Swiss hills like Maria from *The Sound of Music* and warming myself up with some lovely cheese fondue and wine in a wooden chalet afterward, preferably with an entourage of handsome Swiss men? I knew I would have to deal with my disappointment later; right then wasn't the time. I dug my nails into my palms and smiled brightly. "I'll go to Belgium, then."

"We do have several spots there. I just feel we should let you know, though, that more than half of them are in the Flemish-speaking part of Belgium."

Flemish? I had been so sure I was going to Switzerland that I hadn't even considered the possibility of being sent to Flemish-speaking purgatory.

I flashed another smile. "Of course, I would make the most out of any placement," I said. "However, French is Canada's second official language, and growing up here on the West Coast, I have always regretted the fact that I have never learned to speak it fluently. I hope to go to McGill University in Montreal, so obviously French would be a huge advantage for me."

There was no need to mention that French had actually been my worst subject all through high school, and that I'd had to drop it after Grade 11 because it was torpedoing my GPA. Or that I ran out to the quad after my Grade 11 provincial exam for French and yelled, "Thank God! I will *never* have to speak French again in my life!"

A slighter, bald man piped up. "You may not be aware of this, Miss Bradbury, but there is no way for us to guarantee where you will be placed. We send over the files for the incoming students, and it's up to our Belgian brothers to allocate them as they see fit."

I struggled to maintain my bright-eyed demeanor.

"There's always France, I suppose," mused the head man, as though thinking aloud.

My head snapped in his direction. "I understood there were no exchange spots available in France."

He cleared his throat. "That *was* the case, but there has been a...ah...development."

My heart began to somersault. *France?*

A tall man at the opposite end of the table, who had been picking something fascinating out from under his thumbnail, jerked his head up. "With good reason!" he said, paying attention now. "Every exchange we arranged in France has ended in disaster. The families didn't even bother to come and pick up our students from the airport, or they suddenly decided that they were sick of hosting and locked the child out of the house or left on vacation without them. We couldn't possibly jettison another student into—"

The chair cleared his throat meaningfully. "I have a letter here from the Ursus Club in Beaune, France." He waved the letter, which from what I could see was written in elaborate cursive with a fountain pen. I longed to get a closer look—it possessed a tantalizing whiff of the exotic. "They say that one of their students is being hosted this year by our district, so they would welcome one of our students. Just one student you see. It would be on a trial basis. They sound sincere."

"Don't believe them," snarled the tall man. "I was president of our club the year our poor student was abandoned at the airport in Paris. He had to take a plane back to Seattle the next day. Try explaining *that* to his parents!"

"We must believe them," the chair insisted. "Ursus spirit demands we have good faith in our French brothers. Besides, Miss Bradbury here strikes me as a competent sort of person who can deal with extreme situations. I wouldn't even mention the possibility of France to most of our outgoing students."

"I...I...," I stuttered, wondering how I was going to disabuse him of this notion. I couldn't imagine any horror worse than leaving for a year abroad only to have to return to Canada the next day with my tail between my legs. Yet...France! I had always wanted to see Paris and the Eiffel Tower and learn how to drape scarves properly.

"George"—the tall man's voice was stiff with displeasure—"throwing this nice young lady here to the French would be like throwing a lamb to the wolves, and I for one—"

"Neil," the head man said in a quelling tone, "there is an open space for France and it needs to be filled. Miss Bradbury has explained how urgently she wants to learn French. She is mature and full of positive energy. I have complete confidence in her."

What is the word for "shit" in French? Merde? My mind whirred as I tried to find a way to extract myself from this fix.

But then I thought about red wine. Little cafés. Baguettes. French men were supposed to be very charming, weren't they? In any case, they had to be an improvement on Canadian boys. It could be a disaster, or it could be even better than Switzerland. In any case, I decided, it was definitely better than spending a year learning Flemish.

"I'd be delighted to take that spot in France." I straightened my shoulders.

All the men except Neil nodded approvingly at me as though I had just performed a selfless and heroic act. Darn. Had I?

The chair erased Switzerland and Belgium from my application and wrote "FRANCE" on it in large capital letters. He scrawled something in his notes.

"That settles it, then! You'll be heading to France in August, Miss Bradbury. I hope you have an excellent year, or shall I say a *bon voyage*?" He chuckled at his own joke.

"Thank you," I said, "or shall I say *merci*?" This got a laugh out of all the men, and they stood up and stretched their polyester-clad legs to indicate that I was dismissed.

I must have missed the sound over the whir of the fan and the muffled scrape of chairs against the carpet, but when I think back to it now, I am convinced there must have been a mighty creak. There had to have been, because at that precise moment my entire life shifted on its axis.

chapter two

The Air Canada 747 jumbo jet was nearing Charles de Gaulle airport. I remained plastered to my oval window, admiring the patchwork of fields below the airplane's wing. They were dotted with what looked like little villages.

France. I had done it. I had left my little mossy island in the Pacific to explore the world. The farthest I had ever travelled was to Hawaii for our yearly spring vacation. I had never been to a place where English was not the native tongue. I sensed that I possessed an adventurer's soul but had never been able to test my theory.

The pilot had already lowered the landing gear. My palms were sweaty, but my chest felt as though it was not big enough to fit my heart. The fields grew so close that I could see the cows on them, munching away. Not just any cows! *French* cows! I caught a glimpse of the runway.

Just as I was anticipating the wheels touching down, the whine of descent was replaced by the roar of engines, and the nose of the airplane tilted vertiginously back up toward the sky. I put a hand to my chest. My heart was ready to explode. I began to shake and look around for answers. The terror in the faces of my fellow passengers made me want to vomit. Was I going to die before getting to France after all? The airplane roared away from the airport and then carved a steep, curving circle in the clouds.

"Sorry about that," the pilot said over the speaker. He sounded calm, but then again pilots always remained calm...didn't they...even when their plane was seconds from crashing into a field full of French cows? "Turns out there was another plane on our designated runway. We're going to wait here for clearance to land from air traffic control." There was a click and the pilot's voice once again filled the cabin. "Goddamn Frogs. Will they ever get their act together? They're probably all on a goddamn coffee break." There was a louder click. Nervous laughter spread through the cabin.

What had I gotten myself into? What if France was total anarchy just as the man in the Ursus interview had argued? What if there was no one to meet me at the airport because my host family had changed their mind and decided they didn't want to be bothered with some strange Canadian teenager? Such a thing would be unthinkable to a Canadian, but then Canadians would never just leave a plane sitting in the path of an incoming 747 while they took a coffee break, either.

I smoothed a hand over the collection of pins on my navy blue Ursus blazer. I was not used to anarchy. Everything in Canada is governed by certain unspoken rules, which are understood and adhered to by almost everyone...such as my family at the airport when they sent me on my way that morning...or was it the morning before? With all the various time zones, I had lost track of what day it was. We'd all known that we had to hold back our tears and act stoic about my departure. Emotions didn't follow rules, so they were scary and therefore suppressed.

The pilot came back on again. "Sorry about earlier," he mumbled. "Anyhow, we just received clearance, so we'll get you on the ground in ten minutes or so. Welcome to Paris folks."

Once off the plane, I followed the pack of passengers into a clear plastic tube that had something inside it akin to a flat escalator that was headed downwards. I wondered if I had landed in an episode of *The Jetsons* by mistake. The tube was scorching hot and airless, and I was sweating profusely. Hadn't they heard of air conditioners? Or maybe, I reflected, the person responsible for allocating the runways was also responsible for the temperature control inside the terminal.

As much as I wanted to, I couldn't take off my blazer. It was how my French family, if they decided to come pick me up after all, would recognize me.

At the end of the tube, I followed the crowd to an area dotted with luggage carrousels. In the background, muffled announcements were being made almost constantly, along with the musical series of *ding*s from an unseen loudspeaker. Nobody seemed to be paying attention. I coughed. Everyone around me had lit up a cigarette and was smoking industriously.

A wave of exhaustion caught me by surprise. I had been awake for… I began to count and lost track. The terminal was redolent of urinals and unwashed bodies. I sniffed at myself and crinkled my nose. I was undoubtedly contributing to the latter.

The luggage carrousel remained sullen and motionless. I checked the flight number on the screen above it—AC Vol #805 Toronto. I was in the right place, yet I seemed to be the only one who was staring at the metal oval, willing it to move. The other passengers acted as though they weren't expecting it to do anything any time soon. A lot of the women were wearing linen clothing and strappy sandals in earth tones, and they'd somehow clipped up the most amazing hairstyles that looked both elegant and nonchalant. The men wore crisp, open-neck shirts, and some wore purse-like things over one shoulder. They all smoked in an unhurried manner, as though they were settling in for a long wait.

For the first time in my life, I was completely alone in a foreign country. I wasn't so much scared as intrigued by the idea. Somehow, the sensation wasn't completely unfamiliar. In a way, I'd often felt alone. In a society of logical, rational people, I hid my over-sensitivity, my sentimentality, and my longing for romance. At school, I'd quickly learned how to construct a gregarious front, but underneath that was profound solitude. I didn't show anyone the real me, but I lived in the hope that one day I would meet somebody who would see through all the layers of not-real-me. Not just *see* the real me, but *love* the real me. *A pipe dream*, I told myself. I wanted nothing less than a man who had x-ray vision specially adapted to my soul. Such a person surely didn't exist. In any case, I was certain they didn't exist in my hometown.

After a few minutes of waiting, I noticed that some people were leaning on luggage carts. I located a line of them a few luggage carrousels over. I tugged one out of the line, but it didn't budge. On closer inspection, I saw that it was connected by a chain. It required a coin of some indeterminate value. *Shit.* I had some French bills in my wallet but no change. Why wouldn't the luggage carts be free anyway? I spotted one by an empty customer service desk. As I wheeled it back to the immobile carrousel, I realized why it had been abandoned. One of the front wheels was coming off, and no matter which direction I pushed it, the cart went the opposite way. I commiserated belatedly with the pilot: *Goddamn Frogs*.

The baggage carrousel came to life with the sound of screeching metal. Even though they had been waiting a good forty minutes, everyone around me looked surprised, as though they hadn't expected it to happen so soon.

Still, no suitcases came off. People momentarily looked perplexed then lit up more cigarettes.

In the distance, I could hear another carrousel begin to grind. A few minutes later, somebody shouted something in French, and the crowd turned and took off toward the other moving carrousel. I hesitated and examined the screen again. It still showed our flight number. *This* was where our bags were supposed to come out, not somewhere else. Still, I saw that people from my flight had begun to pluck bags off the other one, so I gave up logic and ran over there too, using every muscle in my upper body to wrestle with my wonky cart. Those French could run fast, even with cigarettes dangling from their lips.

Suitcases tumbled down the baggage chute. I looked up at

the screen—LAN Vol #115 Buenos Aires, it said. That was completely the wrong flight, but contrary to logic, people from my flight continued to grab their bags.

The crowd was thinning out. Soon there were only five of us watching three Adidas bags circle around and around.

After a few minutes of this, the machine clicked off and froze again. An elderly gentleman wearing a silk neck scarf—which I felt was a bit overkill on a stifling summer's day—just shrugged. "*Eh merde*," he sighed.

My French left much to be desired, but I knew what "*merde*" meant. The question was, what did it mean for my suitcases? I remembered checking them in at the Victoria airport. There had been a layover in Calgary, and another in Toronto... My bags could be in the North Pole now for all I knew. *Merde* indeed.

The elderly man with the silk scarf walked toward a sign that read *Sortie*, and because I didn't know what to do, I followed him.

A pair of sliding doors opened and then closed behind me, disgorging me into some sort of arrivals hall, which held what looked like people from every corner of the globe—beautiful African women dressed in brightly colored dresses and head-wraps, a bunch of kids from an American high school wearing matching jackets and chattering in Southern accents...

"Laura!" I heard my name, though pronounced completely differently than I was used to hearing it, with the "r" rolled and the second "a" drawn out at the end.

I scanned the crowd but couldn't place who was calling me. Then I heard it again, coming from a beautiful woman in a knee-length skirt and matching jacket. She had blond hair and turquoise eyes. Beside her stood a man with an irrepressible smile and a girl about my age, whose messily twisted chignon and scarf around her neck marked her as undeniably French, hence light-years more stylish than I could have ever hoped to be. *Could this be my host family—the Beaupres?* My heart leapt with hope. They didn't *look* like the type of people who would abandon a freshly arrived exchange student at the airport, even one without her luggage.

They rushed to me with outspread arms, and all gave me two warm kisses, one on each cheek. I enjoyed being enveloped in a cloud of perfume and cologne and soft fabric, hoping that it overpowered my own stink from travelling for so long.

"Where are your bags?" Sophie, the daughter, asked in stilted English, although it was far more than I could manage in French. "Are they...I cannot remember the word...*perdus*?"

I took out my pocket dictionary and looked up the word. Lost.

"*Oui, perdus*," I agreed. Look at that! I was almost fluent in French already!

My French prowess dried up the minute we arrived at the baggage return office, a place that closely resembled Dante's version of Hell. Luggage was teetering in precarious piles all around the desk, and a sweaty young man appeared completely overwhelmed by the task at hand.

I thanked the heavens that my beautifully attired host parents seemed intent on finding my missing suitcases. Before leaving Canada, I had been informed by my local Ursus Club that I was going to stay with four different Ursus host families during my year in Burgundy. That was quite a few, even by Ursus standards. Two host families generally was the norm. I was daunted by the idea of adapting to four different families and wondered if I could blame their enthusiasm to host me on the multi-year ban on Ursus exchanges to France. In any case, if all the families were as lovely as the Beaupres, maybe it wouldn't be so terrible after all.

Madame Beaupre somehow glided up in front of the crowd to the man at the desk and spoke to him in the most melodious French I'd ever heard. He paused and actually leaned over the desk to take in her statuesque figure, which was highlighted by her beige outfit that revealed tanned legs and feet shod in perfect, dark red pumps. A smile illuminated his face, and he listened to her with rapt attention.

She paused eventually and turned to me, asking me a question in French. I had no idea what she was saying. Pretending to understand occurred to me, but I quickly concluded that I wouldn't be able to play that game for long. I shook my head instead and shot her a look of apology.

Sophie stepped forward and asked, "Your *sacs*...what did they look like?"

My suitcases were standard black Samsonite, but I thanked my father, who'd never let any of us leave the house without a suitcase unless it was all trussed up with at least ten flapping ribbons of neon yellow flagging tape, which he used when moose hunting. I would tell them that there were neon yellow ribbons bedecking both my suitcases.

"They are black, but they have yellow ribbons all over them," I said.

"I'm sorry?" Sophie shook her head. "I do not understand what you say."

They all waited for my answer in French—except for the man behind the desk, who was still staring at my host mother with worshiping eyes.

I opened my mouth. I couldn't remember the French word for "ribbon." I couldn't remember the French word for "yellow." I couldn't remember the French word for "suitcase," even though I was certain Sophie had just said it. I certainly couldn't remember the French word for "neon."

My eyes roved around the room—I was desperate for help. An irate man almost prostrated himself on the desk trying to get the baggage man's attention. He was wearing a bright yellow wristwatch—the kind only a French man could pull off. I jabbed my finger at it and repeated the English word "yellow" several times.

"Your *sacs* are yellow?" Sophie asked.

"No. No." I shook my head. "There are yellow ribbons on them. My two suitcases are black."

I clearly had lost Sophie, as she just stared at me with her brown eyes wide. Again I scanned the room in desperation. I grabbed a luggage tag off a pile on the counter. I flapped it around in front of me. "On suitcase. Yellow."

"Ah!" Sophie conveyed this crucial tidbit of information to her parents, who were wearing identical frozen smiles as if trying hard to not look too appalled at my French, or rather my lack thereof.

I was equally distressed. I had taken eleven years of French in school, for heaven's sake. True, it had always been my worst subject and the bane of my existence, but somehow, I thought that after all those years I would have retained at least the word for "yellow." I remembered my French teacher asking me, "How can you be so terrible at French and so good in your other subjects, Laura?" Maybe Flemish would have been a wiser choice after all. No one would have expected a person to know Flemish.

The baggage man was talking with my host mother again, a regretful hound dog look in his eyes. I divined what he was telling her, even without being able to understand French. He had no suitcases with yellow flappy things to give her, and he was heartbroken about this fact. Madame Beaupre gave him a gracious smile and an eloquent shoulder shrug. She turned on her perfect heel and sashayed out of the tiny room. I glanced back at the last moment. The baggage man was still watching her.

chapter three

We walked for so long in the suffocating building that I could feel another layer of sweat bead through the layers of travel grime encasing my body. There was garbage everywhere—random pieces of paper and food wrappers, and even an abandoned shoe. There didn't seem to be any garbage cans, but there were several sets of ominous-looking guards patrolling the terminal. They were dressed almost entirely in black and armed to their teeth with automatic weapons—the kind of thing I had never seen outside a Hollywood movie. Was France involved in a war that I knew nothing about?

Finally, we reached a multi-story car park. The concrete was crumbling in several places, and what was there was decorated with every style of graffiti imaginable (though showing a distinct predilection for the hastily rendered, oversized penis). *This* wasn't at all how I'd pictured France. I'd imagined that Charles de Gaulle airport basically stood at the junction of the Eiffel Tower and the Champs-Élysées.

We drove at a snail's pace in bottlenecked traffic on roads that were bordered on each side with huge walls covered with yet more graffiti. I craned my neck to see if I could catch a glimpse of anything, but it was impossible to see beyond the concrete barriers.

Madame Beaupre kept turning around and asking me nice-sounding questions, to which I just kept answering *oui*, even though I had no idea what she was asking. Sophie smiled, but seemed preoccupied. I knew from the letters we'd exchanged that she was leaving early the next morning for her year in the United States. I remembered how I had felt a day earlier...or was it two? Scared, excited, overwhelmed... I wouldn't have been up to carrying on a conversation in a foreign language either.

Sleepiness snuck in like a bandit. My head dropped.

I woke up with a jerk at some point en route to Sophie's grandmother's house that, they had written me, was in a village about an hour's drive from Paris. Monsieur Beaupre was navigating the car at breakneck speed through impossibly narrow streets. The concrete walls had been replaced with houses made from pale cream stones and decorated with bright red geraniums.

"Oh my God," I murmured to myself. The village outside my window looked just like the villages depicted in *Snow White* and *Cinderella* and all the other Disney movies I had grown up watching. Somehow it had never occurred to me that the images in those films had actually been inspired by a real place—Europe—and that the real place still existed. "It's beautiful."

Sophie and Madame Beaupre looked over at me and smiled.

I must have dozed off again, because I woke up just as the car was pulling past a worn, blue gate into the courtyard of a rambling stone farmhouse. A snowy-haired, round-faced lady was on the front steps, waving at us with lovely plump arms.

Sophie leapt out of the car and threw herself into the woman's arms. "Mamy!" she said, and promptly burst into tears.

Monsieur Beaupre went over and kissed his mother's cheeks and started crying as well. Madame Beaupre joined them, perfectly formed teardrops running down her exquisite cheekbones.

She beckoned me out of the car. "*Voici Laura, notre petite Canadienne*," she said. Mamy grasped me by both cheeks and gave me a juicy kiss on each.

"*Bonjour*," I said.

She wrapped me in a hug that smelled of lavender and butter. Tears pricked at my eyes. She was so huggable, just like my own grandmother who lived by the beach on a tiny island and swam in the ocean every night.

She hurried us all inside, laughing and crying at the same time. Something was bubbling on the stove. Four scrumptious-looking baguettes were in the center of the table, which was already set with flower-sprigged napkins and mismatched plates.

"*Tu veux te doucher, Laura*?" Madame Beaupre asked me, and I turned to her wide-eyed and quite uncertain of what to answer. Then I remembered the boys snickering in French class back home whenever the teacher mentioned the verb "to shower"—"*te doucher.*"

I nodded. So, I couldn't remember the words for "ribbon" or "yellow," but it appeared that I could remember every French word that had made the rude boys laugh in high school French.

Sophie led me upstairs to a tiny room off the top of the stairs. She showed me an old, white bathtub, which had a shower nozzle attached to the tap with a long metal cord. She opened the cupboard and took out two towels for me.

"Do you need...clothes?" she asked.

I eyed Sophie. She was several sizes smaller than I was, not to mention many inches taller.

"I have a few in my carry-on." I gestured at my backpack slung across one of my shoulders.

"*À bientôt*!" She shut the door behind her.

I dropped my backpack to the floor and surveyed the room. My head felt wonky, as though I was still on the airplane when it was banking steeply. Thank God I had packed a clean pair of underwear, a pair of shorts, and a T-shirt in my carry-on.

I shucked off my clothes and turned one of the knobs on the bathtub. It squealed, and hot water began gushing out of the tap. After a few minutes of consternation, I found a lever under the tap, which I pulled up, and the hot water began running out of the shower attachment in my hand. I turned on the other tap to cool it a bit, then focused on my most immediate problem. How, exactly, was I supposed to wash myself with this set-up? Should I stand up or sit down? How was I supposed to hold the spray handle and shampoo my hair at the same time? There was a bottle of what looked like shampoo and the biggest square of cream-colored soap that I'd ever seen on the ledge of the bath. Well, there was water and there was shampoo and there was soap... I would just have to figure out the rest.

Twenty minutes later, I emerged from the bathroom smelling like coconut shampoo and savon de Marseille (I noticed this was what was stamped on the big block of soap). Although I had soaked both towels Sophie had left for me, trying to clean up all the water on the bathroom floor, the room still looked as though a tsunami had swept through it. How did French people wash themselves like that every day and end up looking so pristine?

I was embarrassed. I couldn't find any more towels and was almost dead on my feet from fatigue. How was I going to explain the deluge that happened in there? No English words came to mind, let alone French ones.

I walked gingerly down the worn wooden staircase in my shorts and T-shirt—which I had also managed to get rather damp—wracking my brain for the French word for "towels." Halfway down, my nostrils began to twitch from the delicious smells coming from the kitchen. My stomach rumbled, demanding food.

"*La voilà*!" Mamy exclaimed as she caught sight of me in the hallway. She beckoned me to come and sit down at the table.

"*Salle de bain...*," I began, remembering the word for "bathroom," but she waved away my attempts at trying to speak and, with a surprisingly strong grip on my shoulder, maneuvered me into one of the wooden chairs. She slid a large piece of quiche onto my plate, along with a healthy portion of bright green salad.

I examined my quiche. Back home in Canada, like most girls my age, I'd developed atrocious eating habits. I'd experimented with vegetarianism, restrictive diets, binge eating, and living off meal supplements. The only food I actually enjoyed eating was food that was "bad" for me. Anything "good" for me—broccoli, poached salmon, or one of my mom's moose roasts, for example—invariably tasted like something that had been left rotting on the compost pile.

The quiche was dotted with green things, but nothing that looked too suspicious. Anyway, I was starving. I put a forkful in my mouth and chewed. The quiche, even the green things—which I suspected were leeks, though I had only ever tried them a handful of times—was creamy and delectable. The salad made me entirely rethink my prejudices against salads. It was fresh and satisfying and covered with tangy vinaigrette.

Mamy poured red wine into my tumbler.

"*Pour moi?*" I asked. I sat up straighter and tried to look nineteen, until I realized I was no longer in Canada but in a country where there was no minimum legal drinking age.

She nodded and said something very quickly in French, and then laughed.

"*Merci!*" I said.

Having forgotten my sleepiness momentarily, I gobbled up my lunch. The meal was one of the best things I'd ever tasted. Luckily, eating meant that I wasn't really expected to talk.

Mamy took the empty plate from in front of me and busied herself with all the pots and pans at the stove. I was really hoping for some dessert, thanks to my intractable sweet tooth.

I took a few sips of wine and then a few of water. *Wow. Wine at lunch.* This was fantastic.

Mamy returned a few seconds later and placed a full plate in front of me. I stared down. On my plate lay two beautiful slices of pork roast that were rolled with bacon and some sort of herb butter mixture. To the side were five perfect, little boiled potatoes, and beside them were creamy-looking white beans swimming in a sauce redolent of garlic and fresh rosemary. Sophie passed me the breadbasket, and I took a hunk of roughly sliced baguette, which felt airy soft under my fingers. *So...this is the* second *course of lunch?* I checked in with my stomach. Yes, it could handle the challenge.

"*Merci*," I said, then sniffed my plate again. "*Merci. Très bien.*"

"You are hungry?" Sophie asked me.

I nodded.

"And you are tired?"

I nodded again and picked up my fork. A ceramic jar that appeared to contain some sort of mustard was passed around. I took some, cautiously, but found that its spiciness went perfectly with the sliced pork roast. I had never realized potatoes could be so delectable. They were the texture of silk and soaked up just the right amount of sauce.

The conversation around me lilted along musically in French, but I couldn't make out more than the occasional word. Everyone was speaking so *fast.* I stopped trying to follow and instead used my little bubble of incomprehension to better enjoy the incredible flavors that gave me the odd impression that I was tasting food for the first time.

It was the sound of crying that snapped me out of my reverie. I looked down the table and saw Sophie and her mother and grandmother holding each others' hands across the table and sobbing openly. Monsieur Beaupre dabbed his eyes with the corner of his cloth napkin.

I held my breath. Everyone was crying—that had to mean something terrible was going to happen. Then Sophie said something and started laughing through her tears, and everyone else did the same, and they all leaned back in their chairs, guffawing. Eventually, I observed covertly, everyone dug back into their plates again and carried on chatting and eating as though nothing unusual had occurred. None of them seemed embarrassed or traumatized in the slightest. I finished off my plate, turning this over in my mind like a pebble, considering that maybe, for French people, tears weren't something to be kept inside.

Next, Mamy brought a huge, worn wooden cutting board to the table. On top sat the most gorgeous selection of cheeses I had ever feasted my eyes on. She placed it squarely in front of me, then filled my tumbler with wine again.

There was nothing on the platter that resembled the rubbery blocks of cheddar or mozzarella we found at our local grocery store. There was a large Camembert or Brie, and a crumbly wedge of pale yellow cheese with a thick brown crust, and one that had little pockets of what looked like mold—I'd be avoiding that one. There was also an orange cheese with a pungent smell, which bulged out softly without being runny exactly, and four more that looked equally intriguing. I'd always nurtured a deep love affair with cheese. The sight of this cheese platter was enough to make me suspect that France was in fact my spiritual home.

"*Laura?*" Mamy plopped down a clean, smaller plate in front of me. "*Tu aimes le fromage?*"

I actually understood that. "*Oui!*" I laughed. "*Oui. Oui. Oui.*"

"Serve yourself," said Sophie. Everyone watched. I sensed that cheese was a decisive matter in France.

I took a large slice of every type of cheese on the platter, except the one with pockets of mold. I looked up as I passed the cutting board along. My tablemates were staring at me with round-eyed amazement.

"You like cheese," Sophie said. It wasn't phrased as a question this time.

"I *love* cheese."

My host mother helped herself to three delicate slices—roughly a quarter the size of mine—off the platter, and Sophie and Monsieur Beaupre took only two each.

Oh no. A faux pas *already. A second one, actually, once they discover the state of the bathroom upstairs.* My cheeks burned, but it wasn't exactly like I could put the cheese back. I scraped a hunk of the creamiest looking cheese with the pungency of unwashed socks onto my slice of baguette and took a bite. I sipped the red wine and marveled at how the two tastes went so well together. I should have felt embarrassed about having the table manners of a bumpkin, but the cheese was so delicious that I didn't really have it in me to be repentant.

The family continued to slide covert glances of amazement at me as I polished off my plate of cheese and a second glass of wine, as well as two more slices of baguette.

"You were much hungry," Sophie observed.

"It's a long way from the West Coast of Canada." I smiled. "Not to mention airplane food is revolting."

Mamy seemed thrilled by my prodigious appetite. She squeezed my cheeks and then gave me a wet, lavender-scented kiss on each one. "*Elle est superbe, cette petite Canadienne*," she remarked. I wasn't certain exactly what that meant, but I knew from the warmth in her kisses that it was a compliment.

She cleared away the plates again and busied herself with an ancient-looking coffee maker that sat on the worn, stone kitchen counter. My host mother reached over and patted my hand. She had such beautiful aqua eyes. I detected sadness in them though. Her only daughter would be leaving for a year the next day. Sophie had two older brothers, but she was the youngest child and the only girl. Words of comfort popped into my head in English. I realized only then just how frustrating my lack of French was going to be.

Mamy whipped a dishtowel off something on the counter to reveal the most stunning strawberry pie I had ever seen in my life. She put it in the center of the table. On closer inspection, I saw it wasn't exactly a pie—it was a proper French strawberry tart with fat, glossy, whole strawberries nestled against one another atop a layer of custard.

I felt as if I was going to explode after the cheese course, but I couldn't say no to *this* creation. Maybe just a *petite* slice... I suppressed the thought of the number of calories I had just consumed.

Mamy served me a portion as generous as her upper arms and said something quickly to Sophie.

Sophie turned to me. "Mamy wants me to explain that she made this especially for me. Her *tarte aux fraises* is my favorite." Sophie teared up again. I was amazed by how the Beaupres could move from tears to smiles and then back to tears again in a matter of seconds, without anybody appearing the least bit unnerved by these shifting sands of emotion.

I applied myself to my tart. The custard was lightly infused with vanilla, and the berries were perfectly ripe and tasted like strawberries that had just been picked after a morning basking in the sunshine.

While I was scooping up the last crumbs, Monsieur Beaupre placed a small espresso-sized cup of coffee in front of me.

"*Merci.*" There was no more room in my stomach, but I reasoned that the coffee could flow between the cracks.

By the end of the cup, I was nodding off, despite the infusion of caffeine. All of a sudden, I could no longer keep my head upright on my neck. Madame Beaupre came over and took my arm, saying something gently in French that I didn't understand, but which I reasoned must have had something to do with me going to bed. I nodded, hard-pressed to keep my eyes open. Madame Beaupre led me upstairs to a little room just down the hall from the bathroom, which had two beds, both covered with well-worn floral fabric. A lovely, old porcelain statue of the Virgin Mary with a kindly looking face smiled down at me from the antique wooden dresser.

Madame Beaupre pulled back the sheets to reveal a long, thin cushion shaped like an enormous sausage, instead of a rectangular pillow. Some different-sounding French birds were cooing outside the window. Madame Beaupre stroked my forehead and motioned at me to get into bed. She closed the door softly behind her. I shucked off my shorts and collapsed onto the bed in my underwear and T-shirt. After dreaming of it for so many months, I was finally there, in France—eating French food and sleeping in a French bed and listening to French birds. *Maybe I'll also meet a young Frenchman this year—someone whose soul understands mine.* Before I could dream any more about that, sleep, along with the soft duvet, enveloped me.

chapter four

When I opened my eyes, the light was still pale—early morning sun. I could hear the shower, or rather the bath with the strange shower attachment, running. Surely, Sophie was getting ready to leave for the airport.

On the chair beside her bed was a matching underwear and bra set, confectioned of delicate, multicolored flowered fabric and trimmed with pale blue. If I were going to have a love affair with a Frenchman, as per my wildest fantasies, I seriously needed to consider upgrading my underwear.

I rolled over, dozed off again, and dreamed of French lingerie.

When I woke up again, the sun was shining brightly through the linen curtains in the bedroom. I checked my watch. It was just past ten o'clock. I had been sleeping for almost twenty hours. I had never done that before, but then again, I had never traveled to France before either.

I pulled on my clothes from the night before and headed downstairs. The chill of the worn stone steps under my feet, the smell of furniture polish and old wood, and the coo of the birds outside all reminded me I was far from home. Instead of feeling sad, I felt a shiver of excitement run through me.

Sophie's Mamy was bustling around in the kitchen.

She heard me. "*Bonjour, ma belle.*" She grasped my shoulders and kissed me soundly on each cheek.

"*Tu as bien dormi?*" It took me a few seconds, but I recognized the verb "*dormir.*" Sleep. She was asking how I slept.

That's what one did when guests first got up, whether in Canada or France or Uzbekistan, right?

"*Bon*," I said, smiling back.

She pointed to the clock on the wall that said ten fifteen. "*Café?*"

I nodded. "*Merci.*"

She sat me down as she had the day before and passed me a wicker basket containing two croissants. I knew lunch was not far away, but I had missed dinner the night before—and besides, I could never say no to a croissant. I took one.

She served me coffee in a big china bowl with pale pink roses painted around the rim and a few chips on the well-loved edges. *Why do we drink coffee only from mugs in Canada? Why don't we drink hot things from bowls?* She poured in some warm milk from a beaten-up casserole with a worn wooden handle. The bowl warmed up my hands so nicely as I drank. If there ever was a country that could use warming up, it is Canada.

I buttered my croissant with butter from the fresh block that Mamy had set on the table and topped it with a spoonful of delicious-looking jam that came in a glass jar. I took a bite. The thin layers of the pastry melted on my tongue. The butter was unsalted and tasted like cream, and the jam had the strongest, purest strawberry taste that I had ever experienced in my life. It had to be homemade.

"*Bien!*" I said to Mamy, gesturing with my croissant, even though that word woefully fell short of describing the nirvana of my first French breakfast. She nodded. *Bien.* That was a useful word.

"*Regarde*!" she said and took my croissant and dipped it in the *café au lait*. She took it out and passed it to me. I'd always been told dipping food into liquid is considered rude, but maybe that wasn't the case in France. Anyway, the end result was too delicious to argue the point.

Just as I was finishing up the last of my *café au lait*, my two croissants having been conveyed tidily to my stomach some time beforehand, I heard car tires crunch across the gravel of the courtyard. Seconds later, Monsieur and Madame Beaupre walked into the house. They looked as though they had aged ten years since the day before. Their faces were tear-stained and their eyes were red.

"*Bonjour, Laura*!" They greeted me with what I could tell, despite the language barrier, was forced cheer. I wished more than anything that they felt comfortable enough around me to know they needn't bother hide their sorrow for my benefit. I gave them both a kiss on each cheek as Mamy had given me.

Half of me felt self-conscious about all the kissing, but another part liked it. In any case, unlike hugging, where it was often unclear whether it was appropriate to hug or not to hug, the protocol with the kissing seemed relatively straightforward so far.

"*Elle est partie*?" Mamy clasped her hands tightly against her pale green housecoat, and a few tears escaped from her eyes. She and the Beaupres began to talk in such rapid-fire French that I couldn't make out a single word. They all began to cry.

I realized for the first time how it must have been for my parents after I had disappeared through security at the Victoria airport, what they must have felt as they left the airport, got in the car, drove back home…

I wanted to let the Beaupres know that, even though they felt then as if Sophie had departed into a dangerous and far away world, just like me, she would be fine. That even if she was crying the last time they saw her, by the time she boarded her first flight, she was most likely filled with the thrill of the adventures that lay ahead.

I couldn't tell them this, of course. Why didn't I work harder at French in high school?

"Sophie"—I tried—"*elle est bien.*" My three tablemates stared at me, trying to decipher what I meant.

I pointed at myself. "*Moi, je suis bien,*" I said. I am good. "Sophie. *Elle est bien* in the United States."

Madame Beaupre's eyes glistened, and she reached out and covered my hand with her own. I think she was touched that I had at least tried.

"*Oui,*" she whispered. "*Sûrement.*"

It wasn't until I had gone back to the bedroom—after inundating the bathroom floor yet again in an attempt to wash myself—that I saw my two suitcases festooned with their yellow flagging tape standing like sentinels at the far end of the bed. *My stuff!* Even though I longed for my clean clothes, seeing my suitcases felt oddly foreign for an instant. They were my Canadian life, and already I was living something new in France.

Still, twenty minutes later, I floated down the stairs, freshly showered and wearing a clean pair of jean shorts and a linen shirt.

Madame Beaupre and her mother-in-law were at the kitchen table.

"*Merci.*" I gestured upstairs toward my suitcases, and promptly blanked on the French word for those same objects. "For my suitcases." I made a sweeping gesture over my clean clothes and sighed dramatically in relief. They smiled at me and launched into what I had to assume was an explanation for how my suitcases had arrived, while I nodded and said *oui* at what I hoped were appropriate intervals. I was just going to have to live with the mystery of never knowing exactly how my suitcases had materialized.

After another scrumptious lunch of roast chicken with *herbes de Provence* and the potatoes from the day before mashed up with heavy cream, I climbed back into the back seat of Monsieur Beaupre's car. Mamy cried as she waved us off, and I hoped I would see her again soon.

Quickly, I noticed that the car seemed to be missing a crucial feature, or at least a feature I had been brought up to believe was crucial—seat belts. I tapped Madame Beaupre on the shoulder after we left Mamy's village and motioned to where a seat belt should be across my lap. Madame Beaupre rattled off a charming explanation, which finished with her smoothing down her impeccable pale blue skirt and matching jacket. Nobody wears them, I understood. Something about them wrinkling clothes. I recognized the word "*vêtements*."

Having not quite yet emerged from a three-year-long hippie phase, I didn't own anything that was in danger of wrinkling, but I did feel naked without a seat belt. I would choose being wrinkled over being catapulted through the windshield any day.

Going south on the autoroute, Monsieur Beaupre cranked the speed to over 150 kilometers per hour. Cars around us zoomed past. Both my parents would have had a heart attack if they'd known I wasn't wearing a seat belt. Luckily, they didn't. Or wouldn't, unless my host father crashed in a high-speed pile-up.

I considered asking Monsieur Beaupre to slow down but couldn't find the courage to do so. I needed them to like me, and I'd been sent there to adapt to a new way of life, hadn't I? Maybe that just included driving far too fast.

Madame Beaupre turned on the radio and tuned in to a French radio program that sounded to me as if it involved a lot of shouting. I tried to pick out familiar words, but there weren't very many. *Surely, we don't speak English that fast at home?*

I leaned my head against the window and watched the green fields with the occasional fairy-tale stone village fly by. I wondered what time it was back in Canada? My eyelids drifted southwards.

I was woken by the soft calling of "*Laura…Laura…*" from the front seat. I wiped the drool from my chin. How charming—I hoped I hadn't snored too. I sat up and massaged my temples.

"*Nous sommes presque arrivés*," Madame Beaupre murmured.

We passed funny-looking fields, which I belatedly realized contained row upon row of vineyards. They were a deep green. Madame waved a perfectly manicured hand. "*Les vignes*," she said.

So, "vineyard" *is* "*vigne*"*?* I stored that away. Given the number of well-tended rows we were passing, it looked as if that word could come in handy.

Just a few minutes later, we went through a tollbooth, where Monsieur Beaupre flashed a card and the barrier lifted. We took a few turns through windy streets until we arrived at a well-kept, white house. I smiled and nodded as they chattered on to me in French. The front door opened and a beautiful golden Lab leapt out, followed by a handsome, olive-skinned Frenchman. My host brother Julien, I guessed. The other brother lived in Grenoble.

"*Bonjour, Laura.*" He gave me a kiss on each cheek before moving on to his parents. He had the same high cheekbones and curved smile as his mother but had his father's brown eyes. He wore an immaculate pair of pressed jeans, a pink-and-blue checked button-down shirt, and what looked like expensive leather loafers. I'd never before realized that people *could* iron their jeans, much less want to.

He ushered me into the house while the dog leapt around our feet. My new brother patted the dog. "This is Biscotte."

I patted Biscotte and she licked my hand. It took me a few moments to realize that, for the first time since that morning, I had understood what was being spoken.

"You speak English?" I asked. I knew I had to speak French at some point, but I was feeling jetlagged and confused.

"I do," he said, "but I won't speak English with you after today. You're here to learn French."

So...he was the didactic as well as the impeccably dressed sort of man. "Understood," I said.

Julien beckoned me farther into the house, which was decorated elegantly with gold-hued wallpaper and bunches of flowers, as well as antiques that glowed with age and polish. "Your bedroom is upstairs. Would you like to rest for a while?"

"That would be perfect," I said. Adjusting to a new language and a new culture was surprisingly exhausting. Also, retreating to my bedroom for a while would give the Beaupres a little time to process Sophie's departure as a family, without them feeling the need to be polite or to include me in a conversation I was light-years away from understanding.

I was shown up to my room on the top floor—Sophie's room, Julien explained with a thoughtful look. A poster of very French-looking people playing guitars was taped to the wall. The single bed looked inviting. The bed also contained one of the enormous sausage pillows like the one I'd slept with earlier. It was actually extremely comfortable to sleep with, almost like an extra body to hug.

"I'll leave you to rest now," he said. "Can I get you anything before I go?"

"No, thank you," I said. "*Merci.*"

After he closed the door behind him, I wandered over to the window. I peered out to the tile rooftops beyond. I heard a soft cooing and spied two pigeons perched on the roof outside.

"Hello," I said to them. "I mean, *bonjour.*" I was way more used to crows, seagulls, oystercatchers, and the occasional raven. The pigeons seemed well-behaved compared to the West Coast birds with their constant cawing and squawking.

There I was. In my room in Burgundy. Part of me still couldn't believe it.

My heart ached, an ache I knew well. It had nothing to do with missing my family or my home in Canada, which would have been the most logical explanation. No, it was the same familiar feeling I'd experienced at random intervals since early adolescence.

It was difficult and embarrassing to try to express—my heart ached for someone I hadn't met yet. It made no sense, and I'd never contemplated attempting to explain it to anybody else. They would have said, surely, that it was just another manifestation of my overactive imagination. Sometimes, I tended to agree. I often tried to conjure up an image of the person I missed so acutely, but he remained elusive. Still, I couldn't help but be aware of his absence any more than I could help but be aware of a missing limb. Sometimes I wondered if we'd met in a previous life and were trying to find each other in this one.

It was all so fanciful that I often tried to reason myself out of my feelings. It never worked. The need for that missing person remained, as solid and tangible as a mountain.

My body, exhausted as it was, tingled with questions. Could he be someone that I had already met but hadn't recognized right away? The idea that maybe he and I could miss each other entirely in this life, or worse yet, that we would cross paths but somehow not recognize each other, fanned panic in my throat. It was possible he was in France. Somewhere nearby. My heart started to beat faster at the thought.

chapter five

An hour later, and after some more daydreaming on my new bed and a bit of desultory unpacking, I ventured back downstairs.

At the bottom of the stairs, there was a little den-like room with two puffy chintz couches and a TV positioned on a polished antique table opposite them. Julien was stretched out on one couch, his eyes glued to the screen.

The house had a far more dignified feel than my Canadian home, which was a 1970s creation with drop ceilings and a surfeit of brown shag carpet. I was a bit shocked to find Julien there—my sisters and I were never allowed to watch TV during the day, especially a gloriously sunny summer day.

I glanced at the television briefly, then did a double take, my eyes wide. Across the screen strutted twelve or so bare-breasted and gorgeous ladies dressed in elaborate confections that consisted mainly of feathers and sequins. Was Julien watching *porn*? I'd heard the French were more liberal about nudity and sex, but... I began to slink away before Julien noticed me.

Just then Madame walked in, and rather than hurriedly turning the TV to another channel, Julien pointed to the screen and said something in an admiring tone of voice to his mother.

"*Elles sont magnifiques*!" Madame agreed, then turned to me and rattled off a question in French.

"I didn't catch that," I said to Julien, hoping he would rescue me, but at the same time wondering how I could escape this awkward situation.

"She wants to know if you have cabaret dancers like the ones at the Crazy Horse and the Lido in Canada too."

I nodded at the screen. "Is that what those women are doing?"

"Yes. They are a cultural institution in France, the showgirls. Look at their figures! Look how they dance! It is magic. They are magnificent."

"No, they don't have that in Canada," I said, briefly imagining a Canadian version with the women in snowshoes and toques. "Definitely not."

Julien translated this piece of information to his mother.

She clicked her tongue. "*Quel dommage*."

"What a shame," Julien translated off-handedly. "That's what she said." His attention was again riveted on the TV.

It made me feel unnerved to watch these women and their multiple pairs of bare boobs bounce across the screen with my host family, so I gratefully followed Madame into the kitchen. I could only handle so many cultural differences at once, after all.

I had already looked up the translation for "Can I help?" in my pocket dictionary before coming downstairs. "*Puis-je vous aider*?" I asked, feeling inordinately proud of myself.

"*Aider*?" she asked. "*Non, ma puce*."

Puce...what did that word mean?

She then rattled off another sentence that I didn't understand. My confusion must have shown on my face, because she took my hand and led me back to Julien, who was still watching the showgirls. She repeated what she had asked me.

"She wants to know if you'd like to go into town with her to pick up a few things for dinner."

"I'd love that!" I answered then remembered to speak directly in French. "*Oui. Merci*!" I said.

Five minutes later, I found myself walking briskly into the main cobblestoned street of Nuits-Saint-Georges alongside Madame. We stopped several times along our route, as we kept running into people she knew, and they would all stop and kiss and exchange a few words. Everyone carried one or more baguettes underneath their arms or in baskets. I was introduced and was sometimes kissed, sometimes offered a hand to shake. I understood nothing apart from "*bonjour*" and "*au revoir*" from the chattered conversations.

We finally made it to the *boucherie*, as was announced by big red letters painted on the storefront. Also, an entire pig's head in the window was somewhat of a giveaway that it was the meat shop.

Madame was greeted warmly by a stout man in an impressively bloodied white apron. I watched the transaction as she took her time selecting a few cuts of meat that looked like some cured sausage cut into slices and several different types of pâté.

After that, we went to the cheese store, the *crémerie* according to its sign, and bought two gooey specimens. Next, we went to the green grocer and bought a head of butter lettuce and two bunches of leeks.

Finally, we ended up in the *boulangerie*, where the most delectable-looking pastries filled up the display case. Each one was a work of art. *Éclairs* of three different colors, delicate squares of flaky puff pastry and cream and chocolate, and intricate miniature fruit tarts with the fruit glowing and the cream underneath flecked with black dots of vanilla.

Madame came up beside me, preceded by the enchanting scent of what smelled like expensive perfume.

"You like?" she asked me.

"*Oui.*" I nodded. How could anyone answer anything else?

She pointed to one particularly delectable-looking confection of alternating layers of chocolate and meringue. She said, "*Something-something Sophie.*" I deducted that *that* type of pastry was Sophie's favorite.

"Delicious," I agreed, with what I hoped was sort of a French accent. It worked, because Madame Beaupre nodded and ordered four of them. The shop lady placed the quartet in a beautiful box, which she tied artfully with a piece of pink ribbon. She handed it to me. "*Merci*," I said.

A half hour later, after I'd set the table outside, we were sitting down to dinner on the Beaupres' outdoor patio underneath an old wisteria. Even though it was seven o'clock, the sun still beat down, and the shade was a welcome respite from the dry heat. Biscotte lay at my feet, his tongue hanging out of his mouth. He reminded me of my childhood dog Heidi, who used to station herself under the table and eat all the bits of broccoli and salmon I didn't want.

Monsieur Beaupre filled my wine glass with a white so chilled that it created a film of condensation on my glass. Clearly one did not have to ask for wine in Burgundy. It just appeared.

One of the pâtés we had picked up at the butcher sat on a white china plate. I followed Julien's example and took a slice of the fresh baguette and spread a bit of the stuff on it. I didn't know what the pâté was made with, and wasn't sure I really wanted to find out, but I was cautiously optimistic.

I sunk my teeth into the pâté on baguette. The bread was like a soft pillow under my teeth and the pâté was like silk against my tongue. It had a salty, savory taste that was perfectly balanced and deeply satisfying. I let out an involuntary sound of satisfaction.

"You like?" Julien asked me. He looked cool and collected as usual...not the type to groan at the table by accident.

I nodded.

He pushed forward a little ceramic bowl filled with what looked like mini gherkins. "Try it with *cornichons*."

I picked a few and took a bite of the crisp, vinegary mini pickle. Then I took another bite of the pâté on baguette and a sip of the crisp, cool white wine. Why weren't the clouds parting and an angelic chorus singing? The flavors, the textures...they were a revelation.

"Try one of these." Julien pushed another slightly larger bowl filled with paper-thin slices of dried sausage toward me. I copied Monsieur Beaupre, who'd peeled off the powdery skin around the meat.

"What is it?" So many things could be hidden in a sausage.

"Saucisson sec."

That didn't help at all, but I decided to take a leap of faith and bit into one. It was salty, dry, and perfectly spiced with garlic and oregano. I took anther sip of white wine. *Perfection.* "This is *so* good." *That*, I realized, was a vast understatement.

"Do you want to know how to say that in French?" Julien asked.

"It's '*c'est bien*,' right?"

He shook his head. "*C'est bon*," he said. "Not '*c'est bien*,' like you've been saying. '*Bon*' is for food and wine and other things in life that give pleasure."

So, would "bon" be used for, say, diving into cool water on a hot day, or a kiss? I might need to know these things, I thought hopefully. Still, I wasn't quite comfortable enough with Julien to ask.

"What would you call food that doesn't taste good?" I asked instead. I thought of boiled cauliflower, diet health shakes, low-fat yogurt, skim milk...

Julien frowned at me. "Why would you eat anything that didn't taste good?" he said. "The whole point of food and wine is pleasure. It has to be '*bon*,' otherwise, what's the point?"

My whole worldview turned on its head. Food had been a boring necessity when I was younger, and then as my body became curvy during my teens, food became a source of guilt and shame. It was something I either resisted or binged on, but it wasn't something I'd ever viewed as a source of unmitigated pleasure. Things either tasted good and were bad for me or tasted bad and were good for me. The idea that food should always taste good, no matter what, and that guilt had no role to play in eating sparked a mini revolution in my mind.

The rest of the meal was equally delicious. After the pâté, *cornichons*, and *saucisson sec* came thin veal cutlets in what Julien explained was one of the simplest sauces that all French people knew how to make—a dollop of Dijon mustard with a bit of thick cream called *crème fraiche*, mixed directly in the pan along with the meat juices. There was fresh tagliatelle pasta and baguette to sop up the delectable sauce and a little pot of spicy Dijon mustard to eat with the meat. A beautiful green salad with homemade vinaigrette came next, followed by the gooey and smelly cheeses we had purchased in town.

I slathered my slice of baguette with the soft cheese as the family looked on in approval. Monsieur Beaupre filled my glass with some red wine. Madame said something, but unfortunately, I didn't understand a single word.

"That one is my mother's favorite," Julien translated. "It is not a well-known cheese and it is made locally. It's called l'Ami du Chambertin. She's surprised you like it, as it is quite strong."

The cheese was indeed redolent of old socks, but in a strangely appealing way that I couldn't quite explain. I took a bite. The flavor was both pungent and mild, and the texture on the outside creamy, with a more solid, milder middle. I sipped my wine, which matched the cheese in strength and complexity.

"*C'est très bon*," I said.

They all nodded, pleased.

Next came the delectable little pastries that made Madame Beaupre a bit teary as she told me she always bought one for Sophie to cheer her up. I bit into one. The crumbly layers of meringue were the perfect foil for dense, creamy layers of chocolate ganache. I thought about Sophie, who I sincerely hoped wasn't eating at McDonald's or Kentucky Fried Chicken for her first American meal. I sent thanks out to the Universe that I had been sent to France at the last minute. I couldn't, at that particular moment, see why any other country in the world would have any appeal whatsoever.

chapter six

That night, and the several nights that followed, I had bizarre dreams where people talked French all around me, and I just kept answering *oui, oui, oui, oui* until my mouth ached.

I helped around the house, reveled in the delicious meals, and wandered around Nuits-Saint-Georges. School would start in a few days, so I was, for the most part, content to have free time to explore.

I always took my camera with me to capture photos of mossy, old stone walls, French cats lazing on windowsills, worn French shutters, and the lovely clock tower, which was built in 1610 and the pride of the town. I spent a lot of time standing at the base of the clock tower, peering up at its face and trying to let its age penetrate my mind. It was difficult to fathom for me, as my hometown in Canada doesn't possess any buildings that date before 1900. I also sneakily tried to take photos of locals sitting in cafés, so picture-perfect French wearing their berets and puffing on their Gauloises cigarettes that I sometimes wondered if they were not, in fact, employed by the Tourism syndicate.

I'd been there almost a week when, one night, Monsieur Beaupre flew in the door from work and announced he was taking us all to dinner at a favorite restaurant in a hilly area above town. "It's *très rustique*," he said, loosening his tie.

I wasn't certain what constituted "rustic" in this land of ancient and beautifully worn buildings, but I was curious to find out.

I put on an ankle-length denim skirt and a large leather belt, as well as a cotton top that was cool in the sultry air, which was so different from the constant ocean breeze I was used to. In the warm evenings, a scent filled the air that reminded me of the delectable smell of baking bread. I wasn't sure where it had come from, but it was a completely different smell from the air redolent of seaweed and salt water at home.

We hopped into Monsieur Beaupre's sporty little Renault and shot out of the driveway. He seemed to have only two speeds when he was behind the wheel—either Formula 1 racer or parked.

"Slow down, Robert," Madame said. "You're going to scare Laura." It dawned on me several seconds later that she had spoken, as she always did, in French and that I had actually understood.

"*Non, non, c'est bon*," I said.

"*Bien*," corrected Julien. "Being in the back seat of the car when my father is driving is certainly not a pleasure."

"*Bien*," I repeated. In fact, Monsieur Beaupre's driving wasn't *bon* or *bien*. I was merely being polite. I was also desperate for them to like me. Hurtling along the narrow streets without seat belts was terrifying.

We quickly—*très* quickly—wove out of Nuits-Saint-Georges and began driving up a series of switchbacks through the vineyards.

"Robert! Slow down!" Madame clutched his arm.

He did not slow down. Instead, he sped up. The road, I noticed as we climbed ever higher, was narrowing. It became too tight for even two small French cars to pass each other. *It must be one way*, I reasoned, ignoring the panic growing behind my sternum. *This must be the way up, and there must be another road down.*

I looked out the window to distract myself. Vineyards whizzed by in their row upon perfect row of greenness. Luscious, tight bunches of grapes, so deeply purple they actually looked black from a distance, dotted the vineyard leaves. I glanced back at the road just in time to see a small, white van hurtling toward us.

"Robert!" Madame hid her eyes.

My whole body braced for the collision. Dead after only five days in France, and entirely my fault—I should have spoken up and demanded he slow down. Ursus had been wrong to send me to this lawless country.

There was the grinding sound of metal against metal. I winced. We sped onwards. I grasped my thigh, mainly to make sure it was still there. I was alive!

Monsieur peered out his window where his rearview mirror was now hanging off the side of his car by only a few exposed wires. "*Merde alors*," he exclaimed, sounding more annoyed than alarmed. Madame subjected him to a rapid-fire diatribe that made me wish once again I understood French better. Even in my shocked state, I could tell that it sounded highly entertaining.

Julien chuckled beside me in the back seat. "That is not the first rearview mirror my father has broken that way."

My hands shook from the burst of adrenaline, so I trapped them between my denim skirt and the leather of the car seat. The road had leveled off, and we seemed to be driving along gently undulating hills covered with vineyards. We passed through a little stone village clustered around its church, and I saw another village in the evening haze in the distance, nestled into a little valley between a large hill and a rise on the other side. I focused on it and took a few deep breaths to try and slow my racing heart. It was a tranquil sight. Like most Burgundian villages, it looked freshly plucked from the pages of a fairy tale.

"What is that village?" I asked Julien, freeing a hand to point ahead of us.

"It's called Villers-la-Faye. We're in an area called the Hautes-Côtes now," he said. "In English, I think that means 'the high coast.'"

"It's lovely."

"It is a much higher elevation, and the wine they produce here is quite different. These villages are different too. A little more...how do you say it? Rough around the edges? Less sophisticated. More authentic." Julien was a valuable tour guide, especially as he had forgotten about his vow not to speak English to me.

Monsieur Beaupre finally slowed down, probably because there were some children tooling around on bikes on the road just after the red, white, and black sign that marked the entrance to Villers-la-Faye.

We turned up a street where there were more children and a cluster of three people—who looked closer to my age and were smoking cigarettes—in front of a brown wooden gate, across the street from a tiny *boulangerie*. I stared at them. There was a striking girl with long black hair and a short man who looked a few years older than I was.

My gaze, though, was drawn to a taller man leaning his back against the gate. He was wearing a denim jacket, and his close-cropped dark hair gave me a clear view into his eyes. They met mine and didn't look away. His eyes seemed to be smiling at me, even though his mouth merely twitched. At the top of the hill, I looked over my shoulder and out the rear window of the car. He was still watching. I sat back against the seat of the car, my cheeks burning. It felt as if a cage of butterflies had been released in my stomach. I fought the absurd urge to shout at Monsieur Beaupre to stop the car. *Don't be ridiculous, Laura. You will never see those people again. None of your host families live anywhere near Villers-la-Faye. It's just your overactive imagination...*

Monsieur Beaupre was chastised about the rearview mirror by Madame clear to the far side of the village. She stopped only when he parked in front of a large building with la Maison des Hautes Côtes written in cursive on a large sign outside.

"Here we are!" Monsieur declared and hopped out of the car.

Inside the building, we were welcomed by the hostess and led into a darker room with curved stone ceilings.

"This is a wine cellar," Julien explained to me. "Have you ever eaten in a wine cellar before?"

"I've never *been* in a wine cellar before."

We were given seats at one end of the longest, biggest table I had ever seen. It belonged in a medieval château or something.

"You see?" Julien said. "Communal tables. Very rustic."

I couldn't make much sense of the menu, so asked Julien what he recommended.

He frowned at the menu, his concentration deep. "*Escargots*!" he said, finally. "You are in Burgundy. You must have snails!"

I recoiled. "Must I?"

"*Ah oui*!" Madame Beaupre chimed in, then rattled on, saying something to the effect that snails were delicious—or she could have been informing me that snails were hermaphrodites. She was talking so fast, I honestly didn't think I would have been able to tell the difference.

"So, snails are the local specialty?" I asked Julien.

"*Oui*. There are no snails in the world as delectable as Burgundian snails. You simply must try them."

Oh God. Here was the moment of truth I had been dreading since learning I was coming to France: I was going to have to eat something disgusting. I sent up a prayer that I wouldn't vomit.

I figured it couldn't get much worse than snails, so I just let Julien order my entire meal for me. I was exceedingly grateful to see a large earthenware pitcher of what appeared to be red wine land on the table.

Next, the waitress brought us all strange-looking utensils. They resembled the metal clamps used during abdominal surgery in the Middle Ages. Monsieur Beaupre became animated as he held his clamp up to demonstrate how it opened and closed. "You see?" he said. "For the eating of the *escargots*."

So, I had to capture the snails and trap them with these clamp thingies? Dear God, maybe they weren't even dead when they brought them to us. They might expect me to kill *them too.*

Luckily the light was so dim in the wine cellar—which was lit only by large, torch-like candles mounted on the curved stone walls—that nobody noticed, even though I could feel all the blood draining from my face. My wine glass was filled, and I drained it at record speed.

Soon the waitress brought us each a circular tray containing twelve piping-hot snail shells. The air was redolent of garlic and parsley. They smelled good...good if I didn't think about the fact that they were snails. *At least, if they're this hot, they* must *be dead...surely?*

My thoughts inevitably traveled to the massive banana slugs that emerged from the dirt before a rainfall back home. They squished and popped under my shoe whenever I stepped on one by accident. I swallowed hard.

"The *escargots* they serve in this restaurant are huge," Julien said, a smile from ear to ear.

"That's a good thing?"

"The best thing," Julien confirmed.

Monsieur Beaupre mimed how I needed to clamp on to the shell with my pinchers and then use the tiny fork to extract the creature inside. He pulled out a shriveled gray thing, which he dabbed in the sauce that had spilled in the ceramic plate below and popped into his mouth.

"*Délicieux*!" he declared. "Your turn."

I followed his example but took my time in the hope that they would lose interest in watching me eat my first snail. That was not to be. I finally managed to extract my snail from its shell.

"Dip it in the sauce," Julien suggested. I gave my snail a few desultory dabs in the melted parsley garlic butter.

They were still watching. I was riveting entertainment, apparently. Waiting would just make it worse. The only way out of this thing was through. I closed my eyes and, trying very hard not to grimace, popped the snail into my mouth. The flavors of garlic and freshly snipped parsley and creamy melted butter distracted me to the point where I bit down on the snail, giving these flavors a satisfying meaty edge.

"Oh my God," I muttered to myself, my eyes flying open. "I think I actually like snails."

I swallowed. "*C'est très bon*!" I smiled at my host family members, who were all watching me with expressions of delight. I felt as though I had just passed a crucial test. My parents were going to be shocked when I told them during our next phone call. Maybe I wasn't a picky eater after all. *Maybe I was just never surrounded by delicious enough food...until now.*

I polished off my dozen *escargots* in record time, and after that, the meal continued to be yet another orgy of pleasure.

Next came a plate filled with *boeuf bourguignon*—beef stewed in a red wine sauce, another local specialty Julien informed me. The meat was so tender that it fell apart as I tried to fork it up, and the sauce was earthy and satisfying. Homemade buttered noodles and toasted baguette slices rubbed with butter and fresh garlic were provided to soak it all up.

Next came the most massive cheese platter I had ever seen, so extensive that it had to be rolled over to us on a trolley. I let Monsieur Beaupre choose a generous selection of cheeses for me, one in particular that he called Comté and urged me to nibble while sipping the earthy, strong house red that flowed liberally. The flavors complemented each other beautifully.

Then came a creamy Camembert from Normandy, an aged goat's milk cheese, and several more whose names I couldn't remember but which were equally delicious.

Lastly, chilled dessert cups, each filled with the darkest, deepest chocolate mousse I had ever seen and topped with a dollop of whipped cream, were placed in front of us. I extracted my first spoonful and let it melt on my tongue. It was more chocolaty than sweet, and so satisfying.

The Beaupres took obvious and explicit pleasure in eating, and they seemed overjoyed this was a pleasure they could share with me.

By the time we got back in the car, night had fallen. We were all in a contented, deeply relaxed mood.

Monsieur Beaupre seemed to have completely forgotten about his rearview mirror, and as we drove back through the now-deserted streets of Villers-la-Faye, Madame didn't even chastise him for his speed.

I was hoping to catch another glimpse of the group of young people, but they had vanished. I felt a pang of disappointment. It must have been because I missed my friends back home. I would be starting school in three days, I reasoned. There, I would make some friends of my own.

chapter seven

I woke up early for my first day of school. I tried to think positively and remember lessons from Dale Carnegie's book *How to Win Friends and Influence People*, which my father had made me read when I was ten. Inside, though, I dreaded leaving my French family cocoon to strike out into uncharted waters. I had always been shy, but after reading Dale Carnegie, it dawned on me that shyness wasn't valued in North American culture. I developed an extroverted shell and hid my real self. The reality remained, however, that nothing drained me faster than acting outgoing.

Madame Beaupre was going to drive me to school. As I gave Biscotte an *au revoir* pat, Julien explained to me that normally I would take the bus, as all the other high-school-aged children from Nuits-Saint-Georges did, and as he had done up until four years earlier when he'd passed his *baccalauréat*. Madame wanted to escort me on my first day, though, to be sure I found my way and didn't end up wandering aimlessly around Beaune.

The drive to Beaune was only twenty minutes from Nuits-Saint-Georges, but I hadn't seen the village yet. I'd read, however, that it was a stunningly preserved, fortified medieval town, which also happened to be the spiritual, cultural, and economic heart of the winemaking trade in Burgundy. Sounded promising.

As we drove along, I watched Madame's elegant hands shifting the gearshift of her sporty Peugeot with ease.

After about fifteen minutes, the traffic began to thicken and the vineyards were replaced with boxy, newer-looking buildings, which eventually gave way to older stone fronts. A miniature Arc de Triomphe appeared in front of us. Cars drove underneath it in both directions. We turned right before we reached it, though, then a sharp right again into a parking lot clogged with cars, most of them honking.

As far as I could tell, the parking lot was complete anarchy. Thank God one of the Ursus rules for exchange students was "No Driving." Even though I'd had my license since the day I turned sixteen, I had absolutely no desire to drive among all these crazy French people.

Madame, however, looked completely cool as she shifted gears and parked her car up on the sidewalk. The undercarriage scraped against the curb in an alarming fashion. Car repair would be an excellent career choice in France. I followed her across the parking lot, paying close attention to how she strolled with utter nonchalance in front of moving cars and smiled beatifically at all the drivers.

She slowed down a bit to wait for me. "*Nerveuse?*" she asked me, which I actually understood.

I shrugged. "*Un peu.*" A little. That was a lie. I was *a lot* nervous.

She slid her arm around my shoulders and gave me a squeeze. "*C'est normale, ma puce.*"

I reminded myself again to look up in my pocket dictionary what "*ma puce*" meant. She often called me that in the same tone my parents used to call me "sweetie" or "honey."

We walked through the school grounds, which were rather shabby and, disconcertingly, featured many statues of the Virgin Mary and large crosses. Having been brought up in a lapsed Anglican household, I knew less than nothing about religious things, especially Catholic things. Was I supposed to genuflect at some point, or sprinkle holy water on myself, or perform some other mysterious ritual?

We entered the far end of the building and turned into an office at the end of the hall. We sat in the empty chairs and waited. I had no idea who we were waiting for, but Madame

Beaupre seemed to know what she was doing.

A few minutes passed before a figure in black burst into the room, full of apologies. It wasn't until she took her seat behind the desk that I digested the fact I was sitting across from a real-life nun. She wore a shapeless black robe, inset with a white panel running down the front. It was accessorized with only a massive wooden cross on a piece of twine around her neck and a little necklace of beads hanging off the thicker rope encircling her waist. *A rosary?*

Thank God she wasn't wearing one of those wimple things. I would have been questioning if I had unwittingly landed in a re-enactment of *The Sound of Music*.

Madame Beaupre reached out and shook her hand. "*Bonjour, ma soeur.*"

Sister? That's right. Nuns are called sisters.

How did an agnostic Canadian greet a nun? Madame introduced me and I stuck out my hand. The nun raised her eyebrows, but shook it.

She urged us to sit down and slid a pile of papers over to Madame Beaupre for her to fill out. She kept pointing out spots where I needed to sign too. I passed the nun my passport, which she passed off to some underling—maybe a nun-in-training?—to photocopy.

The nun gave me a sheet of paper with a list of what looked like foreign-sounding school supplies, none of which I had in my backpack, which contained only a pencil case and a clipboard with lined paper.

Another sheet was placed in my hands. This one looked like a timetable, with courses such as *mathématiques*, *philosophie*, *lettres modernes*, etc., printed in a grid.

I realized that the nun had been asking me a question while I had been trying to decipher what was written on my piece of paper. She repeated it again, but I had no idea what she was saying. I looked at Madame Beaupre for help, shrugging an apology.

She repeated the word "*bac*" several times and then used the longer form "*baccalauréat*," until I figured out she was asking me if I wanted to write the French exams at the end of the year.

I most certainly did not. I'd worked hard during my last two years of high school. My course load had been full (even with the French class I'd dropped) and I'd taken six advanced placement courses. I'd worked on Saturdays and during vacations since I was twelve years old at a ladies clothing store downtown, first in the stock room and, from the time I was fourteen, as a salesperson on the floor. This year in France was the reward I had been working toward all those years. I refused to sign on for another year of intense studying. School this time around was about meeting people my age. It was merely a means to an end.

"No *bac*," I said. I wanted to expand on this and explain my reasoning but unfortunately didn't know the words.

The truth was my primary goals were to go to a lot of cafés, drink wine, fall in love, and learn French—not necessarily in that order. After giving it some thought, I decided that even if I were miraculously able to speak French, it was probably wise not to share those goals with the nuns. The only subject I was truly excited about at school was English. It was a life-long fantasy of mine to attend a foreign language class and to effortlessly do well. I spent many a French class back in Victoria fantasizing about that. I glanced down at my timetable to see "*anglais*" marked in the grid three times during the week. I chuckled inwardly. *Me in an English class? Awesome.*

The nun frowned at me. "*Pas de bac*? Are you sure?"

"*Oui*," I answered.

She stared at me some more, but finally nodded and wrote something down on the papers in front of her.

My BC high school diploma, my driver's license, and my Grade 12 report card were all taken to the photocopier. Just when I began to believe that we would be spending the whole day in the nun's office, she stood up and motioned for us to follow her.

We climbed a staircase that, judging from the looks of its dirty white paint and splintering wooden steps, had seen better days. At the top, the nun opened a door to a classroom. It was packed full of desks, and at least twenty-five French faces turned to examine me. French high school students apparently missed the memo about it being rude to stare. They looked me up and down, exchanged questioning glances with each other, and then went back to more blatant staring. I wasn't the type of girl that was stared at in high school. In looks and behavior, I specialized in middle-of-the-road, likeable but not riveting. I squirmed under their collective gaze. The nun rattled something to the rotund, perspiring teacher at the front of the class. I caught "*Canadienne*" and "Ursus." He pointed to an empty desk at the front and center of the classroom that, *quelle surprise*, no one else had deemed fit to claim.

Madame Beaupre squeezed my hand and whispered in my ear something about picking me up after school. I could tell she was nervous about leaving me, but I gave her a confident smile so as to appear the absolute opposite of how I felt.

I made my way over to the seat, feeling all eyes on me. I opened my backpack and extracted my pencil case.

"Est-ce que tu as un cahier?" the teacher asked me.

Shit. Un cahier? What the hell was a *cahier*? Unless it could be contained in my pencil case, I was pretty certain I didn't have one. I shook my head. The teacher frowned at me. I pulled out my clipboard.

"*Tu auras besoin d'un cahier.*" He sighed, already fed up with me.

I was so lost that I couldn't even figure out what class he was teaching. I snuck a look at the timetable. *Histoire*. History. OK. That was a start.

The other students were feverishly taking notes, writing so fast that they barely looked up or at me, thank God. How could I take notes if I didn't understand a word? I began to doodle 3D cubes, a constellation of stars, then hearts.

The teacher walked over to my desk and raised a brow at my artwork. Maybe doodling wasn't a good idea. I decided to mark down odd words I could catch to look up in the dictionary later that night. It was deceptively difficult, like catching grasshoppers.

Although the course seemed to last a long time, at the end of it, I had a list of only five words. I was doubtful whether I had heard and written even those down correctly. Before I got up, the teacher dropped a heavy textbook onto my desk and asked me a question in French.

"*Oui*," I answered, even though I had no idea what he had asked. I concluded that ninety percent of the time, *oui* was a decent answer. Ten percent of the time, it was surely a disastrous answer, but I liked my chances.

He nodded, satisfied. I slipped the textbook into my bag and walked out of the room. When I was halfway down the stairs, I realized I had absolutely no idea where I was supposed to go next. I took out my timetable: *Anglais. Ah-hah! English class. My salvation.* That was, if I could find the room.

Students pushed past me on both sides. The girls all seemed petite and intimidatingly chic with their hair clipped back in messy twists and scarfs tied around their necks with such skill that I wondered if in France they started learning this in toddlerhood. No one stopped to help me, or even smiled. They just jostled me as if I didn't exist.

I looked for a room number on my timetable. Nothing. Was I just supposed to *know* where the room for English was, or was that something else that had been lost in translation? I blinked back tears. This had somehow never been part of my exchange student fantasies.

I felt a tap on my shoulder and whipped around. A girl about my height with wavy hair and piercing blue eyes stood there. She wasn't smiling but didn't look mean…not exactly.

"You are lost?" she demanded with a very heavy French accent.

I nodded.

"*Moi, Sandrine.*" She pointed to herself and then extracted the timetable from my hands.

"Laura," I said.

"*La Canadienne*?" she asked. I nodded in confirmation. "*Ah! Anglais*," she said. I nodded again. "*Moi aussi.*" She pointed to herself. "I have English too. Follow me."

I followed her down the stairs, back into the courtyard, then up another different but almost identical set of stairs. We slipped into a classroom that boasted a huge map of the British Isles covering half of the chalkboard. She slipped into a desk and indicated for me to sit down in the one beside her. I gave her a wide smile. She didn't smile back and her manner was brusque, but I wasn't in a position to be difficult.

I was wracking my brain for something to say to her in French in a desperate attempt to cement our friendship when a young man with completely round glasses came into the room. At first, I thought he was a student.

"Hello," he said. "Welcome to English class." He spoke slowly and with the oddest accent. I couldn't place it as either British or Irish or Australian...there was definitely some French in the mix, as well. He consulted a list of names and said, "So...who do we have here?"

He called out the names and pronounced mine in what I was coming to recognize as the French way. The second syllable of "Laura" was emphasized instead of the first, and the two "r's" in "Bradbury" were rolled as only the French can do.

"Where did you learn English?" I asked. "I just can't figure out your accent."

He stared at me, stunned.

"You speak English?" He pushed his glasses up his nose.

Now I had the full attention of the other students in the class, but this time I didn't mind the staring so much.

A tall, husky guy leaned back in his chair and began to laugh. "*Trop bien*!" he said. I didn't know exactly what that meant, but he said it the same way I would say "awesome."

"Yes," I said. "My French is still pretty pathetic, but I grew up on the West Coast of Canada, near Vancouver. I'm here in Beaune on an exchange with the Ursus Club—"

"Slower, please." The teacher motioned at me to slow down. I probably *was* speaking rather quickly. After days of feeling as though a crucial limb had been cut off, I could finally communicate. Also, I had a language class where I was actually better than the teacher! *Trop bien*, indeed.

"Are you sure you want to be taking this English class?" the teacher asked. "What could I possibly teach you?"

They were not going to take this away from me. "It's the only class where I understand anything," I said. "Besides, I could help my fellow students if they need it—that would be an excellent way for me to make friends."

The teacher pursed his mouth, giving the distinct impression that he was not thrilled about having a fluent Anglophone in his class but wasn't quite sure of how to eject me.

Sandrine, at last, smiled at me. "*Génial*!" she whispered to me under her breath. I wasn't sure exactly what that meant, but it sounded good.

I was supposed to stay for lunch at school but realized I'd brought no money to pay for it—somewhat of an oversight. Besides, I had no idea where the cafeteria was even located, and while Saint Coeur school had a plethora of nuns and crosses and Virgin Mary statues, it appeared to be completely devoid of directional signs.

I couldn't even be annoyed. The whole lunch thing had probably been explained to me and I'd probably answered *oui*—one of those ten percent of the times when *oui* was a disastrous answer. I found an empty classroom and composed a couple of letters to friends back home to make myself look busy and to distract myself from my grumbling stomach. I was starving by the time the end of the day rolled around.

Thankfully, Madame was there when I emerged from the big wooden door. She asked me how it went.

"*Bien*!" I nodded cheerfully.

She looked at me with an air of skepticism, but didn't press the point. "Are you hungry?" she asked.

"*Oui.*"

She drove underneath the mini Arc de Triomphe and down a

busy, narrow thoroughfare. Beaune was as lovely as it was described in the guidebooks—cobblestoned streets, old storefronts, picturesque-looking people buying bread and doing other French-looking errands. We ended up on a big circular *place*, or "square," that had a merry-go-round on it surrounded by several different cafés.

She got out of the car and beckoned me across the street. "*Une petite crêpe*?" she asked.

"Super," I said, with what I hoped sounded like a French spin on the word.

I gobbled down my *crêpe* with Nutella and sucked back a *café* as well.

Next, we went to a stationery store, where Madame Beaupre bought everything on my school supply list. I was thrilled to realize that in France, instead of using ballpoint pens, high school students used actual fountain pens with little refillable ink cartridges. It was the little differences that enchanted me even more than the big differences between France and Canada.

On the way home, I reasoned that even though the day had been tough, school would become slightly less disorienting with each new day. I needed to be brave and give it time and enjoy the fact that I was, for the first time in my life, the top student in a foreign language class.

chapter eight

When we got back to Nuits-Saint-Georges, Madame Beaupre reminded me that there was an Ursus meeting that night and that we would be eating dinner there. How had I missed that important chunk of information?

My face ached from smiling at strangers all day long. I wanted nothing more than to collapse in my bedroom to recharge my batteries.

"What did you have for lunch?" Julien asked, patting Biscotte, who'd come to give me a warm welcome.

"Um." I kneeled down to give Biscotte a hug. "I didn't have lunch."

"Are you sick?" he asked, alarmed.

"No. I just couldn't figure out where the cafeteria was, and I didn't have any money to pay for it. I'm sure it was explained to me. My mistake."

Julien translated this to Madame Beaupre, who was horrified and assured me that it would all be taken care of the next day. She talked to Julien some more and then waved at him to translate.

"You do understand that you have to give a speech at the Ursus meeting tonight?" he asked.

My head snapped toward him. "What?"

"I suspected you might have missed that part as well." He looked at me with pity.

"A speech? In French?"

"Yes."

"I can't do that. My French is atrocious."

He turned and asked his mother a question. Madame was looking at me with concern in her lovely aqua eyes.

"It need only be a few minutes," Julien said, as though *that* was going to console me.

Just like the snails, the only way out was through. Somehow, though, I couldn't envision how this speech scenario could end as well as the *escargots* incident had. "I'd better go up to my room and write it then," I said, giving Biscotte a final kiss.

"Maman says you'll be leaving the house at twenty minutes to seven," Julien called after me as I left the room. I consulted my watch. It was already six o'clock.

I ran up the stairs to my bedroom, where I feverishly consulted word after word in my French-English pocket dictionary. No lounging in silence for me.

Within a few minutes, I was sweating. How was I supposed to give a speech to the whole Ursus Club of Beaune in French? Me, the French dunce...how had I gotten myself into this?

I wrote the speech in English first—generic stuff that should be easy to translate, such as saying how happy I was to be there, that I found France beautiful so far... It felt so good to be writing again that I forgot myself and began to wax poetic about local wine and snails. I was running out of time by the time I'd started to translate everything. I had no idea how to conjugate the verbs and, frankly, no time to look them up, so I figured that I would just leave verbs in their infinitive. Desperate times called for desperate measures.

At seven o'clock, as was his habit, Monsieur Beaupre arrived home late from work, and we sped off in his car. It must have enjoyed an interlude at the garage because the rearview mirror was reattached.

We sped off toward Beaune, past my new school, and under

the mini Arc de Triomphe.

Monsieur Beaupre stopped in front of a spot on the street that looked far too small for his car. He began to wedge it in, though, using his bumper to push the cars in front and behind him so that he could squeeze in. Is that what bumpers were really for? If so, we had been under-utilizing them back in Canada. How he was going to extract his car when the evening was over remained a matter of fascinating speculation.

I carried my Ursus blazer over my arm. Even though it was now early September, the hot summer weather hadn't loosened its hold on Burgundy, and I didn't want to have to don the itchy wool until the last possible moment.

Monsieur Beaupre led us to the doors of what looked like a charming hotel on a cobblestoned street not far from where he had parked. The antique street lamps illuminated the storefronts and stone buildings with a yellow light.

When we got into the hotel lobby, I reluctantly pulled on my blazer. How was I going to get through the evening? Muscles around my mouth that I didn't even know existed already ached from smiling so hard all day. My role as an Ursus exchange student was to be outgoing, though, so I let Madame launch me into the crowd to begin the introductions.

On my way to my table I was introduced to about twenty people, who chattered away at me in French. My head swam with French words, none of them connecting or making any sense. I was not seated at the same table with the Beaupres because, as an Ursus exchange student, my job was to interact with everyone.

I was the only woman at my designated table. I smiled at the men while wondering to myself what the hell I was going to talk to them about in my limited French. Luckily, a beautiful entrée of some kind of silky pâté adorned with lettuce leaves and artfully cut vegetables and *cornichons* arrived at the table—it would stay my anxiety about awkward silence.

The man to my right lifted the bottle that had been placed on the table in front of him and asked me in French, "May I serve you wine, Mademoiselle Bradbury?"

I thought briefly back to the "No Drinking" rule—this was an Ursus meeting after all, so my behavior here had to be impeccable. However, I could sense that he wanted me to answer yes. I concurred.

"*Oui. S'il te plaît*," I answered.

"*Ah, on se tutoie alors?*" he declared. "*Sympathique!*"

Crap. I was probably supposed to use the more formal "*vous*" when addressing him, as he had done for me. The distinction between "*vous*" and the less formal "*tu*" had never been successfully beaten into my head during French classes. The English way just made so much more sense—using "you" whether addressing the Queen of England or a five-year-old child. *Why complicate things?*

To hell with it. I was a foreigner, and if it was considered *sympathique* to address everyone with "*tu*," then that sounded like a good thing. Besides, "*tu*" was far easier to conjugate.

He poured me a glass of red wine.

"You know to drink wine?" he asked in fractured English.

"Yes," I answered. I had been a fan of wine ever since I was fifteen or so and my friend Gordon absconded with a bottle of his parents' Blue Nun, which we drank behind a bush. It was safe to say I had mastered that skill. I tipped my glass back and gulped down several mouthfuls of wine.

"*Non! Non! Non*!" He shook his finger at me. "Not *drink* wine. *Taste* wine."

I felt my forehead wrinkle. There was a difference?

He pointed at himself and spoke slowly. "*Je suis un oenologue*, a professional wine taster." He pointed to his various tablemates. "Louis is a *négociant.* Simon and Maxime make wine." He pointed to the last man at the table. "Gaspard exports wine."

"Ah," I said. I was surrounded by wine experts. Now this

wasn't at all intimidating.

"*Regardez*!" he said to me. "Look! I show you."

He held his glass up to the light and swirled the wine around.

"You see? First, the color. This one...lovely. Garnet with rust tones." His English became much more fluent as he described the wine.

He took my hand and wrapped it around the stem of my glass. "Now you."

I followed his instructions and swirled my glass around, then examined the color. It was still red, of course, but it did warrant a closer look. The ceiling lights shone through the wine to show different shades, from almost black to brown to ruby.

"*Joli*," I said. The men all laughed and I joined in.

My teacher lowered his glass so that he was looking at it from the side. "Next, we need to examine its legs."

"Legs?"

He spun his glass around, then put it in front of me so that I could watch where he was pointing to on the inside of the glass. The wine was viscous and ran back down to join the rest of the liquid in distinct rivulets.

"These are legs," he explained, pointing to the rivulets. "They indicate the sugar content in the wine. All good wines need beautiful legs, just like women."

I was still thinking up a suitable response to that when Simon, the winemaker with the reddest nose of the two, said, "Next is the smell."

"Not smell! Smell is for...how do you say...skunks! The *bouquet*," my teacher said. "Like flowers." He swirled his wine around in his wine glass and stuck his thin, hooked nose in it as far as it would go. Then he swirled some more. Wasn't he worried about getting wine up his nostrils?

All the men at the table did the same thing. There was much sniffing and swirling. I picked up my glass. The wine smelled good. Then again, wine always smelled good to me.

"Black currant," my teacher concluded.

"*Cerises*," said Louis. That was one of the few French words that my brain had retained from my eleven years of school French. "*Cerises*" means "cherries." I sniffed again. The wine certainly smelled good but...cherries? Maybe...or was that just the power of suggestion?

"An undernote of leather," Gaspard the wine exporter declared.

The men seemed to take exception to this statement and plunged their noses deep into their glasses once again. "Not leather," said one. "*Sous-bois.*"

"*Sous-bois?*" I quickly leafed through my French-English pocket dictionary. Much to my surprise "*sous-bois*" was there. It roughly translates as "earth."

I took a deep sniff of my wine again. *There* is *a deep earthy smell, but I wouldn't say it smells like* dirt. Anyway, wasn't that considered an insult?

I was forgotten for several minutes as a debate broke out in rapid-fire French—first about *sous-bois* versus leather and then about a wide range of other wine-related subjects from what I could tell—which wasn't much. They could have been arguing the merits of mistresses versus wives for all I understood.

Then Gaspard took a sip and swished his mouthful of wine like a swig of Scope before swallowing it. How could all this not be considered appalling table manners? Rather than objecting, however, the rest of the men joined in and seemed to be in competition with one another for who could make the most noise and contort his face into the most comical grimace as he swished the wine around. Suddenly my teacher must have realized he had forgotten about me.

"Now," he said, as though there had been no interruption, "you must taste the wine. You mustn't just gulp it. You cannot properly taste it that way. You must let it sit on your tongue for a time, then roll and swish it in your mouth. Give it time to play in there. This is the only way to taste the wine's nuances and to start having a relationship with it."

I had drunk wine before—mainly bad wine. This was the first time it dawned on me that maybe I needed to develop a *relationship* with my wine. I swished the wine around in my mouth as all the other men were doing. It actually did taste different. There was the first spark of it on my tongue and then a mellow warmth that ran down the back of my throat.

"What do you taste?" Simon asked from across the table.

"Black currant," I said, repeating what somebody had mentioned in regards to the bouquet. I did not want to reignite the debate over *sous-bois*.

"There *are* strong notes of cassis," my teacher said. "We have a prodigy!" With that, the entire table erupted into a song that consisted of "la laaaas" and applauding, which I couldn't really make heads or tails of but which sounded definitely on the celebratory end of the spectrum.

For the next hour and a half, I was plied with a myriad of different wines and taught the fine Burgundian art of wine tasting. The courses of food came and went, each as delicious as the last. With each course, the men had me taste a new wine and start the process from the beginning. Color. Legs. Bouquet. Taste. When I was busy selecting a stinky Époisses, among other cheeses, from the cheese trolley, Louis disappeared from the table and returned with three dusty, cobwebbed bottles of unlabeled wine.

"You must try these," he said.

"Where did they come from?" I asked, mystified.

"The boot of my car."

"*Fantastique*!" said Gaspard. "We all need to try. Louis is a winemaker in Gevrey-Chambertin. Sublime wine, although he should watch his tannins."

The table erupted in hilarity at this jest. I joined in, even though wine humor was still a bit of a stretch for me. Everything seemed hilarious all of a sudden.

Louis's wine was my favorite. It was sublime. In the end, we had tasted so much wine that I had completely lost my nerves about my speech. In fact, I pretty much forgot about it altogether.

As I was polishing off the final crumbs to my chocolate-and-raspberry pastry, I thought I heard my name amid a jumble of other French words being spoken up front by a man at the podium. I squinted in his direction.

"Your *discours*, Mademoiselle Bradbury!" My neighbor patted me heartily on the back. "It is time for your speech! *Allez-y*!"

I grabbed my index cards on which I had nervously penned my English to French translations only a few hours before. The room swayed... *Oh my God*, a sober voice in the back of my head observed. I was drunk. How did that happen? More importantly, how was I going to convey my already unintelligible French in this state?

I took my place behind the podium, knocking the microphone askew. There were at least eighty or so expectant faces turned to me. I had to steel myself not to turn and simply hightail it to the nearest washroom, or outside, or anywhere but where I was standing—front and center. My cheeks were on fire, but I managed to smile at the crowd. Then, I was overtaken with a sincere wave of love for everyone in the room. I *loved* Burgundy so far. Then the wave drew back, and I was left with frustration. How on earth was I going to get this point across?

No way out but through, I reminded myself. I launched into my speech, peppering it with *merci*s while being vaguely aware that I was completely butchering the French language as I lurched along. I got to the end and lifted my head to see everyone in the room observing me with stunned expressions. They hadn't, I could tell, understood a word.

"*Merci*!" It must have been the wine, because I lifted my fist and did an air pump. "*Vive la Bourgogne*!"

The men at my table burst into a round of applause, which segued into the celebratory song they had been singing. The entire room joined in, and I stayed behind the podium, laughing. I may have even given the crowd a royal wave.

When I made it back to my table, my wine tasting teacher squeezed my shoulder. "You have a Burgundian spirit, Mademoiselle Bradbury. I knew it the second I met you."

chapter nine

I was given a cafeteria card by the head nun the next day, although I still had no idea where I was supposed to go when lunchtime rolled around. I was in the hall staring at it when Sandrine, the kind girl from the day before, stopped in front of me.

"*Bonjour, Laura,*" she said.

"*Bonjour.*"

She leaned in for *les bises*, which took me by surprise. Luckily, I clued in just at the last moment and didn't botch it up entirely. *So...friends kiss each other every day?* Was it just reserved for good friends? Sandrine had just met me... She scowled so much that I wasn't certain whether she actually liked me or resented having to take me on out of pity. This whole kissing thing was turning out to be a minefield. In France, hugs are basically reserved for people you know very well or for family—way less complicated.

"*Cantine?*" she asked me, pointing at my card. I remembered that word from Julien and Madame Beaupre the day before. It is French for cafeteria.

"*Oui.*"

"Come with me," she said in heavily accented French.

I followed Sandrine like an obedient puppy. We crossed the courtyard with its statue of the Virgin Mary and climbed up three flights of an extremely steep spiral staircase that looked like some sort of remnant from the Middle Ages. Then it dawned on me—the stairs could actually *be* from the Middle Ages.

At the top of the staircase, there was a long and very noisy room under the eaves. There didn't seem to be any trays. *Strange.* Instead, places were set with china plates, silver knives, forks, and spoons, and squat glasses at long monastery tables.

I wondered what the food was going to be like. Gross soups thickened with too much cornstarch and a salad bar, like the cafeteria food in my high school? Also, I wondered how much time we had to eat. In high school in Canada, we had half an hour—just enough time to bolt our food, but so fast we got a stomach ache.

Sandrine sat down in the middle of a group of other students, mostly guys, at a table that was almost full except for two empty places. She kissed a few of the students, and then she said my name. "*Laura. La Canadienne.*" She waved over at me and introduced me to the group.

Should I go around and kiss everyone? No. That would be too weird. We had just been introduced. I stayed at my seat and smiled instead. Why did no one have any food?

The people at the table studied me with undisguised curiosity. I was grateful that at least my clothes blended in. I was wearing a pair of Levi's jeans, a loose linen top, and a pair of sandals. My hair was pulled back in a simple ponytail.

"Do you speak French?" The burly guy with brown eyes who had said *trop bien* in English class the day before was sitting across the table from us.

I made the hand motion that meant "not much," as if I was squeezing a tiny atom of air between my thumb and my forefinger. The boy grinned at me. He had a contagious smile that made it seem as if he was inviting me to share in a joke with him, or maybe the joke was on me... I couldn't be sure. I smiled back.

He flipped his glass over. "What number do you have?"

My confusion must have been evident, because he reached and flipped over my glass and pointed to a little number engraved in the bottom. Apparently each glass had a different number.

I read mine. "Twenty-seven. I mean, *vingt-sept.*"

The boy read his and then turned his glass back upright. "Mine is *soixante-neuf*," he said. "Sixty-nine. Do you know what that means?"

I did, and I suspected, given the boy's sneaky look, that it meant the same thing in France.

Sandrine, who must have been listening to the exchange, snarled at him. "It is not." She grabbed his glass and flipped it over. "Yours is seventeen. Thibaut is an *idiot* sometimes," she explained to me while still glaring at him.

Thibaut just laughed. "*C'est vrai*," he admitted. It's true.

I felt a stab of despair as sharp as an ice pick. If Thibaut was anything to go by, French boys were no different than Canadian boys—obsessed with sex. Had I crossed the Atlantic only to be confronted with more of the same bullshit?

A bunch of people wearing white clothes came out from behind a partition, bearing plates of colorful but unidentifiable food. One of them placed a plate in front of me.

"*C'est quoi*?" I asked. What is it? That, although probably not grammatically correct, was another one of those multipurpose phrases. Maybe not polite, but serviceable.

"*Trio de salades*." Sandrine pointed at her plate. "Carrot, celery, and beet."

A trio of salads? That was all we got for lunch?

Wicker baskets filled with sliced baguette were placed in the center of the table. I tucked in. I didn't want to go through the whole afternoon starving as I had the day before. This was a bit of an odd lunch, as well as a bit on the sparse side, but maybe I had just solved the mystery of why French people tend to be skinnier than North Americans.

The salads were surprisingly satisfying. They were all dressed with different dressings—a vinegary one for the carrots, a creamy one for the celery, and one that had the heat of Dijon mustard for the beets.

I bolted my food as I always did back in Canada, only to look up and see that my tablemates were taking their time, pushing food onto their slices of baguette and using the bread to mop up the sauce on their plates. They were all in what sounded to me like involved conversations, punctuated with laughter and debate. In Canada, we all usually fell silent while eating—we had no time to eat, let alone talk and eat.

After what seemed like a long time, the kitchen staff came back, whipped away the plates, and disappeared back into the kitchen. I couldn't figure out why my fellow students weren't collecting their backpacks and getting ready to leave. I knew meals are longer in France than they are in Canada, but surely not at school.

Just as I was flipping through my dictionary to find the words to ask Sandrine what was going on, the kitchen staff appeared with new plates, filled this time with artfully presented breaded meat of some kind and long, thin green beans.

"There's more food?" I asked Sandrine. She looked at me, her eyes wide.

"*Bien sûr*!" she said. "Of course there is more food. That was just our *entrée*."

"Lunch...?" I asked. "*Combien de temps*?" How long do we get for lunch?

"Two hours," she said.

"*Deux heures*?" I answered. "We get two hours for lunch?"

"Of course. All over France." She flicked her hand around to encompass the whole country. "Two hours for everybody."

The meat turned out to be chicken cordon bleu—chicken breasts stuffed with cured ham and melted cheese, then breaded and baked. I had never thought I liked green beans, but these ones were crisp and redolent of butter and parsley.

I liked green beans, I realized, with the same shock I'd felt a few days earlier when I discovered I loved snails.

After the main course came bowls of what looked to me like thick cream.

"*Fromage blanc*," Sandrine said, pointing at mine with her spoon. "Delicious."

I sprinkled some sugar over mine, copying Sandrine, and dug in. Where had *fromage blanc* been all my life? It was like heavy yogurt, but tarter and creamier. I had found yet another Favorite Thing.

I figured the *fromage blanc* was dessert, but as Sandrine explained to me in a mix of English and French, it had in fact only been the cheese course. There is always a dairy course before dessert, Sandrine explained.

Next came a trio of miniature *éclairs*—one chocolate, one vanilla, and one coffee-flavored.

We actually get to eat this kind of stuff for lunch every day? Not only that, but have time to unwind and chat with friends? I had no idea what was being discussed most of the time, but I picked up on the relaxed, social vibe.

After dessert was cleared, surely it was time to go, I reasoned. We had been there well over an hour and a half already. But no. Coffee arrived for each of us, served in white, china espresso cups. Even Thibaut, for all his muscles and juvenile taste in jokes, drank from his diminutive espresso cup with a sort of unstudied nonchalance that I had never before seen in a North American guy.

Sandrine took out a pack of Gitanes from the pocket of her jean jacket and gestured that she was heading outside for a smoke. Did I want to come? I grabbed my backpack and followed her.

My friend Alice had smoked in high school and she was forever looking for a new hideout to do this forbidden act—in the showers, behind a clump of trees, even in the bathroom stalls. Smoking was something I occasionally did at parties, mainly to give myself something to do with my hands when I was feeling awkward. The truth was cigarettes made my chest wheeze and my mouth feel like the bottom of a birdcage.

I followed as Sandrine and the rest of the lunch gang made their way down the medieval corkscrew stairs and out into the courtyard.

At the first windowsill at the base of the stairs, we stopped, and more than half of our group whipped out packs of cigarettes and lit up. Thibaut, I noticed, wasn't smoking.

Sandrine extended her pack to me and nodded for me to take one. I shook my head. Maybe I would feel more French if I smoked, but if I established myself as a smoker, then I would feel pressure to *actually* smoke.

"Non, merci."

"You no smoke?"

"*Non.*"

Still, I hung out with them in the balmy air and enjoyed watching the blue smoke from their cigarettes curl up over our heads.

I spied one of the nuns in full habit coming out the far door. I squeezed Sandrine's arm and gestured toward the nun. I needed to warn her to stub out before she was caught in the act.

Sandrine raised her eyebrows. "*Quoi*? We are allowed to smoke here."

"You are?"

"Of course," Sandrine shrugged. "We are eighteen, *après tout*."

I surveyed the courtyard more closely and noticed for the first time that the ground was festooned with cigarette butts.

A two-hour, multi-course lunch and sanctioned post-meal cigarettes… I was on a steep learning curve here.

The weekend came quickly. Back in Canada I would have worked at my part time job in a women's clothing boutique and made plans with friends, but in France I had no friends yet.

On Saturday, I helped Madame get ready for lunch—melon wrapped with a type of prosciutto-like ham for starters, then barbequed sausages studded with pistachios from Lyon, and a large salad that she called *tabouleh*, which was made with tiny round grains and chopped vegetables mixed in a lemony dressing. She also asked me to wash some tender buttercrunch lettuce that, she told me via Julien, she had bought at the market the day before.

"Can you make a vinaigrette?" she asked me, as I separated and carefully washed the lettuce leaves.

"Vinaigrette?" Like...a salad dressing? The only kind of salad dressing that I have ever seen came from a Kraft bottle.

"Here, I'll show you," she said...I think.

She added a dollop of Dijon Mustard from the ceramic mustard pot that always sat on the kitchen counter. Then she poured in a little bit of white wine vinegar and stirred it around quickly with her fork. Then she put in a bit of olive oil and mixed that with similar vigor. The ingredients merged together to make a pale yellow emulsification that looked and smelled delicious. She added a twist of freshly ground pepper directly from the pepper grinder, mixed that in, and then stood back and said, "*Voilà*!" I nodded. I thought I could handle that. She minced a shallot and scraped the little bits into the vinaigrette and mixed it again.

That actually wasn't that hard. How many other things had I been eating from bottles or boxes or cans that weren't that difficult to make?

During our *cafés*—which Madame Beaupre and Julien always drank from a clear glass because they swore it tasted better that way—after yet another delicious lunch, Julien said, "I'm going to visit my friend Adalene. Would you like to join me?"

Adalene came up often in Julien's conversations as the reference for all that was feminine and beautiful. I was curious to meet this paragon.

"I'm going to change," Julien said, getting up from the table, which I found odd, as he was already wearing one of his pairs of ironed jeans and an impeccable checked shirt. Was she his girlfriend? Or did he want her to be? "Do you want to go and change too?"

I looked down at my Birkenstock sandals and tie-dyed T-shirt. I shrugged. "No. I'm good."

Earlier that morning, I had finally finished unpacking and had found my crystal necklaces at the bottom of my suitcase. I had put three of them on, one on top of the other, and was feeling very loose-limbed and bohemian in the way that hippy crystals make you feel.

I accepted a second cup of espresso while Julien changed. He was certainly taking a while, I thought. This made me even more curious to meet Adalene.

Finally, he returned wearing pressed Bermuda shorts and a different checked shirt, this time a lovely madras plaid with pastel colors. He had also added a pair of sunglasses, which were strategically placed on his head. He looked so meticulously dressed and one hundred percent French that I almost burst out laughing. He was also wearing loafer-like shoes that looked expensive and Italian-made, with no socks.

"Are you ready?" he asked. I didn't understand the question. Of course I was ready.

We walked through the center of town and through some winding streets on the opposite side of the main street. Julien led us to a huge wooden door that was built into a massive, ancient-looking stone wall.

Mounted just beside a brass doorbell was a modest plaque that said Domaine Hudelot.

"She's a winemaker?" I asked Julien, after he had rung the doorbell.

"Her father is," Julien said. "She is an only child. It would be very unusual for an unmarried woman to take over a wine domaine. Her father insists she marry a winemaker so the vines stay in the family line."

That sounded highly chauvinistic. "So, you're out then," I quipped.

Julien cast me an affronted look. "Adalene and I are just friends."

"I was joking. Sorry."

The door opened and a stately elderly man who looked very proper was on the other side. *Adalene's father?*

Julien didn't greet him as such. There was no handshake or *bises*. He just said a polite *bonjour*, and the man said that Mademoiselle Adalene was to be found in the living room. The man, I did notice, was casting curious glances at me.

I followed Julien across a pea gravel courtyard and into the grand, ivy-spangled house. He opened the main door and led us down a wallpapered hallway and then turned right. The air smelled of old money and prestige.

Adalene was ensconced in an antique armchair, which was upholstered with blue and gold silk. "Julien!" She jumped up, gave him *les bises*, and, still holding on to his arms, started talking in rapid-fire French. Julien said something and I caught my name. She pulled back and gave me a welcoming smile. "Ah! So, you are the *Canadienne* that the Beaupres have been waiting for all these months!" Her English was excellent.

"*Oui*," I said.

She reached out and fingered my crystals. "I love your necklaces!" she exclaimed. "So original!"

I wasn't sure which element of Adalene's appearance I should praise first. She was stunning—a petite, green-eyed blond with perfectly manicured nails, wearing tailored capri pants, a snug-fitting but perfectly elegant cotton shirt in a lovely shade of jade, and the most exquisite, black leather flats that, like Julien's shoes, looked as though they had been hand tooled by some Geppetto-like person in an obscure Italian village.

"*Tes chaussures*!" Julien exclaimed, admiring Adalene's feet. He obviously knew and cared about shoes. She did a pretty little spin, modeling them for him. "*Magnifique*!" he concluded.

"I knew you would love them," she said, linking her arm in mine and traipsing us to the kitchen, where she plied us with homemade *madeleines*.

"It is not everywhere that you meet a man who knows his shoes," she whispered to me, but loud enough for Julien to hear. Julien blushed.

I looked down at my standard two-strap, suede Birkenstocks and, for the first time in my life, doubted their aesthetic appeal. Adalene was warm and welcoming, but beside her I felt completely out of my element.

We stayed at her house for a good hour. She and Julien chattered in a mix of fast French and English, which she switched to occasionally just enough for me to cotton on to what they were talking about before the conversation flew off in an entirely new direction.

Not being able to understand and speak French reduced me

to an almost infantile state. I went from being a quick-witted, competent, intelligent seventeen-year-old to someone who needed to be babied. I was humbled by how my entire personality felt buried under my lack of French.

When we took leave of Adalene, she kissed me warmly and invited me to come and visit with Julien again.

"She's lovely," I said to Julien as we walked home.

"She is. It will be a lucky man who marries her. She has such style, such elegance. Did you see her shoes?"

"They were exquisite."

"You can tell all you need to know about a woman by her shoes," Julien rhapsodized, a dreamy expression on his face. "Does she have good taste? Does she take good care of herself? Look at a woman's shoes and you know all."

If there had been a way I could have hidden my Birkenstocks while walking, I would have, but unfortunately it was physically impossible. My eyes were drawn down to my feet. Not only was I wearing one of the ugliest forms of footwear known to man, but my toenails were in dire need of a pedicure. Even though my suspicion had been growing since I'd arrived at the Beaupres, I knew at that moment with absolute certainty that, while Julien may be someone else's soul mate, he would never be mine. I could never pay that much attention to my footwear.

Julien followed my glance down to my feet. There was a sudden stiffening of the atmosphere around him. He wasn't an unkind person, I knew, and I could tell he was wondering how to backpedal. I prickled with embarrassment on his behalf.

"Of course, there are always cultural differences," he said. "One has to account for that, naturally."

"Naturally." I wished he could laugh at his *faux pas*, but his features were rigid with mortification.

I needed someone who could face such a gaffe head on, apologize, and laugh. I just had to find *that* person.

chapter ten

By the time the third week of school rolled around, I was definitely understanding more French, enough to follow about a third of what was said in my classes and at home. Sandrine had taken me firmly under her wing. Thank God, because the boys in Sandrine's group of friends, led by Thibaut, took it upon themselves to find sly ways to trick me into saying pretty much every dirty word and expression in the French language. I wondered if this was what the Ursus members back in Victoria had in mind when they rhapsodized about "cultural interactions."

After school that Friday, Madame Beaupre was doing errands in Beaune and came to pick me up with a big smile on her face. "How would you like to do *les vendanges* tomorrow?" she asked.

I was proud that I knew that the word "*vendanges*" means "grape harvest." It was all anybody in the Beaupre household or at school had been talking about for the previous several days. The harvest was later than usual because of the cold spring, and everyone was impatiently waiting for it to begin.

"Really?" I said. "I'd love to!"

As we drove back to Nuits-Saint-Georges, she explained it slowly and simply in French. I was amazed that I understood the gist of what she said.

My second host family, the Girards, whose house I would be moving to in mid-December and who I had, according to Madame Beaupre, met at that Ursus dinner and wine-tasting lesson in Beaune, were winemakers. Their vines spanned the nearby villages of Comblanchien and Corgoloin. They were beginning their wine harvest the next day and thought it would be an excellent way for me to have this quintessential Burgundian experience. It was exactly the kind of cool thing that I'd daydreamed about in my bedroom back in Canada.

I glanced out the car window, where the buildings of Beaune were giving way to the vineyards. Just as we passed the sign for the village of Chorey-les-Beaune, I caught sight of wine harvesters dotting the vineyards.

"*Regardez!*" I pointed, barely able to contain my excitement.

"*Oui.* It's started!" Madame Beaupre said, reflecting how I felt. Everyone in Burgundy talked about the grape harvest with barely contained glee, like kids looking forward to a huge ocean storm back in Victoria. The harvest was central to the life of every Burgundian, it seemed, even those like Madame Beaupre who were not directly involved with the wine trade.

I would be dropped off at the Girards' wine domaine before dawn the next morning and would join the harvesting team for the weekend. I needed to dress warmly, Madame Beaupre told me with maternal anxiety. The vineyards were full of mud. Rain was a distinct possibility, so I needed to have some waterproof outerwear too. She could lend me some of Sophie's.

I sat back in my seat as we passed Corgoloin, and then Premeaux-Prissey, and began to daydream. That familiar ache in my heart returned. I wondered if I'd finally meet the person I knew was out there somewhere for me. Somebody who wouldn't draw any ironclad conclusions based on my shoes. It was possible. If so, would I know him? This question kept my mind occupied for most of the evening.

I had been brought up to be an ambitious and independent woman. I shouldn't need a man. I felt guilty about my lurking feelings of loneliness, but I couldn't convince my heart to pay heed to my head.

The next morning, Madame woke me up, still in her silk *peignoir* and with rollers in her hair. I could have turned over and slept for several more hours but forced myself to get out of bed and stagger downstairs to the bathroom and take my shower.

I dressed in jeans, a heavy cotton sweater, and running shoes. I carried a K-Way jacket and Sophie's grape-harvesting rain pants in my arms. Apparently, the one place Burgundians could dispense with elegance was in the vineyards.

Madame emerged as I was sipping my big bowl of *café au lait*. She located the car keys and, with a kiss on my head, told me it was time to leave.

We headed out to the car just as the sky was beginning to turn from black to a dark shade of blue. Already there were a lot of tractors and utility vehicles on the narrow vineyard roads that Madame Beaupre had opted to use between Nuits-Saint-Georges and Corgoloin, where the family's wine domaine was located in the center of the village.

It was intimidating, this idea of being dropped off among a bunch of new people. Madame told me that the wine harvesters were always made up of family members, close friends who came back every year, and hired hands, often young people who were traveling and wanted to pick up a few days' work.

I donned my gregarious Ursus front as we entered the village, just like Clark Kent changing into his Superman costume.

Madame pulled up to park in front of an ancient stone house attached to a large garage-like building. People of all ages, dressed in versions of what I was wearing, were mulling around the open door of the garage. They were drinking from plastic cups.

Madame took me over to a small, round man with a pleasant face, who, as it turned out, did not look entirely unfamiliar. *This must be my second host father, Monsieur Girard.*

"*Bienvenue, Laura.*" He kissed me roundly on both cheeks. "Did you come ready to cut grapes?" He spoke in slow, methodical French that was surprisingly easy to understand. Thank God for that.

"*Oui.*"

He handed me a pair of *sécateurs*, big metal clippers that were slightly rusty and looked, unlike me, as though they'd seen other harvests. I noticed almost everyone else was holding a pair. "Don't lose these. They will be yours for the weekend."

A woman with abundant white hairs growing out of her chin, who looked almost as ancient as the house, came by bearing a tray loaded with more plastic cups. Monsieur plucked one off and handed it to me.

"You do like wine, as I recall," he said.

Merde. Monsieur Girard must have heard my tipsy speech at the Ursus meeting... My eyes darted to his face and I was relieved to see he was smiling, and not angry. "*Oui,*" *I answered.*

"This is our white aligoté," he said. "Those will be the first vines we harvest this morning."

Somebody shouted, and a noisy tractor pulled up in front of the crowd. "Hop on!" Monsieur told me. "It will take you to the vineyards."

I hopped on, coughing from the gray diesel fumes that bellowed out the back. The tractor did not contain anything as pedestrian as seat belts, or even, it seemed, any more than two seats at the very front. One of these was for the driver, who happened to be an extremely handsome young man, with chestnut curls and huge dark eyes with lashes that I felt were unfairly bestowed on a guy.

I ended up standing on the ledge of the door at the front of the tractor, clinging for dear life. I seemed precariously high off the ground. I jammed my *sécateurs* into my back pocket and clung on to my plastic glass of wine with one hand and the frame of the tractor with the other.

Once we got going, I realized that, although the tractor lurched and hopped along the pitted vineyard paths, it didn't go very fast. I felt slightly more at ease and glanced behind me. There was a wooden trailer attached to the back of the machine, where most of the other harvesters sat. *Beginner's mistake.* I would sit there on my way back.

The tractor lurched up to a patch of vineyards on the upwards slope of the Nationale road, just outside the village limits of Premeaux-Prissey. A grizzled man who must have been pushing sixty-five and who, had he been dressed in military garb, could have passed for a general in a World War II movie, gave me a large plastic bucket with a metal handle. He led me to a section of the vines and shouted a set of instructions at me in staccato French. I didn't understand much but...how complicated could it be? I needed to snip off the bunches of grapes. I could handle that.

I began, and within seconds the General was beside me again and motioned at me to kneel down. I studied the ground... It was muddy.

I knelt. Luckily, as a coastal girl, I was not intimidated by a bit of mud. It squelched under the denim covering my knees. Maybe I should have sacrificed vanity and put on Sophie's rain pants after all. I had left them, as well as my change of clothes, back at the domaine.

The General put his face so close to mine that I got an excellent view of his patchy, white facial hair. He demonstrated exactly how to snip the bunches of grapes. Apparently, there was a very specific spot on the vine that allowed for maximum grapes and a minimum of green vines. I nodded and said a few enthusiastic *ouis*!

He grunted and stalked off to berate someone else.

I began snipping the grapes off the vines. The clusters were different from any grapes I had ever seen in the supermarket. They were fat and fit together so snugly that I almost couldn't distinguish most of the individual grapes.

The first few landed in my basket with a satisfying thump, and quickly my basket was half full, then completely full. Just when I was going to stand up to stretch my legs and figure out where to empty it, a strapping young man with a large, white, inverted plastic cone strapped to his back like a backpack came down the row. He stopped beside me.

"*Bon travail*," he said. Nice work.

"*Merci*," I answered, standing up with my basket.

"Ah. You are the *Canadienne*?" he said, in English.

"You could tell from my *merci*? I thought I was pronouncing it better."

"Still a slight accent," he said. "But it's charming."

"Charming? I'd rather be able to pass for French." I said honestly.

"Give it time. I'm Florian. I'm from Switzerland. Nice to meet you." He stuck out his hand.

"Laura." I wiped mine off on my jeans and shook his. "You guessed right. I'm from Canada. The English-speaking part, obviously."

Florian had white-blond hair and looked as though he had been brought up exactly like Heidi had, on fresh milk and huge wheels of cheese made from cows that roamed the green pastures of the Alps. He leaned forward and gave me *les bises*. I was surprised. I had never had a handshake and *les bises*. I blushed. To cover up my awkwardness, I lifted up my basket of grapes. "What should I do with these now?"

He turned around so that the cone he carried on his back was turned toward me. "Pour them in here," he instructed. "Gently. We don't want to bruise the precious grapes."

When he turned back, he was giving me a sly smile. He was flirting with me. I couldn't believe it. Here I was, flirting with a cute Swiss guy in the middle of the grape vines during the grape harvest in France.

Someone else tapped me on my back. I turned to find a young boy who looked around twelve. He thrust a bottle in my hand. It was a bottle of white wine, unlabeled and chilled in the cool morning air.

I gestured with the bottle to my new Swiss friend. "What am I supposed to do with this?"

Florian laughed. "Drink from it, of course. You will find there are bottles of wine passed up and down the rows all the time. It wouldn't do to let the harvesters go thirsty, you know. They wouldn't come back the following year."

I took a swig. It was the same delicious white wine I had sipped from the plastic cup before leaving the Girards' domaine. I passed the bottle to Florian then wondered if I should have wiped the neck off with a bit of my clothing first to clean it. I looked down. I was absolutely covered in mud. A patch of clean clothing would be challenging to find.

Florian accepted it and, without taking his eyes off me, took a deep drink. "Ah!" he said. "That was particularly good." We stood staring at each other.

Just then, the General started yelling something about "*fainéants*" and "*AU BOULOT!*" in our direction.

Florian winked at me. "That was for us. Back to work. I'll save you a seat at lunch though. Would that be all right?"

"That would be great," I said.

I nestled down again, farther down the row of vines, and happily snipped off grapes.

My back was soon cramping, as were my thighs and my knees, from being bent over in an awkward position for so long, but I was so caught up in daydreams of Florian the Swiss Grape Harvester that I barely noticed. I didn't feel my soul reverberating, but I was flattered and a bit thrilled. That was a start, wasn't it? I needed to be open-minded, I thought to myself.

I had never been particularly attracted to blond men. I'd always found them bland, a bit like the plastic Ken dolls I'd played with as a child. Or maybe it was that I knew for a fact I was no Barbie and never would be. *Don't get so ahead of yourself, as usual.*

A cowbell rang out over the vines, and we were all summoned to a white utility van, where slices of baguette with different types of pâté were available for a midmorning snack. I ate several, as I was already starving. Florian also took a few, then stood talking with a group of male harvesters. He did catch my eye, though, and winked at me again.

Florian was very...wholesome. It wasn't that I went for crack addicts or Hells Angels biker gang types, but I did like a guy to have a bit of an edge. All these thoughts and conjectures swirled through my mind as I sat back down after the snack to snip many, many more clusters of grapes.

Florian wasn't sent to my row again to pick them up. The General must have assigned him elsewhere.

Bottles of wine, first white and then red, kept being passed to me as I worked, and I took a swig out of every one until the sky started spinning. There was no water, and the work made me thirsty.

The smell of the earth in Burgundy was completely different than back home—it had a mineral scent, overlaid with the smell of decomposing leaves. My stomach began to rumble again.

Finally, the tractor engines began to rev up, and somebody rang the cowbell. Lunch! We all took our buckets over to the tractor that was hauling the grapes and dumped them in the back. Florian appeared beside me. "Don't forget about sitting together at lunch."

I shook my head. "I won't." Even if Florian didn't have that Han Solo edge that I always appreciated in a man, I was seventeen and far away from home for the first time in my life—what was wrong with having a little fun?

Florian then lifted himself, in a notable display of arm muscles, up onto the wooden rail that surrounded the trailer piled high with grapes. I couldn't decide which was more impressive, Florian's biceps or the mound of grapes.

To think all those clusters would be squeezed to make delectable wine... During the previous few hours, I'd gained an entirely new appreciation for wine and the work that went into making each bottle. I was pretty sure I wouldn't be able to drink it again without remembering the feel of my knees squishing into the Burgundian mud.

I found a spot in the back of the white utility van where fifteen or so of us harvesters had piled in. Seat belts didn't appear to be a high priority for the French at the best of times, but during the grape harvest, road safety rules seemed to be abandoned in their entirety.

We were dumped out in a tumbling, muddy mass back at the domaine. There was a pail full of with water and a couple of sponges for us to wipe off any removable mud before taking our spot at the two huge monastery tables that had been set up in a vaulted cellar that was attached to the winemaking hangar. Everyone seemed to be referring to the hangar area as the "*cuverie*."

I tried to remove some of the mud that covered me from

head to toe, but the water in the pails was already dark brown by the time it was my turn, and I only ended up smearing it more extensively over my clothes. I settled for washing my hands—and hopefully most of the mud off my face—in the bathroom. As there was no mirror, whether I had succeeded or not was anybody's guess.

By the time I got to the tables, Florian had already claimed our seats and was waving me over.

I sat down. "I'm soaked," I said.

"Are you cold?" he asked. "Would you like me to warm you up?"

I looked across the table and down a few seats to where Monsieur Girard was sitting. My second host father's eyes were not looking as good-humored now, and they kept shifting back and forth between me and Florian.

In English, I said to Florian, "Monsieur Girard is my second host father during my year here. One of the rules for exchange students such as me is 'No dating.'"

"What!? But that is simply unnatural! How old are you?"

"Almost eighteen."

"They cannot possibly tell an almost-eighteen-year-old girl that she has to be celibate for a year."

I tended to agree. Telling an eighteen-year-old girl she couldn't fall in love was like telling the tide it couldn't come to the shore.

"How old are you?" I asked, almost as an afterthought.

"Twenty-one," he said.

That was good. I'd always liked guys who were slightly older.

"I don't really know what to think about the Ursus rules," I admitted. "I'm not clear on how strictly they are applied."

"What are the rest of the rules?" Florian asked as he passed me a basket full of delectably warm cheese puffs.

"No Drinking," I began.

"Well, you broke that one," Florian observed. Indeed, my glass was already filled with wine.

"As far as I can tell, that particular rule doesn't seem to

apply to exchanges to Burgundy."

"*Logique*," surmised Florian.

"No Dating."

"Like I said—unnatural."

"No Drugs."

Florian shrugged over this one. "That shouldn't be too much of a problem."

"No Driving."

"Even a vineyard tractor?"

I shrugged. "I guess so. I'm not sure."

I had barely noticed that my plate had been whisked away, but another—heaping with tiny round grains and delicious, steamed carrots and other vegetables with hot sausage—had been placed in front of me. A delectable spicy sauce soaked into everything.

I took several bites to take the edge off my hunger. "This is delicious," I said, changing the topic. "What is it?"

"*Couscous*. It is a North African specialty from Morocco and Tunisia."

"It's fantastic."

"Back to this 'No Dating' rule," Florian said, not to be distracted, "I'm Swiss. Compared to the French, we *love* rules. This is why Switzerland is so much cleaner and the trains always run on time, and why my whole country is so much more *pleasant* than France. Still, I cannot agree with this no dating nonsense."

"France is pleasant." I felt defensive of my adopted homeland.

"Have you ever been here when they are in the streets striking over something or other? They are always striking." His lips twisted with disdain.

Maybe France wasn't perfect, but the anarchy there had a certain chaotic energy that I found invigorating. France, at least, was never boring. I couldn't say the same for Switzerland or Canada.

"What if I stole a kiss?" Florian leaned closer so he could whisper in my ear. "Would that be dating?"

"I'm not sure," I said, but I found myself wishing that Florian would stop flirting for a few minutes. The food on my plate was delicious and deserved my full attention. "Monsieur Girard is watching us pretty closely," I added, forking up another bite of *couscous*.

Florian glanced his way. "So he is. Then we'll just have to find a place where he can't see us."

"I just met you. Maybe I'm not ready to kiss you yet."

"You look to me like a girl who is ready to be kissed."

That was a bit presumptuous. "We'll see. In the meantime, I'm loving this *couscous* stuff."

Luckily, Florian didn't appear to be easily offended. "It's delicious," he agreed. "They always feed us well. That's why the same people come back year after year. For the wine too." Florian refilled my wine glass, which I had drained almost without noticing. There was a definite dearth of water during the harvest—it appeared to be assumed that we got all of our hydration though wine.

When the *couscous* plates were cleared, two enormous cheese plates were passed around the table.

Florian insisted I serve myself first.

"I take it you like cheese," he surmised, after watching me make several selections.

"You must love cheese too, being from Switzerland."

He passed the cheese platter on to the person on his other side. "Actually, I don't like cheese."

"What?"

He shrugged in apology.

"Never?"

"Never. My mother kept trying, but I've hated the taste since I was a baby."

I began to entertain grave doubts about Florian. I didn't think I could trust someone who didn't like cheese, let alone fall in love with them.

He took my hand under the table then and squeezed it. "It leaves my hands free to do other things."

Perhaps that sounded like a good idea for him, but I had plans to enjoy *my* cheese, and trying to eat it one-handed was decidedly awkward.

Still, his hand was warm. It felt nice to be touched. So, I ate my cheese with one hand while Florian held the other under the table and carried on a conversation in French with the guy beside him, perhaps for the benefit of Monsieur Girard, whose gaze was still riveted in our direction.

The cheese plates were whisked away shortly after I had finished. I wasn't sure who was working in the kitchen, but the service there would have put most five-star restaurants to shame.

Out of the kitchen came four huge glass bowls of what appeared to be chocolate mousse—yet another one of my favorite things—carried by two chattering, middle-aged women. Along with that were baskets of fine, lacy little biscuits shaped like rounded roof tiles and which Florian called tuiles.

"The old grandmother makes these every year," he said, "as well as the chocolate mousse. You will never taste better, I guarantee it."

After tasting both, I decided that I may be able to trust Florian a bit, even though he didn't like cheese. The wine kept flowing, even through the dessert course. It stopped only after the dessert was cleared away, when we were all served tiny cups of espresso so strong and bitter that I had to grit my teeth to get it down. It was perfect.

A few minutes later the cowbell rang again, so loud that I jumped.

Florian gave my hand a squeeze under the table and let it go. "Back to work." I suspected from his expression that he was considering sneaking a kiss as well, but luckily he glanced at Monsieur Girard first. He was still watching us.

The harvesters were lining up to use the various bathrooms in the house, and Florian came to find me as I was climbing into the back of the now-empty trailer attached to one of the tractors. He squeezed in beside me and, in one fluid movement, dipped down and dropped a quick kiss on my lips.

"Oh!" I breathed, surprised. Nobody around us seemed to have noticed or, if they had, found it anything unusual. I had been surprised, so the kiss was difficult to evaluate. The spontaneity was nice. No lightning bolt, but I was intrigued enough to investigate further. Besides, wasn't it wiser to enjoy what was right in front of me rather than saving myself for some fantasy man I'd concocted in my overactive imagination?

"I wanted to do that throughout the entire lunch," he said, and then he leaned in and whispered into my ear. "I'll try to get assigned to your row."

I chuckled. "We'll probably get yelled at again."

"It would be worth it," he said.

chapter eleven

Unfortunately, seconds after I'd been deposited back in the vineyards, the clouds opened and the vineyards became a pit of squishy, pale brown mud. The pouring rain put a distinct crimp in any planned dalliance. I regretted my decision to leave my rain pants back at the domaine yet again.

The festive mood of the morning shifted into something more subdued, reflecting the weather. Everyone worked hunched over, knees inches deep in the ever-increasing mud. We still drank from the bottles being passed up and down the vineyards—but I would have gladly traded them for a piping-hot coffee or a hot chocolate, as the damp cold penetrated my bones.

The afternoon dragged on forever. I began to count each clump of grapes that went into my bucket to pass the time. I counted to one hundred and then back again several times. I could not remember ever having felt that exhausted, even after the lunch at Mamy's house when I was freshly arrived from Canada. Madame Beaupre was right. Wine was the result of hard, backbreaking work.

Florian had not managed to be assigned to my row. In any case, all the carriers had their hoods drawn tightly around their heads and were pretty much indistinguishable from one another.

About three hours after I thought I couldn't go on any longer, the cowbell rang. I tried to stand up on shaking legs. I slipped and landed flat on my back in Burgundy's prized limestone-rich earth, which had been cultivated for winemaking since Roman times. The rain splattered on my cheeks and hair. I had no idea how I would manage another day. Even Florian wasn't enough of a draw for that.

I unstuck myself limb by limb and didn't even try to brush myself off before heading over to the vehicles—there was so much mud on everyone that nobody would even notice. I climbed back into the back of the tractor, my muscles protesting with every movement. Florian was nowhere to be seen, and I was too tired to look very hard for him.

I'd brought a change of clothes for myself, but we were all made to change in the utilitarian bathroom off the *cuverie*, which had only a sink and a toilet. I could hardly blame them—I wouldn't let people as muddy as me into the house either.

My fellow harvesters were silent, wrapped in their own thoughts or catching a catnap, sitting on the floor or in the few chairs that were scattered around the room, with their heads either in their hands or rested on one of their arms. I yawned. I wasn't sure I would be able to make it through dinner without falling asleep in my plate. I had already learned that while dinners were many things in Burgundy, one thing they were not was fast.

In the bathroom, I peeled off my soaking, muddy clothes and shoved them in my backpack. I'd have to do this laundry myself. I couldn't in all good conscience allow Madame Beaupre to undertake such a monumental task. My skin had taken on a distinct brownish tinge from the mud. I tried to wipe it off with a little mitten-like facecloth, but that only appeared to push it deeper into my pores. Grape harvesting wasn't quite as idyllic in reality as it had been in my daydreams. Which of my other French fantasies were, in fact, part delusion?

I gave up and slipped on a clean pair of jeans and a turquoise cotton sweater. I managed to wipe some of the mud off my face, though there was still a healthy quantity in my hair and on my scalp. I raked my hair back into another ponytail with my fingers.

I returned to the *cuverie*, where the grape pressing machine was humming and clunking. Monsieur Girard beckoned me over.

"So, Laura," he asked me in his bashful way, "how did you like your first day of grape harvesting?"

"I loved it." Granted, the aching muscles and the endless mud hadn't been part of my initial daydream, but I felt a deep satisfaction from being a part—albeit a small one—in this year's Burgundy vintage.

"Are you sore?" Monsieur Girard talked slowly and articulated his words with extreme care. If he had been speaking in English, it probably would have driven me bonkers, but in French, it was perfect.

"Very," I admitted.

He smiled shyly. "Just wait until tomorrow morning." He looked me up and down. "The mud is the sign of a good day's work. Burgundy's mud is prized around the world, you know."

"Then I must be extremely valuable at the moment," I said as I watched the churning of the press. "How do the grapes look?"

He peered in and then nodded back at me. "Winemakers never like to admit when they look good. We're an extremely suspicious lot, you know, but...they don't look bad, shall we say? I was worried about getting them in quickly when it began to rain. I had to assign a few more people to the sorting table, of course, but overall, I am satisfied. *Tiens*, do you want a taste?"

He went over to a nearby table where there was a tower of plastic glasses piled up. He plucked one off the top and then went to the front of the machine, where the freshly squeezed grape juice was pouring out the spout. He filled a glass about halfway and passed it to me.

"It will taste sour but will still give you—or it will give me—*de toute manière*, an idea of the personality of this year's vintage."

I took a sip. I fought to keep my lips from puckering from the sour taste. It was intriguing though. I took another.

"Are you interested in winemaking?' he asked, watching me.

"Of course," I said. "There is so much I want to learn. I know next to nothing."

"Really?"

"Why are you so surprised?"

He shrugged. "I wish I could get my children interested, but all this generation of Burgundian children want to do is move to Paris. They don't seem to care much about tradition or the land."

"How could you not be interested in wine?" I asked, more to myself than anyone else. I didn't know much then but was hungry to learn everything I could. To me, winemaking, especially in Burgundy, seemed as much an art as a science, and one imbued with century-old traditions and rituals. With wine, my love of gastronomy, creativity, and history were merging together to create what was fast becoming a true passion.

"When you come and live with us, I will teach you," he said. "It would be my pleasure."

And with that, he launched into a detailed explanation of the workings of the grape press. I tried hard to follow, but the language became highly technical, and he lost me. I kept nodding, trying to ignore my grumbling stomach and shaking legs as he waxed on about pumps and filters.

Finally, the clang of the cowbell made Monsieur break off his explanation. He looked disappointed but told me to go and find a place at the table. He said he still had one more load of grapes to see safely crushed before he could think about eating his dinner.

He caught my arm as I turned around to leave.

"That Swiss boy...Florian...is he bothering you?" My heart beat a bit faster in my chest.

"Florian?" I said. "No. We just enjoy talking to each other. I'm merely interested in learning about other European countries." I lied. No way was I admitting to enjoying Florian's attention.

"You are all of our responsibility," he reminded me. "You are young and *charmante*, not to mention very far from home."

"It's nothing like that," I assured him, feeling instant guilt at my duplicity.

"I have a daughter of my own," he said. "I am a protective father. My daughter would surely say overprotective, but I feel a responsibility as your host father to make sure that you stay out of trouble."

Florian was waiting for me at the table and waved me over. I didn't want to give Monsieur Girard grounds for any further suspicions, but then again, I *had* hopefully reassured him. This was a cultural exchange after all. I was learning about life in Switzerland and, well...getting a better feel for Swiss people...

I slid into the seat beside Florian.

"I thought he was never going to let you go!" he said.

"He was showing me how the grapes were pressed. He asked about you too. He reminded me about the 'No dating' rule."

"What did you tell him?" Florian's blue eyes widened with alarm.

"I told him you were teaching me interesting things about the customs of Switzerland."

Florian laughed and I joined in, struck by the irony of it all. In Canada, I had been free to date, yet not many guys had ever lined up for the opportunity.

A jovial, round-faced fellow on my other side was already hoisting a glass filled to the brim with what I recognized as kir to his mouth. "What is so funny?" he demanded in a heavy German accent.

"Nothing," I said. "We were just joking about the mud."

"It was terrible," he said. "I got so stuck at one point, Florian had to come and rescue me." He patted his rotund gut as if it was a beloved friend. "This makes it difficult to get up and down easily."

"You could drink less beer and lose it, Heinrich." Florian leaned across me, ensuring as much bodily contact as possible, and poked his German friend.

I wasn't sure if Heinrich was going to be offended, but he chuckled and patted his stomach again. "Why would I do such an absurd thing? I do not usually roll around in the mud like I did today, but I enjoy drinking beer and eating delicious food all year round. Now speak some reason, please, *mein Kumpel.*"

The dinner that night, Florian told me, was going to be *coq au vin.* "The grandmother makes it herself," he added. "Just like the tuiles and the chocolate mousse we had at lunch."

"How many years have you been coming here to do the harvest?" I asked.

"About four. My father buys quite a lot of wine from Girard every year."

The dinner progressed much as the lunch had, but even more leisurely. The wine being served warmed my blood and made me feel sparkling, despite the drying mud on my scalp and various unwashed parts of my body.

Florian and Henrich joked and flirted with me, and when I got up after the cheese course to use the washroom, Florian followed me. I was both alarmed and intrigued. The wine had caused a certain madness in my blood that made me want to be alone with him just to see what would happen. I was vaguely aware that Monsieur Girard's warning merely compounded that desire. There was nothing, I was discovering, that made me want to do something like having someone forbid it.

"I'll wait." Florian gestured at me to go in and use the bathroom.

There was a mirror inside, but the light bulb was dim. I tried to freshen my teeth with a finger dipped in water and to rub the most visible splotch of caked mud from my hairline. When I emerged, Florian took my hand and led me to a little closet-like space underneath the wooden staircase. It was pitch dark inside once he had shut the small door behind us and smelled as I imagined cobwebs would smell. He pulled me to him and smashed his mouth against mine in a kiss that was forceful and highly reminiscent of pinot noir and red wine sauce. I vastly preferred the light kiss he had surprised me with after lunch.

Part of me was caught up in the covertness of it all, but another part of me remained detached and observing. The latter part registered that Florian was either drunker than he appeared or simply not a very good kisser. His technique—if that was what one could call it—involved a wide-open mouth like a grouper fish and lots of tongue. His big teeth banged against mine. No lightning bolts. At one point, I actually began to worry about missing out on dessert.

There was a knock on the door. I jumped. *Oh God. Monsieur Girard?*

"*Merde*," the French word slipped out of my mouth and, for a flash, I was impressed with the fact that a French swearword came out of my mouth before an English one. If it was Monsieur Girard, would the Ursus Club send me back to Canada? All of a sudden, I was furious with myself. Those sloppy Swiss kisses hadn't been worth it.

"Who do you think it is?" Florian whispered.

"I have no idea," I hissed. "Be quiet."

Maybe the person knocking would believe that there was no one inside and go away.

We waited, barely touching now.

The door creaked open and there stood the wizened grandmother, the very one responsible for the *coq au vin* and *mousse au chocolat*. She looked about a thousand years old, but her eyes were a bright amber and sharp enough to cut diamonds. "You're missing the *tarte aux fraises*," she said calmly.

"We were just—" Florian began in French.

"Do you honestly believe that you are the first people who have had the idea of using this closet during the *vendanges*?"

I thought about it. "Uh...*non*."

She narrowed her eyes at Florian. "As a matter of fact, *jeune homme*, I remember catching you in this closet last year. I have been keeping an eye on you. I do not think I should allow you to get this *petite Canadienne* into trouble... She just arrived freshly off the airplane." She shooed Florian away with an imperious flick of her claw-like hand. He gave my arm a quick squeeze and scuttled off.

Coward.

This left me caught in the impenetrable net of her gaze. I stumbled over words of apology in French, making a complete mull of it. She sputtered her lips not so much with disgust as with impatience. "You are seventeen," she said. "Of course I was going to find you in here with a man. Now go. Eat your dessert."

I scurried around her imperious finger and back to the table. Florian was already digging into the tart, and I could tell he was purposely not looking at me as I sat down. Monsieur Girard, on the other hand, most definitely was. I could feel my face burn.

A wave of despair washed over me. *Risking my year here for a few terrible kisses was epically stupid.* Why had I done it? I despaired yet again that no man would ever live up to my imagination. Maybe I had just watched too many romantic comedies and read too many romance novels. Was there a man out there who was worth breaking the rules for? I was starting to entertain serious doubts.

chapter twelve

It was inevitable, perhaps, that I came down with a humdinger of a cold after my weekend grape harvesting. Once I told Florian that I was simply not willing to take the risk of getting into trouble with my host families or the Ursus, or, God forbid, of being sent back to Canada, things between us cooled off.

In the end, I met with a few other wine harvesters and made some new friends, ate delicious food, drank copious quantities of wine, and basically had a thoroughly Burgundian experience.

However, I woke up Monday morning with what felt like razor blades in my throat and my nostrils pouring like an open faucet.

Madame Beaupre's eyes opened wide when I dragged myself down for breakfast. "*Ma puce*!" she exclaimed. "I should have known. Sophie gets a terrible cold every year after the harvest."

"I'm fine," I reassured her, my nose honking.

"No, you're not!" She felt my forehead. Her fingers felt cool and lovely. "You've got a fever. You're not going to school."

"I'll just take some aspirin," I said, giving the word a French spin and hoping she would understand what I meant.

"You are going straight up to bed. I am calling the doctor."

"You don't need to do that. I'm fine." Doctors always made me nervous, and a *foreign* doctor added a whole new level of anxiety.

"No arguments." She pointed upstairs. "*Allez, ma puce*!"

I made my way back upstairs and collapsed into bed. I'd been brought up to believe that colds are just inconveniences one soldiers through. One could drink a bit more orange juice than usual or pop a few aspirin, but a mere cold shouldn't stop anybody from going to school or work. That would be...wimpy. Un-Canadian. We all like to think of ourselves as tough lumberjacks. As I lay in the bed, though, I noted that my body did seem to want to be horizontal instead of vertical.

I dozed off and was awakened by my bedroom door opening.

"*Comment ça va, ma puce*?" Madame asked, hovering over me. She had brought me a mug of something hot that smelled like lemons.

"*Ça va*," I said.

She moved farther into the room, revealing a man in a black suit and tie behind her, who was holding a black leather doctor's bag as if he had stepped straight out of a Dickens novel. Julien brought up the rear.

My heart skipped a beat. A foreign doctor. He was probably going to want to give me a bunch of shots or do other weird, painful stuff. Anyway, what was he doing there? *Since when did doctors still make house calls*?

I sat up in bed and fought off a wave of dizziness. The doctor strode over to my side and strapped on a blood pressure cuff before I could formulate a protest. I scrambled to remember Grade 10 Biology to think if blood pressure was even impacted by a cold.

He listened to my chest and back with his stethoscope, peered down my throat and in my ears and up my nostrils, and instructed me to cough, via Julien, who acted as translator. I waited nervously for the verdict, but instead he extracted his prescription pad from his bag and wrote on it for what seemed like an unusually long time, filling up several squares of paper.

"Julien," Madame Beaupre instructed, "can you go to the pharmacy and pick up these medicines for Laura?"

"There's no need," I said, in English to Julien. "I'm sure I don't need any medicine. I'll be fine."

"Don't be silly," Julien said, not even bothering to translate this for his mother and the doctor. "Of course you need medicine. How else are you going to get better?"

The doctor patted me kindly on the head and said something in French that sounded reassuring, although I had no idea what it was.

"Go back to sleep," Julien instructed. "When you wake up, I'll have your medicine ready for you."

After they left, I lay back in bed but couldn't fall asleep right away. What were they going to get at the pharmacy? Something foreign, no doubt. For the first time since arriving, I longed for my own bedroom and my own bed and my own bottle of extra strength Tylenol. It wasn't homesickness exactly...more a longing for everything to be familiar and comfortable until I felt better. I loved France, but I had been thrown into unfamiliar situations on a daily basis since my arrival. Most of the time, I found that exhilarating, but in my current state it just seemed more than I could cope with.

I reached over for my pocket dictionary that was sitting on my bedside table. Madame Beaupre kept calling me "*ma puce.*" What could that mean? I flipped through the pages in the French section and found the word. "*Ma puce*" means "my flea." *That* was an endearment? She also called me *mon chou* sometimes, so I went to that word. It means "my cabbage." I closed my eyes, trying to fight off nightmares about what kind of strange medicine they would prescribe me in a country where people used "flea" and "cabbage" as terms of endearment.

I woke up with a grumbling stomach. I checked my watch. Ten minutes until noon. I staggered downstairs, feeling rested, but still sick. Julien and Madame Beaupre were in the kitchen making lunch.

"*Enfin,*" Madame said when she saw me. "I'm so glad you slept. Julien has all your *médicaments.*"

My medications? As in plural?

I watched in awe as Julien plunked two very large, white, plastic *pharmacie* bags on the kitchen table.

"I will explain everything to you," he said.

"Great," I replied, thanking God he'd chosen to speak English.

He opened the bags and poured their contents on the kitchen counter. The array of bottles, or bottles and boxes, made me begin to wonder if Julien hadn't in fact brought the entire pharmacy to me.

"Those can't all possibly be for me," I said.

"What? Do you not take medicine in Canada?

"Not this much!"

"What do you do when you get sick?"

"With a cold?" I shrugged. "I don't know...nothing, I guess. Just wait until it passes."

Julien stared at me, incomprehension coloring every finely carved feature on his face. "That seems silly. Why feel sick when you can use medicines to feel better?" I remembered his parallel comment from my first meal *chez* les Beaupre. *Why would anyone bother eating food that wasn't delicious*? I wondered if we North Americans weren't indeed making life much harder for ourselves than necessary.

Julien had already launched into his explanation. There were three cough syrups: one for daytime, one for the evening, and one for night-time.

He held up the biggest bottle. "Do you know what this one is made out of?" he asked.

"No." Something from the curve of his sculpted lips told me I didn't want to know.

"Snail slime!"

Madame must have seen my eyes widen in horror and chided Julien.

"That is not the only ingredient," he said, "but it is one of them. You see, it is called 'Helexia' and 'Helix' is—"

"Latin for snail," I finished for him.

"Bravo! Did you take Latin in school?"

"No. I just read a lot...but I'm not drinking snail slime." Just then, I was caught out by an untimely coughing jag.

"It is very effective. You must take it," Julien said, brooking no opposition. He continued to go through the medications like a collection of greatest hits. He reminisced about ones that had been particularly helpful and others that had not seemed to do a lick of good at the time but in the end had been a wise decision to prescribe on the doctor's part. This affection for both doctors and medicine was novel for me.

I wondered how I would ever remember to take such a mind-spinning array of pills and potions. Julien opened a long, flat box and drew out some pills that I was supposed to take three times a day. They were huge, like regular pills on steroids, and were shaped like torpedoes.

"I'll never be able to swallow those!" I protested. "I'll choke."

Julien blushed. It was the first time I had ever seen him do so. "They are not for swallowing."

I stared at him in confusion. "How am I supposed to take them?"

"They're suppositories."

My blood ran cold. "I've never taken a suppository in my life," I said. "We don't do that in Canada." What sort of barbaric country had I come to?

"I will drink the snail slime," I bargained. "But there's no way I'm using suppositories."

"Hmmmmmm." Julien shared the problem with Madame Beaupre and they talked in rapid-fire French for several minutes. I gleaned that the French word for "suppository" was "*suppositoire.*" This piece of knowledge, it seemed, could come in handy in France. *Non suppositoires. Non suppositoires*, I practiced in my head.

Julien finally turned back to me. "We think you can probably do without those," he said.

"I *will* be doing without those."

We sat down for a lunch of quiche Lorraine with a lovely green salad and a type of chocolate pudding called Danette for dessert. It was the one food, Madame said, Sophie always wanted to eat when she was sick. I could find no fault with that program.

Then they mixed and coaxed a vast array of medicines, including the cough syrup with the snail slime, down my gullet and ordered me back to bed.

I fell into a deep sleep until dinner. Maybe the snail slime worked, or maybe it was just the fear of those suppositories.

chapter thirteen

When I finally returned to school on Wednesday, I was touched that Sandrine and her gang—even the brawny Thibaut—seemed to have noticed I had been away.

I told them as much as I could about the grape harvest, and as they were mostly from winemaking families and had been doing it all weekend as well, we had a satisfying commiseration about the epic mud.

The next week, as we gave each other the obligatory *bises* outside the school doors in the morning, Sandrine asked me if I wanted to go out to a café with her during lunch instead of to the cafeteria.

"We will grab a *jambon beurre*," she said.

"What's a *jambon beurre*?" I asked.

"It's a sandwich. You know, ham and butter on a piece of baguette."

I didn't know actually, but it sounded good.

"Which café do you want to go to?" I asked, delighted that my dream of hanging out in the cafés of France was finally about to come true.

"There's a café called Le Square." She pointed around the ring road that passed in front of the school. "A lot of kids from the public high school, Clos Maire, hang out there. I've arranged to meet my friend Stéphanie. I've told her about you."

"Does she go to Clos Maire?"

Sandrine nodded and dropped her cigarette as the school doors opened and ground it out with the heel of her leather boot. "She's from the same village as me. Villers-la-Faye. We've known each other forever. We try to meet up at Le Square for lunch at least once a week."

"Villers-la-Faye?" I remembered that village. "I've been there before."

"You have?" Sandrine's eyebrows flew up. "Are you sure?"

"Yes. Why?"

"There are many people who live in Beaune who have never been to Villers-la-Faye. They think it's too out of the way. Not important."

"How far away is it?" Granted, we had been driving at Monsieur Beaupre's habitual speed the night we had been there, but I didn't remember it being very far.

"About ten minutes from Beaune."

I laughed. "That's funny. The university I will be going to next year in Montreal is a six-hour plane ride from my home in Victoria."

"Really? And it's still in the same country?"

I nodded. "I guess the whole concept of distance is different for us Canadians. I went to a restaurant in Villers-la-Faye, and I ate snails for the first time in my life."

Sandrine's surprised expression did not abate one iota. "*Quoi*? You never ate snails before?"

"No."

"Now *that's* crazy."

I remembered the group of young people in the road by the brown gate across from the bakery. I examined Sandrine more closely to see if I could remember her being there that night. No. Still, it was an interesting coincidence, her being from Villers-la-Faye.

"I have to get to class," Sandrine said. "I'll meet you at the gates at lunch."

"*Super*." I now pronounced this word the French way and found it to be a multi-purpose way of expressing agreement or pleasure.

I strolled to my first class, *philosophie*—mandatory for all students—feeling pleased. Here I was, not only able to make plans in my stilted French but able to make plans to hang out in a café with actual French people my age.

At lunch I hurried out of my science class and toward the heavy wooden doors that let the students in and out of the walled schoolyard. There was quite a crowd of older students huddled around, also waiting to leave.

"Do you have your student card?" Sandrine asked. She had already lit a cigarette, as had most of the people in the crowd.

I extracted the card from my backpack. "*Oui.*"

"You have to show it to le Dragon."

"Who?"

Sandrine rolled her eyes. "The woman who controls the doors. We all call her le Dragon. She's evil."

I laughed.

"I'm not kidding," Sandrine said, scowling.

Just then a woman with shellacked brown hair and dark eyes reminiscent of a shark stalked up to the doors with a large ring of ancient, long-handled keys jingling around her wrist. The crowd of smoking students parted for her like the Red Sea for Moses. She narrowed her eyes, as if she hated us all.

There is nothing I dislike more than people who abuse positions of authority, and it looked as though I had a prime example in front of me.

"Don't smile at her," Sandrine warned. "It will just make her angrier."

"I smile at everybody," I hissed back.

"I know," Sandrine whispered back. "I've been meaning to talk to you about that. It makes you seem a bit simple, or demented."

I shrugged. "It's the Canadian way. I can't help it."

It was our turn. Sandrine showed her card to le Dragon. Le Dragon took her time inspecting it, then imperiously shooed Sandrine on her way. Sandrine motioned at me to show my card. I did. Le Dragon inspected me and—dammit—I caught myself smiling at her. She looked down her nose at my card. "You are not allowed out," she said, with what looked like an immensely satisfied smirk.

"What?" I asked. "Of course I am. I'm almost eighteen."

Sandrine was now on the other side of the door, wildly motioning at me to shut up.

"You don't have the permission square ticked on your card." Le Dragon thrust it back into my hand. "You must stay inside the school during the school day. Go away."

Rage erupted inside me. I would not be treated like a five-year-old, even though I might speak French like one. I stood my ground. "There must be some mistake."

"There is no mistake," she said, "except for the fact that you are still standing here in front of me. Go to the *cantine*."

I glanced at Sandrine, who was staring at me with wide eyes now. "You go ahead," I called over to her. "I'll get this fixed tonight and we can go some other time. Sorry."

"Move!" le Dragon shouted at me.

I stared at her and then, with a defiant toss of my head, turned around and stalked back toward the *cantine*, my blood boiling. I flopped down in a chair across from Thibaut. His other friends were chattering away about an upcoming history test.

"What's wrong?" he asked. "I was wondering where you were."

I told him the saga of le Dragon as best as I could, and he laughed. "She's a witch," he said. "You don't want to cross her."

I dug my fork into the *tabouleh* salad that had just been placed in front of me. "*She* does not want to cross me. Trust *me* on that."

Thibaut's fork froze midair. "Did you really just say that?"

"Yes," I said darkly, still possessed by righteous anger. "You'll see."

I stared at Thibaut then, not smiling for once. Nothing gets me riled up like injustice, especially injustice created wantonly and willfully by tyrants like le Dragon. I am usually an easy-going person, but if I feel that I or somebody I care about is being wronged, I transform into the most stubborn person in the universe.

He smiled at me then, a slow, sincere smile as if he was actually seeing me for the first time. "*Ma petite Canadienne*," he said, "I do believe that I may have underestimated you."

"You wouldn't be the first."

That night I explained my dilemma to Madame Beaupre, who blamed herself for not signing the correct permission form that first morning at school.

"There were so many papers," I reassured her. "It would be a miracle if you even knew what you were signing."

"I didn't exactly," she admitted. "There *were* quite a few."

The next morning, she came back into the school with me and explained the problem to the secretary at the front office. Within minutes, le Dragon was there, staring us both down with her predatory eyes.

Madame Beaupre turned up her considerable charm to full voltage, but for the first time ever it failed. It was as if le Dragon was her kryptonite—and le Dragon kept insisting that nothing short of written permission from my parents back in Canada would suffice to enable her to tick that permission box on my school card. I could tell that she had no intention of *ever* letting me out of that gate during the school day.

"*Mais, c'est ridicule*," Madame Beaupre protested. "We are acting as Laura's guardians during her time in France, we and her other Ursus host families."

"Do you have the paperwork to prove it?" demanded le Dragon.

"Well...not exactly, but—"

"I'm late for a meeting," le Dragon said, then turned on her heel and stalked off.

"Well!" Madame Beaupre exclaimed. "Of all the ——." Madame Beaupre used one of the extremely rude words that Thibaut had tricked me into saying at the beginning of the year.

I never thought I would hear something so vulgar come out of her exquisite mouth. She turned to me, guilt stealing over her features. "I'm so sorry, *ma puce*."

"Thank you for trying. I wasn't expecting it to be easy. I'll phone my parents tomorrow."

"That woman!"

"It's fine," I said. "I'll figure out a way."

She watched the receding figure of le Dragon walking across the courtyard.

"I'm not so sure," she said. "She is a disagreeable woman, and she has taken a disliking to you."

"Yes," I agreed.

"But how could anyone not love you?" she asked. "You are charming."

The next morning before going to school, I called my parents and asked them to mail me a letter via priority mail giving me permission to leave the school grounds during the school day. They were astounded that the school would not just allow soon-to-be-eighteen-year-old students free reign during their spare time, but agreed to do so right away. So, high school students were allowed to smoke with abandon all over the school grounds but weren't allowed out in a picturesque, crimeless, little winemaking town with a population of 20,000 people? It made no sense.

A few days later, during which time I had actually celebrated my eighteenth birthday with a delicious meal and my favorite pastries *chez* les Beaupre, Sandrine asked me if I could go to Le Square with her again. "Do you have your permission yet?" she asked. "I told Stéphanie about your run-in with le Dragon, and she wants to meet you even more now."

"Soon," I said. "Very soon."

"I'm going away with Stéphanie and her older brother, Franck, next weekend," Sandrine said, looking pleased. I wouldn't have been able to detect the shine in her eyes and slight quirk of her upper lip during my first few weeks at Saint Coeur, but I could now.

"Where?" I asked, feeling a tug of jealousy. I would love to be planning fun weekends away with my friends, but for the moment, I couldn't even leave the grounds of the school.

"A town up in Northern Burgundy. We're going to celebrate the arrival of their cousin's baby. Another friend of ours, Olivier, is coming too, and a couple of Stéph and Franck's other cousins will be there. It's going to be *super.*"

Again, I marveled that the word "super" sounded so much cooler and nonchalant in French. "How old is her brother?" I asked, more to be polite than because I was really interested.

"He's twenty-three," Sandrine said, and her upper lip twitched a bit. "Franck is *génial.*"

I had learned the day before that in French the word does not mean "genial" as it does in English but rather "awesome." "Cool." "Amazing."

"He's doing his military service this year in Dijon with the Air Force," she continued. "You'll have to meet him too."

"Sure," I agreed, absent-mindedly, but I was already fantasizing about my moment of triumph when I showed le Dragon the letter from my parents. I would take such pleasure in waltzing in and out of that stupid wooden door she guarded like a sentry at a prisoner-of-war camp.

The letter from my parents arrived a few days later, and I brought it in first thing in the morning. Le Dragon took it from me with an expression of distaste, as if it was sprinkled with arsenic.

Her eyes roved over the text, and within a few seconds she passed it back to me. "This is not acceptable," she said. "It is not in French."

"Of course it's not in French," I said. "My parents speak only English."

"It needs to be in French," she said, her eyes glittering.

"What does it matter?" I protested. "You wanted a letter of permission to have on file. Here it is."

She leaned closer to me and said under her breath. "This letter is not acceptable, Mademoiselle Bradbury. That is my final word."

"It isn't mine," I snapped, and stormed off. Was there anyone I could appeal to above le Dragon? From what I could tell, she seemed to be in complete control of the gates, answerable to no one.

My next class was English. The teacher had put a new seating plan into place in an attempt to wrest control of his class from rowdies such as Thibaut. I was, I saw, sharing a double desk with that very miscreant.

"I'm going to kill her," I muttered in English as I sat down beside him.

"Kill who?" he asked in French.

"Le Dragon."

"Ah," he said, looking amused. "Rumor has it that she has taken a disliking to a certain little *Canadienne*."

"Rumor would be true." I took my textbook out of my bag and banged it down on the wooden desktop. We were reviewing contractions that day, which meant I could spend the entire class concocting revenge scenarios, as I already grasped English contractions better than the teacher.

Thibaut laughed and then watched me with a thoughtful expression as I mentally flipped through various outrageous—but highly satisfying—methods of thwarting le Dragon.

"You are even prettier when you are furious," he observed.

"What!?" I looked at him, startled and annoyed. "Shut up, Thibaut." In the previous week or so, I had adopted the same callous treatment Sandrine doled out to the boys in our gang, especially to Thibaut.

Thibaut's eyebrows flew up. I didn't say it to be mean, but couldn't he see that I was in no mood for flirting? Besides, since when was he interested in flirting with *me*? Up to then, all Thibaut had seemed interested in was tricking and baiting me.

"You mean you wouldn't go out with me if I asked?" he asked.

I turned and subjected him to a frank inspection—the exact kind that he gave me, often. He was tall and muscular, with light brown eyes and a contagious smile. He wasn't handsome exactly, or even cute, but he had charisma, buckets of it actually. There was a certain chemical fizz between the two of us, especially when we were bickering, which was increasingly often now that my French was improving. Still, I didn't think I would go out with him given his reputation. Sandrine had warned me that he was a notorious womanizer, and I had no intention of falling into his toils.

My inspection appeared to unnerve him. Perhaps not many girls served him up his own sauce, though I couldn't imagine why.

"No, I wouldn't," I concluded. From what I knew of Thibaut so far, his emotions didn't run deep enough for me to fret about his reaction.

The teacher walked in, and I turned to the front of the room to listen to his instructions.

"Laura," Thibaut hissed at me after I had ignored him for a few minutes, "I'm hurt."

I stared at him, skeptical. "You'll get over it." I patted his arm.

"Why won't you go out with me?"

"I'm not even sure I like you even as a friend," I said. "Besides, you're not my type."

"What is your type?"

"Thibaut!" The teacher pointed his wooden pointer at my deskmate. "Mademoiselle Bradbury can afford to be distracted in this class, but given your last few test scores, you cannot. Pay attention!"

I snorted, and Thibaut cast me a hurt look. Sandrine, a few desks ahead of us, turned around, and we shared a satisfied look. High school boys in France could dish it out but, just like those back in Canada, they couldn't take it.

At the *cantine*, Sandrine caught me and pulled me down in the chair beside her. "What was going on with you and Thibaut in English?"

"Nothing. He was just asking me stupid questions."

"Such as?"

"Would I go out with him if he asked, that sort of thing..."

Sandrine shot Thibaut, who was seated a little farther down the table, a murderous look. "What did you say?"

"I said no! What did you think I'd say?"

"Thank God. Trust me, you should stay away from him. He's a fun friend but—"

"Don't worry. We have his type in Canada," I said. "A lot of them, as a matter of fact. I'm not naïve."

"Good. Did you get your permission? Can I finally take you to Le Square with me?"

I shook my head. "She turned me down again because my parents' letter wasn't in French. Can you believe that?"

Sandrine frowned. "Of her? Yes. You shouldn't have challenged her like that. She's taken one of her dislikings to you. Honestly, I don't think you'll ever be able to get the permission now."

"I won't stop until I do."

Sandrine examined me to see if I was serious.

"I'm stubborn," I added. "In case you hadn't figured that out already."

Sandrine nodded. "I'm stubborn too. Like a donkey, my family always says."

I reached down to take my parents' letter out of my backpack. "Can you help me translate this into French?"

"If you tell me what it says."

Sandrine took out a pen, and half an hour later we had composed an elegant, forceful letter in French. That night, I dictated it over the phone to my parents and instructed them to send it immediately.

I received it a week and a bit later. On the bus on the way to school, I admired the vineyards that were turning brilliant shades of yellow, scarlet, and orange, while daydreaming of finally being able to best le Dragon and all of her ridiculous rules.

Back in Canada, I was not the type of student that ever butted up against the teachers in any way. There in France, though, I refused to let a despot steal the dream of wasting time at French cafés from me. It was simply too important. If she hated me for it...too bad. I was going back to Canada at the end of the year anyway.

The first thing I did when I got to the school was go to the office, which I now thought of as le Dragon's lair. She was there, chastising a beleaguered student about something. She eyed me with disfavor. "You again?"

"I have the letter here from my parents. In French."

She pursed her already tight lips and jerked her arm at me to sit down. Her office was small and shabby, and had a particularly bloody painting of Jesus impaled on the cross hanging on the wall. I suspected this *chef-d'oeuvre* came from her personal art collection.

I waited as she perused the letter, savoring my moment of triumph. She thrust it back to me. "I cannot accept this."

"What do you mean?" I demanded, slipping into the informal "*tu*" form as I did whenever I got upset.

"This letter is not from France, so it needs to be stamped by a notary."

"Are you joking?" I said. Luckily, I had learned this expression from Sandrine the day before. I used the "*tu*" form again, but this time deliberately as an insult. I was learning.

Just then, the head nun popped her head in the office to ask le Dragon a question. She stopped mid-sentence, though, as she must have noticed the bristling atmosphere or that le Dragon and I were sitting opposite each other like a couple of gunslingers readying for a shoot-out.

"Excuse me." I turned to the head nun and then passed her my letter. "Could you please read this?"

I then launched into the best explanation I could manage of my battle to leave the school grounds. When I was done, the head nun didn't chastise le Dragon as I was hoping, but she did ask me for my student card. I extracted it from my backpack and gave it to her. She found a pen somewhere in the folds of her voluminous robe and ticked off the box that allowed me to leave the school during the day.

"*Merci*," I said, casting a triumphant look at my nemesis. "Now that wasn't so difficult..."

"*Oui*," the nun said. "Now please go to class. We have some things to discuss here."

I walked out but couldn't resist looking over my shoulder. Le Dragon was staring at me with her lips tightly pressed together. I had won this battle, but she clearly intended for there to be a war.

chapter fourteen

That Saturday, Julien had departed to his school in Switzerland, where he was being taught how to manage fancy hotels. We all missed him, even Biscotte, who kept nudging me for extra pats and scratches.

Monsieur Beaupre offered to take me on a bike ride in the vineyards. I longed for my friends at school, especially Sandrine, to call me up and arrange to do something together to fill my weekends. French teenagers, though, seemed to be slow off the mark in making these kinds of overtures. I had heard that friendships in France took much longer to build, but once they were built, they were for life. That was all fine and dandy, but I wanted someone to hang out with on the weekends *tout de suite*. Still, now that I had permission to go to Le Square with Sandrine, I entertained a hope of creating a social life for myself in Burgundy. Maybe I just needed to be patient. *Ugh! Not one of my strengths.*

I set out on Madame Beaupre's bike. I was a bit wobbly—she was several inches taller than I was. Still, very quickly Monsieur led me off the main streets of Nuits-Saint-Georges and onto the rocky paths that wove their way through the vineyards. The ground was ochre, and because it had barely rained since the harvest, clouds of red dust billowed behind us.

I had a hard time not stopping every few minutes to take photos of the vineyards' leaves. Every shade of yellow, scarlet, and orange was represented in every possible combination. It was sublime.

"That is one of the reasons why this department is called the Côte d'Or," he said. "Because of the golden vineyards in the fall. Golden Coast. Also," he added mischievously, "some say it is because of all the wealth generated by the wine industry."

Indeed, everything around us looked ancient but also extremely well tended.

"Everything was late this year," he said as we rode on. "The cold spring and summer delayed the vines by over a month. Usually they are this color far earlier."

We cycled along until we got to an unassuming rock wall with Romanée-Conti carved into a rock lintel.

"Do you know what this is?" he asked.

"A vineyard?" I asked.

"Not just any vineyard." Monsieur Beaupre got off his bike, and I got off mine. We leaned them against the wall, and he motioned me to follow him inside the rock walls. "This is the vineyard that produces the most expensive wine in the world."

"Really?" It was hard to believe. There was nobody around—no guards, no gates, no cameras. How could the most valuable grapes in the world be left alone like this, completely unprotected?

"Do you want to taste a grape?" he asked, looking more like a naughty seven-year-old boy than a suave business executive.

"Is that allowed?"

"Not really," he admitted, "but we French never met a rule that we don't long to break. Do you want me to take a picture of you eating it?"

"Ah...*yes*!" It would be an amazing souvenir, and the fact that it was slightly illicit made it even better.

He picked one of the few unharvested grapes on the vine. It was a little shriveled looking, but I wasn't going to turn my nose up at one of the world's most valued grapes.

I passed him my camera, and he positioned me beside the vine and instructed me when to eat the grape. It was definitely a little sour and perhaps had an aftertaste of mold, but all in all, it was quite edible. He snapped several pictures, and I took the camera back and we continued on our way. Soon, a huge stone building that was too boxy to be a castle, but far too large and majestic-looking to be a house, loomed in the distance.

"What's that?" It didn't appear to be part of any village but rose, solitary, from among the carpet of vineyards.

"That?" he said. "That is Clos de Vougeot!"

I stared at him blankly.

"You don't know Clos de Vougeot? You haven't heard of it back in Canada?"

"*Non.*" French people often think that things that are famous there, such as Nuits-Saint-Georges' bell tower or the French singers that Julien would watch on his French variety shows, are famous all the world over. I always felt bad disillusioning them on this front. "I don't think so."

"It is the heart of winemaking in Burgundy," he exclaimed with a grand hand gesture. "In fact, it is the birthplace of winemaking. It was built by Cistercian monks in the twelfth century when they began to cultivate wine here. We'll bring you back to visit. I cannot believe we have not done that already."

"I'd like that." The sun warmed my shoulders, and I breathed in that unique scent of limestone and mineral that penetrated all of the Côte d'Or, but especially the vineyards and the cellars.

We rode on and cycled underneath the imposing stone gates of the Clos de Vougeot. The building was massive up close—huge swaths of golden stone anchored by blocky, incredibly solid-looking, angular towers on its four sides.

Further on, a stone village appeared in the distance. "Which village is that?" I asked.

"Vosne-Romanée," Monsieur Beaupre said. "That's where one of my favorite winemakers lives. *Tiens!* Let's go for a wine tasting!"

The village was stunning. Late-blooming geraniums punctuated the golden stonework of the houses and stone crosses dotted the streets.

Monsieur Beaupre pulled his bike up in front of a rambling house. "Here we are," he said. "We'll go straight into *la cuverie*. I know Henri well."

He opened two heavy doors in the barn-like building attached to the main house. There were four huge wooden vats soaring about twenty-five feet off the ground. The air was heady and instantly made me feel drunk.

"Don't breathe too deeply," Monsieur Beaupre advised.

"What's that smell?"

"Macerating grapes. They give off a lot of carbon dioxide. Sometimes enough to make a person pass out, or worse."

"Henri?" Monsieur Beaupre called. "Henri? Are you in here?"

A man's faint voice called back. "Here! I'm in here!"

We both peered around the *cuverie* but saw no sign of the elusive Henri.

"Where?" Monsieur Beaupre shouted.

"*Dans la cuve*," the man responded after a slight pause. "Swimming."

"Swimming?" I looked to Monsieur Beaupre for an explanation, but he just grinned.

"Climb up the ladder!" the voice instructed.

Monsieur Beaupre climbed up a wooden ladder that was hooked on the side of the second vat.

"There you are!" he exclaimed when he got to the top. "I've brought our young Canadian who is staying with us. Can she come up to see you? Are you wearing a bathing suit this time at least?"

"Of course not!" Henri's voice carried down. "But look at the color of these grapes. She won't be able to see anything anyway."

So, Henri was actually *inside* the vat? The air was making me feel light-headed.

Monsieur Beaupre climbed down and told me to go up. "You'll see a surprise inside the *cuve*!" he said, smiling like the cat who had eaten the canary.

I climbed slowly, as my arms and legs didn't seem to be obeying my brain's commands well. At the top, I saw a bare-chested man, whose skin up to his neck was stained a lurid purple. He was moving his arms around in half circles, treading water…or rather grape juice.

"*Allô*!" he said, cheerfully. "So, you are the *Canadienne* I have been hearing about!"

"Yes." I thought I could dispense with the traditional *bises* in this instance, as either I would have to get into the vat to kiss him or he would have to clamber out to reach me. Was he really naked?

"Can you tell me exactly what you're doing?" I asked.

"I'm mixing the grapes," he said. "Punching it down. Some winemakers do it with wooden paddles, but this is the way my father did it and the way that my grandfather did it. I don't think those paddles do as good a job as human legs and arms.

"So, you're swimming in there?"

"Yes."

The smell was even stronger right above the *cuve*. "Aren't you worried you might—you know—pass out, and drown?"

His purple shoulders shrugged. "It happens. Almost every year a winemaker dies from that in France. As for me, I seem to be immune to it. I love the smell. Besides, if I'm going to die, what better way for a winemaker to go than in a *cuve* of his own delicious grapes? Especially in what is turning out to be such a fine vintage!"

"That's a good point."

"Go back down," he instructed. "I'll come. Avert your eyes if you don't want to see me naked, not to mention extremely purple."

I followed his instructions, so hastily that I slipped on the second-to-bottom rung and caught myself just before falling to the concrete floor.

"He's coming," I said to Monsieur Beaupre, turning my back to the vat.

"Go on to the *caveau*!" Henri's voice was louder now. He must be climbing out. "You know where it is!"

"Let's go." Monsieur Beaupre cocked his head for me to follow him and led me through a few passageways until we got to a proper vaulted stone wine cellar that was filled as far as the eye could see with barrels.

"Wow," I said.

"Henri is perhaps a bit eccentric," Monsieur Beaupre said, "but his wine is truly second to none."

"Was that true what he said about winemakers dying every year in their *cuveries* and their vats?"

"Oh yes." Monsieur Beaupre settled on one of five stools that were set around an upended barrel, which made a perfect table. Standing on top were several bottles of unlabeled wine, made distinguishable one from the other in the dim light only by chalk letters and numbers written directly on the green-yellow glass.

"I often worry about Henri drowning in one of his vats while he is mixing his grapes. He should at least have someone watching him so that if he passes out from the fumes he could get immediate help. He will not listen though. He is stubborn that way."

I thought of something that had been niggling my mind ever since we had located Henri. "Is it...you know...hygienic for a person to swim in wine people are eventually going to drink?"

Henri, even through his purple-ness, had displayed an impressive mat of curly chest hair. Were stray bits of body hair from...well...*everywhere* on Henri's body mixed in with his wine? I eyed the bottles in front of me with trepidation.

Monsieur Beaupre burst out laughing. He was still laughing when Henri appeared, now dressed in jeans and a sweatshirt that had the words "Saint Tropez" emblazoned across its front in neon pink. His neck and hands were still purple.

"Henri," Monsieur Beaupre began, "Laura is concerned about the cleanliness of swimming in the vats."

"Not concerned exactly." I lied. "More...curious."

Henri picked up three glasses from the table and turned them so that they were right side up. He made a dismissive sign with his hand. "Pfffssssssssssst. All the alcohol ensures that everything is nice and sterile. Besides, we filter the juice before we put it in the barrels."

I hoped it was a very fine-meshed filter. As he poured us each a first glass of wine, I somehow wasn't looking forward to tasting it as much as I usually did.

My reticence disappeared by the third glass. His wine was truly extraordinary. I thought I tasted a strong flavor of cassis, but this was balanced by cherry notes and a grounding earthiness. So what if a little pubic hair sneaked through? It wasn't the end of the world.

By the time Monsieur Beaupre and I struck out on our bicycles after the wine tasting, Henri was stripping down to hop into another vat.

On the way home, neither of us was riding too steadily. We laughed a lot, and Monsieur Beaupre waxed poetic about the myriad of bottles of wine he had ordered, which Henri had promised to deliver to the house within a few days.

Madame Beaupre took stock of us when we arrived in the doorway and suggested that we both sit down at the kitchen table and enjoy a nice glass of coffee.

Monsieur Beaupre clutched the doorjamb for support. "That is perhaps a good idea."

I could tell Madame Beaupre was torn between wanting to get annoyed at her husband and trying not to laugh. "I take it the wine tasting went well?" she said, taking two little glasses from the cupboard. She filled them with coffee, then set them in front of us.

"It was fascinating!" I gushed. "Henri was swimming in one of his vats when we got there. I heard stories about people stomping on grapes in the olden days, but I had no idea that people actually still did that. In Canada when we want to buy a bottle of wine, we have to go to a special store run by the government that sells only alcohol. It's amazing to actually go and buy wine at the winemaker's house and see how it is made. What a cultural experience!"

Monsieur Beaupre raised his glass of coffee at his wife and hiccupped. "Cultural," he parroted.

Madame Beaupre did look slightly mollified by this, so I figured I would change the topic of conversation. "Why do you always drink your coffee out of a glass?" I asked.

She poured herself a glass and sat down at the table with us.

"That was the way my mother always drank it," she said. "She always said that coffee tasted better from a glass than from a ceramic cup."

I took a sip of mine. I wasn't sure if it was my imagination, but it did seem to taste different—clearer—more pure. I was always going to drink my coffee in glasses if given the opportunity, I decided, as well as buy my wine directly from the maker.

chapter fifteen

Two weeks later, I was able to finally use my checked student card to go to Le Square with Sandrine, who had arranged to meet Stéphanie there for lunch.

I pulled it out and—because I was in a conciliatory mood, and also because I knew she hated smiling as a rule—smiled as le Dragon snatched it for inspection. She scowled at me, having none of my olive branch. She was just biding her time, I suspected, waiting for the perfect moment to exact her revenge.

So be it. I took a deep breath of the foggy fall air as Sandrine and I stepped out to the parking lot. *Freedom.* I had never realized how delicious it was until it was taken away from me.

Sandrine took a minute to cup the cigarette in her hand and light it, then jerked her head for me to follow her. We walked along, hands deep in the pockets of our jean jackets to keep them warm. I needed to think about buying a warmer coat for the next few months.

"I'm looking forward to meeting Stéphanie," I said.

"Ah, la Stéph." Sandrine laughed. "You'll like her. Everybody does."

I found myself unaccountably nervous. Would she like me? Besides Sandrine, I hadn't found French girls were lining up to become friends with me. They all seemed incredibly self-sufficient, as though they had everything and everyone they needed and did not require somebody new, especially a foreigner, in their already full lives. I'd done everything I could to appear open and friendly, but so far Sandrine was the only one who'd actually gone out of her way to spend time with me.

We walked for a few minutes alongside the medieval ramparts of Beaune—which were, just as the tour guides promised, remarkably well-preserved—until a bright red café came into view. "Café Le Square" was spelled out in large plastic letters above the door.

When we got closer, I realized I could barely make out anything through the windows thanks to condensation and smoke. "Looks like a popular place," I said to Sandrine.

"Oh, it is," she said. "Not so much with students from Saint Coeur, but everyone from Clos Maire and, of course, the Viti comes here."

"Viti?" I asked as we jaywalked across the street, narrowly missing being hit by two different cars that honked at us. Sandrine rolled her eyes at them but otherwise appeared unperturbed.

"Viti is short for l'École Viticole, the winemaking school. It's just right down the street from Clos Maire. It's for all the kids who are going to become winemakers or work in the wine industry. My older brother went there."

The idea of having a local school just for winemakers struck me as curious. "Don't they get a degree first? You know, to just learn more general things for a few years? Literature, history...that sort of thing..."

"Are you kidding?" Sandrine said. "The vineyards around here are like gold mines. Nobody wants the next generation of winemakers to be learning about the Fall of Rome when they can be working. My brother didn't even want to go to the Viti at all, but my parents made him. He was brought up to be a winemaker and inherit the family vineyards—he always knew that's what he would do."

I stopped on the sidewalk as Sandrine lit another cigarette and ground out her old one with her heel. I knew she also had an older sister at secretarial school. "What if you or your sister wanted to become a winemaker and take over the family domaine?" I asked.

Sandrine snorted. "That was never even an option. Trust me.

My brother was the only boy, so it was always going to go to him. My sister and I have to figure out something else on our own."

"That's not fair," I said, the feminist inside me bristling.

She shrugged with that air of French fatalism I was beginning to recognize. "Who said life is fair?"

I frowned at that. It wasn't the first time someone had thrown that at me, but I still smarted at the idea. Maybe life isn't fair, but it *should* be. "Just because your brother was born with a penis doesn't mean he is the best person to take over the vineyards."

Sandrine was still laughing at this when she opened the door and pushed me inside the café. I shucked my jacket. The place was so full of young adults, most of them smoking cigarettes, that the air actually seemed to be steaming. Sandrine led me to a booth near the back. Seated there was a striking girl around our age. Beside her was an equally handsome boy, with shoulder-length hair, green eyes, and a definite bohemian air about him.

"*Salut,* la Stéph." Sandrine bent down and gave Stéph *les bises* and then did the same with the boy.

"*Voici Laura, la Canadienne.*" She waved at me, and I said *salut* with as much confidence as I could muster and bent down to give them *les bises* as well. The boy smelled good, like vanilla.

"Laura's just been telling me her opinions about my brother taking over the vineyard," Sandrine said, as we slid into the booth. "She believes that just because Pascal was born with a penis doesn't mean he should automatically be the one to take over the family business."

Stéphanie laughed. "It does in Burgundy." She took a sip of her espresso. "You're right, though, Laura. It shouldn't be that way. Burgundy is so old-fashioned."

I didn't have a brother, just two sisters, but even so, we never considered taking over my father's optical business. Thank goodness, because while I saw myself doing many things for a career, managing optical stores wasn't one of them—but at least I had the choice. If I had been born in Burgundy, and the family business had been wine, would I feel differently? I might.

Stéphanie looked strangely familiar. Maybe it was just that she was so striking. Her hair was shiny black and twisted back in a messy chignon. She wore a bright red scarf around her neck, which set off her olive complexion, and wide hazel eyes that were so full of life they almost gave off sparks.

"The winemakers are all so retrograde," the boy added, casting a longing look at Stéphanie.

Hmmmmm...unrequited love there—or all the signs of it anyway. "Are your parents winemakers too?" I asked Stéph.

She snorted. "No. Definitely not. They're actually two of the few people in the village that are not involved in the business. My father is an x-ray technician and my mother stays at home with my little brother. My grandfather had vines, *bien sûr*—everybody did back then. My parents used to take care of them and harvest them when my older brother and I were little, but they sold them when I was about nine or so. They sold them to Sandrine's uncle, actually."

"Second uncle," Sandrine said. "Or uncle once removed. I'm not sure."

Stéphanie shrugged. "More than half the village is related to you."

A harried-looking waiter wearing the traditional white apron and black jacket came over. We ordered *cafés* and *jambon beurres*.

"Hey Stéph," Sandrine said, "do you think Franck would have liked to become a winemaker like Pascal?"

Stéph stubbed out her cigarette. "Hardly. He's never going to stay in one place for very long."

"Who's Franck?" I asked.

"Stéph's older brother," Sandrine said. "I mentioned him before."

"Franck wants to travel," Stéphanie said, looking an odd mix of sad and proud. "Once he's done his year of military service, he's going to fly off somewhere—God knows where. He's been asking around about *au pair* positions lately." She crinkled her eyes at me. "*Tiens*! He needs to meet you. I'd bet you two would have a lot to talk about."

"Sure," I said, although I didn't think I could help him much in finding an *au pair* position. "Aren't *au pairs* generally female?"

Stéphanie's eyes blazed a bit at this. "Why should they be, any more than winemakers should be male?"

I liked her spark. "Good point. Is his English good?"

Stéph shook her head. "Terrible. He's very good at philosophy though."

"How is he doing with...ah...all that?" Sandrine asked in a delicate, hesitant way that I was not at all accustomed to.

Stéph shrugged. "Not great but...better than he was, anyway."

I had no idea what they were talking about, but before I could formulate a question, the waiter brought our sandwiches. I bit into mine. It was half a gorgeously fresh baguette sliced open, spread with butter, then filled with a few slices of ham and some *cornichons*. How could something so simple be so delicious? I wondered why I had been brought up on rectangular loaves of spongy bread when baguettes were a possibility. What was *wrong* with us North Americans?

"Thibaut has his eye on Laura," Sandrine informed Stéph as she chewed.

"He does not!" I turned to her. "All he does is mock me."

"He asked me to find out what you thought about him," Sandrine said. "I haven't because I don't think he treats women well, but I figured you should at least know. I needed to warn you at least."

"When did he ask you?"

Sandrine shrugged. "I don't know. A few days ago, I guess."

"And you didn't tell me?"

"Why?" Stéph asked. "Are you interested?"

"*Non*!" I answered.

Sandrine shared a smile with Stéphanie.

"Do you know Thibaut?" I asked Stéph.

"A bit."

I couldn't stop thinking about this new piece of information as I finished my sandwich. Something *was* happening between

Thibaut and me—something I couldn't label. Somehow our eyes caught often during the day, and my heart beat a little faster when I spotted him in a crowd. He could be a jerk. I knew that. The problem was he was an oddly appealing jerk. Still, it would probably come to nothing. Right then, in fact, it was still nothing, so there was no point in telling Sandrine any of that.

"Maybe Franck?" Sandrine said to Stéph.

"I can find my own boyfriends, *merci quand même*!" I nudged Sandrine to underline my point. I didn't need her to start matchmaking. Besides, didn't she know that the more she objected to Thibaut, the more I would find him intriguing? I couldn't help that strong contrary streak that often reared its head at the most inconvenient times. "This sandwich is great, though," I added as a consolation.

Sandrine and Stéph accepted my reluctance to be a pawn in their machinations and went on to commiserate about their respective biology classes. I sipped my espresso and pondered further on the conundrum of Thibaut.

chapter sixteen

My time with the Beaupres was almost over, even though I felt as if I had just arrived. I only had ten days before moving to the Girards, my second host family. The Beaupres had truly taken me in as if I were their own daughter, and that was exactly how I felt. From what I had seen of them, the Girards were perfectly lovely people, but I didn't feel ready to move yet.

I was at home in the Beaupres' elegant house. I knew that I had to jiggle the lever on the top of the toilet to make it flush and where Madame Beaupre kept the olive oil and white wine vinegar that I used to make the vinaigrette whenever she asked. A new house and a new family meant starting from square one.

First, though, I was in for a treat. The Beaupres were taking me to Paris for the school break at the end of November. It was a national holiday everybody called la Toussaint, which roughly translated as "All Saints." I knew it had something to do with the Catholic religion, but I wasn't clear on the details.

Madame Beaupre had told me that she was a born-and-bred Parisian, and that her mother died when she was quite young. It was imperative that every year she return to Paris to put flowers on her mother's grave during Toussaint. I found this a little unnerving, but the promise of visiting the Eiffel Tower, the Sorbonne, and the Arc de Triomphe more than made up for it.

I started reading Victor Hugo's *Les Misèrables* as research. It was a thick tome, but that was OK because even though Sandrine, Stéphanie, and I had become quite friendly thanks to our weekly lunches at Le Square, they still hadn't extended any invitations for weekend activities. This left me plenty of free time to fill. I read about the catacombs and the sewers underneath the streets of Paris and the metal Elephant of the Bastille that Gavroche slept in at night.

Julien was also on a break from his hotel school and would meet us at Mamy's house just outside of Paris where we were all going to stay.

I picked through my wardrobe of hippy, tie-dyed shirts and ponchos with my newly Frenchified eyes and found my clothes sorely lacking for Paris. I felt more sophisticated now than the girl who had worn these things before—I could almost carry on a simple conversation in French, after all. I no longer needed to show the world that I was different from the conforming masses. I knew I was different. That was enough.

Madame Beaupre always looked undeniably chic. She favored tailored skirts and jackets accompanied with beautiful silk scarves (often Hermès). I needed to find some clothes like that...maybe not the skirts but at least some tailored jackets and floaty scarves to dress up my jeans. Maybe if I became a little more chic, something would come of the flirtation between Thibaut and me. Right then, I felt as though things were in a holding pattern and wasn't sure they would ever change. I wasn't even sure if I wanted them to progress, but I *was* curious. I picked up my Birkenstocks from the floor of my bedroom. I hadn't worn them since that day at Adalene's house—favoring my Keds instead. I needed to find a nice pair of boots or a pair of flats as well.

In Paris, I could find all of those things, and because I never went out except to Le Square, I had saved up an impressive amount of spending money. I packed extremely light, determined to come back to Nuits-Saint-Georges as a full-fledged French girl.

Sophie, on the other hand, had been calling once a week since she arrived in America. According to her parents, she was beyond enchanted with the cheerleaders and the football players and the daily visits to Taco Bell. It seemed she was as eager to lose her Frenchness as I was to gain it.

Monsieur Beaupre drove at his usual speed, but I had become accustomed to it as well as to the lack of seat belts. We were pulling into the gravel courtyard of his mother's house within three hours, which seemed to gratify him immensely.

Mamy rushed out of her house and greeted us all with *herbes de Provence*-scented hugs and kisses. She grabbed my face between her soft hands and kissed me on the forehead. Of course, she had the most delicious lunch ready for us.

First came a steaming ceramic bowl of French onion soup, topped with garlicky croutons of toasted baguette and grated Emmenthal. The November air outside carried the threat of snow, and I couldn't imagine anything more perfect on a late fall day than this bowl of steaming perfection.

Next came a chicken stew with little button mushrooms in a white sauce redolent of cream and mustard, served over the silkiest mashed potatoes that I had ever tasted. This was all accompanied by delectable wine—first white, then red.

Next came her massive wooden serving board of country cheeses. Even though I was wiser now as to the progression of a French meal than I was the last time I had sat at her table, I still helped myself to generous portions of each of the five cheeses. Life is short—I was determined to grasp every opportunity to eat good cheese.

Slices of fresh baguette were plentiful, and before I knew it over two hours had flown by.

"Your French has come along so well," Mamy said. She passed me the cheese platter for seconds and, after setting it down beside my plate, she grasped both my cheeks in one of her capable hands.

"*Merci*," I said. I hadn't thought about it, but sometime during the previous several weeks, I'd stopped feeling as though I existed inside a bubble of incomprehension. At first, I understood about a quarter of what was being said...then half...and in *that* moment, I realized I understood at least eighty-five to ninety percent of the conversation. Not only that, but I could jump in and contribute most of the time. To think...three months of living in France accomplished what eleven years of school French had failed to do. It seemed I wasn't just naturally bad at French as I'd believed. Maybe I just couldn't learn the way I had been taught at school. Being thrown into the deep end and having to survive seemed a much more effective method for me. Also, I was certain all the delicious cheese played a magical role in my increasing fluency.

"I wonder if Sophie's English is as good as your French," Mamy mused.

"I'm sure it's far better. She spoke more English than I did French."

Mamy's eyes got damp. "It will be an excellent thing for her to be able to speak English for jobs later on," she said. "Still, I don't like having one of my chicks so far from the nest."

I reached for her hand and squeezed it. "She says they are taking as good care of her in America as you are all taking of me." Indeed, from her letters, Sophie seemed to adore her first host family, but I knew she had to move to her second one soon, just as I did.

"You are such a comfort." She squeezed my hand back. "You feel like my granddaughter."

When I thought of a French grandmother, my thoughts went immediately to Mamy. She did remind me of a French version of my grandmother Agnes, who ran a bed and breakfast on a small island in the Pacific and had single-handedly operated a massive farm since my grandfather had died and left her a young widow with four children.

"*Tu es ma grand-mère française*," I said.

She picked up her yellow linen napkin and began to dab her eyes. When she was done, she stood up. "Now! Can you guess what I made you for dessert?"

I couldn't, but the various appetizing possibilities were endless.

"Do you still like sweets?" she asked.

I laughed. "I don't think that will ever change. Especially not in France."

She took four brown, shallow ceramic dishes out of the fridge and put one in front of me. "Do you know what it is?"

I shook my head. I didn't, although it looked delectable and was covered with a paper-thin layer of what looked like caramel.

"*Crème brûlée à la vanille*!" she declared. "Have I managed to make something you haven't tried before?"

"Yes!" I said. I could tell just by looking at it that it was a great oversight I was glad to correct.

"Wait!" she said. "I have the perfect wine to go with it." She went over to the wooden armoire that took up the whole back of her kitchen and turned the large metallic key with a blue pompom on the end. She extracted four of the most beautiful glasses I had ever seen. They were finely etched and handblown into a deep flute shape.

Finally, she produced an oddly shaped bottle.

"What kind of wine is it?" I was always interested in expanding my wine education.

"It's called the *vin de paille*," Monsieur Beaupre said. "It's from the region beside Burgundy called le Jura. Do you know what *paille* is?"

I regretted the fact that I had lost the habit of carrying my pocket dictionary around with me everywhere. "No."

A few explanations later, along with a charade of a cow chewing on something and a lot of mooing sounds, I figured out that *paille* translated as straw, or maybe hay. "Why do they call it that?" I asked.

"The grapes are picked late," Monsieur Beaupre said. "Then they are left to rot on a bed of hay."

"Oh," I said, a bit faintly.

"It's good," Madame Beaupre assured me. "It is a sweet wine and goes well with desserts. It is quite a local delicacy."

I decided anything drank out of these exquisite little glasses could only be sublime.

When Mamy poured us all a glass, I marveled over the dark yellow color of the wine, so intense that it had tints of amber. I took a sip. It was crisp and had the taste of honey. "It's delicious."

I watched as Mamy tapped her spoon on the top of her

crème brûlée, shattering the layer of caramel like a thin pane of glass. I copied her example, and the satisfying crack and shatter of the caramel gave way to a brown-flecked custard underneath. I took a spoonful. It melted in my mouth, and the splinter of the caramel crust that I had managed to scoop up as well crunched between my teeth.

"Why have I never had this before?" I asked to the ambient air. It was unctuous and creamy...would there be any end to new pleasures in France?

"Do you like it?" Mamy asked, looking pleased.

"I love it!" I said. "I love you! I love *France*!"

She grabbed me by the cheeks and planted another kiss on me.

The next few days in Paris were a whirl. We visited the Eiffel Tower and the Arc de Triomphe, then Madame Beaupre led us all into the red-light district as though it was a perfectly tourist-worthy destination.

We strolled along in front of the peep shows and the Moulin Rouge. My Canadian upbringing meant that all of this brought a blush to my cheeks, while at the same time it fascinated me. But the Beaupres seemed to take it in stride, as though it were completely normal to weave between the prostitutes and the striptease establishments. Besides some dodgy-looking characters and a myriad of scantily dressed women, there were also many seemingly regular people, like us. Maybe this was just part of Paris life, I conjectured, and maybe Parisians were as proud to show it off as they were the Louvre.

Julien began to discourse rapturously about the *spectacles* that were put on by the dancers at the Moulin Rouge and the Lido and the other revues.

"Like the ones that you watch on TV?"

"Yes," he said. "It is a magical world of fantasy and beauty.

We should have bought tickets, but you usually need to book months in advance."

Madame Beaupre guided me into a few stores that Sophie liked: one was called Pimkie, and another, Camaïeu. We selected a sky-blue wool blazer and a silk scarf with swirls of yellow and different blues. Julien helped me select a pair of delicate, brown leather boots that proved to be painful to walk in but passed his test of what women's shoes should be. Luckily, he also approved of a pair of flats.

On the third day, we went to the cemetery where Madame Beaupre's mother was buried. It was in the 5th arrondissement, tucked behind the winding streets of the rue Mouffetard, not far from the Panthéon, she'd told me.

It was quite a somber affair, with the gunmetal November sky and frigid air providing a suitable backdrop to the graveyard. Madame Beaupre set down a dark yellow pot of carnations on the grave. Her eyes, I was distressed to see, were full of tears. Julien held one of her hands.

"It was a long time ago," she murmured to no one in particular, "but it is a terrible thing to lose one's mother while still young."

The cemetery was crowded, with many families also using this special day to commune with their departed members and to leave tributes of flowers, and sometimes to leave little marble plaques or other mementos.

I'd never been much in the habit of visiting graveyards. We tend to opt for cremation on the West Coast. Maybe as a result of this, cemeteries have always given me a sense of deep unease, and French versions, I was discovering, were no exception. The contrast between Paris—a city that made me so acutely alive—and the hushed grayness of the cemetery made the inevitability and permanence of mortality sting even more than usual.

It also made me think. Seeing Paris with the Beaupres was a privilege and a gift, but I wanted to one day explore this miraculous city with someone I was truly in love with—that elusive missing person in my life. The familiar ache grew in my chest. Julien was now firmly in the category of honorary brother, and something—though I had no idea what—was happening between Thibaut and me, but still that spot in my heart remained empty. Even though I was only eighteen, I felt panicked among all those graves, believing that I was running out of time. I gave myself a shake. I was letting my imagination run away with my feelings, as usual.

After visiting the cemetery, Julien and Monsieur Beaupre wanted to go and see an exhibit of sports cars in the far northern end of Paris. Madame Beaupre had no desire to go and, as accommodating as I always tried to be, I had a hard time mustering up any enthusiasm for cars. To me, they had never been of any interest besides being an efficient way to convey my body from Point A to Point B.

"Let's go out for lunch," Madame Beaupre said. "There's a special place I want to take you. A place that always cheers me up."

We took the Metro several stops and transferred twice. Madame Beaupre knew it by heart and didn't need to consult the multi-colored route maps on the walls of the stations. I felt like a different person walking through the Metro with Madame Beaupre, like a French girl just out for a stroll in Paris with her *maman*. I loved my own mother back in Canada, but though she had taught me many things, she couldn't teach me how to become more French. Or how to do algebra, for that matter.

We popped out of the Metro and landed in a singularly unpicturesque place. It looked like a shoddily built, extremely rundown mall from the early 1980s.

"This is Les Halles," Madame Beaupre explained. "This whole area used to be a huge market. It was the heart of Paris. They tore it all down to build this monstrosity."

People of every description, color, and race swarmed on and off the escalators that came up out of the Metro station.

"Still," she said, "there are pockets of the old neighborhood, and I'm going to take you to one. This was a restaurant my parents often brought me to as a girl. My father brought me himself after my mother passed away. They serve a delicacy that I'm sure you haven't tasted yet." I hadn't yet tried a delicacy that I didn't enjoy, so I followed with confidence.

We passed by a towering church that could have been built in either the Gothic or Renaissance style—I wasn't sure—maybe a mix of both. Madame Beaupre followed my gaze. "That is Saint-Eustache. It was built in the fifteenth or sixteenth century, I believe. Did you know that Louis XIV was crowned there?"

"*Vraiment?*" I breathed, reverent. How I would love to come back and live in Paris—where centuries and centuries of history were all jumbled together like a huge treasure trove.

Madame Beaupre pushed open the door to a noisy *brasserie.* I looked up at the sign with red writing. Au Pied de Cochon it read. *Pied...cochon...*that was an odd name, but then again restaurants were named all sorts of outlandish things.

The chairs and booths were kitted out in red leather. Touches of yellow made the place cheery. Most of the tables were already full, and the traditionally dressed waiters, in their black jackets and long white aprons, whizzed around the restaurant balancing round serving trays.

"This looks wonderful," I said. The smells coming from the kitchens and from people's plates were welcoming. Madame Beaupre, with her habitual charm, not to mention her stunning eyes, secured us a table for two beside a window looking onto Saint-Eustache.

I felt perfectly Parisian—light-years away from the unworldly Canadian girl I had been a mere three months before.

Madame Beaupre looked around the restaurant and smiled. She reached across the table and squeezed my hand. "I am so pleased to be sharing this place with you. Shall I order for both of us? I know the menu by heart."

"Oh yes." The Beaupres had never steered me wrong as far as food was concerned.

When we lay the menus down on the table, a rotund, elderly gentleman—contrary to the reputation that Parisian waiters have—was at our table in an instant. He acted as though it was an honor to be waiting on us.

We started with a *coupe de Champagne* each and sipped on it as we soaked in the bustling atmosphere of the restaurant.

"I cannot believe you have to leave us next week," Madame Beaupre said, her eyes glistening again. "These few months have gone by far too fast. I actually asked if we could keep you longer, but the Girards and the other families are intent on having their turn."

I would never admit it, but I had also been holding on to a secret hope that perhaps the three other host families would bow out and I would get to stay with the Beaupres for the rest of the year. I loved them already and couldn't imagine having any other French family.

"I don't want to go," I said. "I will miss you all so much."

"I wanted us to have these few days in Paris," Madame Beaupre continued. "And for us to have this lunch together in this place. I cannot tell you how much it helped me to have you after Sophie left. I'm not sure how I would have survived those first few weeks if it hadn't been for you. You've come so far already with your French and your education. I'm proud of you."

"I'm so grateful that you were my first family," I said, tearing up too. "You all were so kind and gentle with me in those first few weeks when I was so confused and didn't understand anything."

We both started crying a bit, but we were quickly distracted by the arrival of a dozen piping-hot *escargots* for each of us. I laughed as the waiter set them down and gave me a pair of tongs. I gestured to Madame Beaupre with them. "Thanks to you, I know how to use these now. Also, I know that I love *escargots*."

"I will never forget that night," she said. "Were you scared to try them?"

"A bit," I said. "But it didn't take me long to realize how good they are."

"You are an adventurous eater," she said, picking up her first one. "I had heard so many horror stories about North American children who only wanted to eat hamburgers and *frites*. It was such a relief to find that you love food as our family does." She popped an *escargot* into her mouth. "Well, actually like everyone in Burgundy...and everyone in France," she said, correcting herself.

"Everything that I've tasted since staying with you is so delicious." It was the truth—so much so that I wondered how I was going to cope with the dearth of good French food when I returned to Canada at the end of the year. I felt almost more French than Canadian already. Maybe I had been born in the wrong country?

"I'm so glad" she said. "I wouldn't have dared bring you here otherwise."

I wondered a bit at that last sentence but was too absorbed in the heavenly garlic, butter, parsley, and snail-y tastes in my mouth.

The first course was washed down by a perfectly delicious house red. Warmth and well-being seeped through every cell of my body. What was it about French food and French eating that seemed to feed the soul as well as the stomach?

Around us were men in sharp business suits and brightly colored shirts and ties, and bourgeois women who were already making the most of the cold snap and wearing their furs, and who all seemed to have tiny dogs in bags near their feet. Everyone in the country stopped to enjoy this kind of lunch—high school students, stonemasons, François Mitterrand... That was knowing how to live. I had no desire to go back to the North American custom of bolting a sandwich in less than four minutes.

The *escargots* dishes were whisked away a few minutes after we were done, and our basket of fresh baguette slices and our wine and water were refreshed. The restaurant ran with military precision.

"Next is my favorite dish in the world!" Madame Beaupre's aqua eyes sparkled. "I just know you will love it. This restaurant is not just something I share with anyone, you know."

"What is it?" I asked, my mouth salivating already.

"Can't you guess?" she asked.

Guess? How would I be able to guess? "Is it something I've eaten before?" I asked.

"*Non*. They are not very common in Burgundy. It is more of a Parisian specialty. Actually, a specialty of the Les Halles neighborhood."

Parisian specialty. Well, that sounded promising.

"You haven't guessed?"

"I have no idea."

"The name of the restaurant is a clue, *bien sûr*!"

Au Pied de Cochon. At the Pig's Foot. My mind whirled with an awful possibility. *Surely one didn't actually* eat *pigs' feet, even in France...*

To answer my unspoken question, the waiter whirled back to us and placed plates proudly in front of us. "Our famous grilled *pied de cochon* with *sauce b*éarnaise and french fries."

The thing lying in front of me looked as though it was too big to be a pig's foot unless it was the foot of an extremely *large* pig. It was breaded and piping hot. Maybe *pied de cochon* was a name for another delicacy that actually wasn't a pig's foot at all but something else entirely, like how a hot dog wasn't actually a dog that was hot but a wiener made of mystery meat.

"*Pied de cochon*?" I asked Madame Beaupre, trying to show enthusiasm that I definitely did not feel. "Is it really a—"

"A pig's foot. Yes. They have been my favorite ever since I was a little girl. This is where they make the best, in my opinion. Why else did you think the *brasserie* was named that?"

I shrugged, trying to press down the tide of panic rising inside me. "I guess I just thought it was a funny name."

There was a pile of golden french fries beside my pig's foot, so I thought I would start with that. I picked one off the pile and chewed it. That, at least, was delicious and entirely unthreatening. Was I actually going to have to eat a pig's foot? And, if I did, how did one eat a pig's foot exactly? Did I pick it up like a chicken leg and gnaw it?

Madame Beaupre dug into hers immediately with her fork, impaling some of the breaded crust and the gelatinous-looking meat underneath. She chewed and a beatific smile lit up her already stunning face. "Try it," she said. "I know you'll love it as much as I do."

There was no escape without hurting Madame Beaupre. Apparently, I *was* going to eat a pig's foot.

The breaded stuff...that couldn't be too bad, right? I took a forkful of that and quickly put it in my mouth before I could think much more about what it had been in contact with. I chewed, but unfortunately underneath the breading were tiny bones that left me in no doubt about what I was eating. Toe knuckles. I hazarded another glance. Small bits of pink meat surrounded by lots of an opaque, gelatinous substance.

"Do you like it?" Madame Beaupre asked me. I shoved another french fry into my mouth to get the breading down.

I hated it, but I loved Madame Beaupre and couldn't bear disappointing her. "Delicious!"

Her eyes filled up with tears again. "I knew you would," she said. "I just knew it."

I tried to extract the pink meat from the gelatinous stuff and the tiny bones, but that proved impossible. I just shoved a whole forkful into my mouth and, with the help of several french fry chasers, managed to swallow the mouthful.

"Do you like how it tastes?" Madame Beaupre asked me eagerly.

I couldn't really consider the taste because every one of my senses was overwhelmed with disgust at the texture, which resembled those huge mouthfuls of mucous one coughs up at the tail end of a bad cold. I steeled myself. I would have to eat enough to make it look as though I had enjoyed it. Every cell in my body was pleading with me to admit that I simply couldn't eat this thing, but I just couldn't find the resolution to say it. As far as I was concerned, Madame Beaupre's feelings trumped mine.

She was polishing off her pig's foot with alarming speed, spitting out the tiny pig toe bones into her napkin and then lining them up along the edge of her plate. It was an image that I didn't think I would easily be able to exorcise from my mind.

I plowed through mine, with each forkful sending up a prayer that the gelatinous mass would not make the return trip up from my stomach. I had finally encountered a French food that I knew, deep in my heart, I would never grow to love, or even like. Pigs' feet were something, I concluded, that you have to be born French to love.

Maybe I hadn't banished all the Canadian-ness from me after all. Especially not the disinclination to wound the people I loved.

chapter seventeen

Three weeks before Christmas, I packed my suitcases again, took a tearful farewell of the Beaupres and Biscotte, and moved to the Girards. I had to hide my heartbreak so as not to distress the Girards.

They didn't actually live beside the family wine domaine in Premeaux-Prissey as I had believed. Instead, they made the wine there, but actually sold it and lived in a little village called Noiron, in what the Beaupres called la Plaine, or the Plain. Although it was no Saskatchewan, it was indeed a flat landscape. When we drove into the village, which consisted only of about twenty or so houses, I also realized it was located more or less in the middle of nowhere.

Within seconds of walking through the door, I was introduced to the Girards' three children. Their eldest was a boy of twenty named Bruno. I remembered him as the tractor driver during the harvest. He had huge dark eyes, ridiculously long lashes, and curly black hair that was a shame to waste on a boy. He was more beautiful than handsome. I was informed that he was being groomed to take over the winemaking side of the family business and was indeed a graduate of the winemaking school in Beaune Sandrine had told me about. He also had a girlfriend in Southern France who was still at university.

He seemed friendly, whereas the other two children—Yves, a weedy boy who was one year younger than I was and who suffered from a very severe case of acne, and Élise, a girl three years younger than I was and who kept giving me the evil eye—

barely spoke a word. They were called forth by their parents to give me perfunctory *bises*, during which they didn't deign to make any skin contact but rather performed the fastest air kisses I had ever received. They immediately retreated to the back of the living room, which was decorated in a gloomy mix of dark wood and crimson leather.

Madame Girard was a tiny, bird-like woman who hadn't inherited the commanding presence of her mother—who, I was still mortified to recall, had been the one to find Florian and I in the cupboard at the grape harvest. Madame Girard called Élise and Yves back to the couches to chat and make me feel welcome, but her orders, unconvincingly delivered, were ignored by her two youngest children.

"Would you like to have a kir?" Monsieur Girard asked me.

"Yes. *Merci*," I said. I had a difficult time believing I would be staying there and not going back later on that night to the cheery familiarity of the Beaupres.

Madame Girard went somewhere and then returned a few minutes later with a bowlful of cut-up cubes of Comté cheese.

"No cheese puffs?" Monsieur Girard asked in what I thought was a pleasant tone.

"I wasn't sure." Madame Girard wrung her hands. "I wasn't sure what Laura would like best, so I brought these. I can take them back though—"

"I love Comté," I said. "*Merci.*"

"It's fine, it's fine," Monsieur Girard tried to assure his wife. "I was merely joking. Come...sit."

Bruno sat beside me and began asking me questions about Canada. He said that he and his girlfriend were planning on taking a year off and traveling around the world after she completed her business degree in Avignon.

"I need you to start working in the vines," Monsieur Girard said, narrowing his eyes at his son.

Bruno rolled his eyes at me, and I smiled back. "I'll be working in the vines the rest of my life, Papa. Surely it can wait for a year. I did my two years at Viti, like you ordered. Surely I am allowed a little freedom before I chain myself to those bloody vineyards until I die."

My eyes widened. He didn't sound too thrilled about the whole "oldest son inherits the vineyards" tradition that I had protested about to Sandrine. That was a side that I had never considered. I thought cutting out the female and younger siblings unfair, but maybe the custom was also unfair on the eldest sons too, especially the ones like Bruno who were given no choice in the matter.

"Let's not argue about that in front of Laura," Monsieur Girard said repressively.

Yes. Let's not. My Canadian upbringing made me want to crawl under the coffee table.

"Has coming to France been a good experience for you, Laura?" Bruno offered me a charming smile.

"Wonderful!" I said. "I've already learned a new language and experienced so many things that I could have only dreamed about before coming here. It's the best thing I have done so far in my life—"

"You see?" Bruno turned to his parents who, I noticed belatedly, were looking strained. "Did you hear what Laura just said? Travel is essential for us young people these days. Why do you believe it for her and not for me?"

God. I had walked right into that trap.

"I'm not inheriting a vineyard, though," I said, attempting to play peacemaker. "And I've already been accepted to a university in Montreal when I return home, so I know what I'll be doing when I get back. Our situations might not be exactly parallel."

"They are *identical*," Bruno insisted with a petulant set to his mouth. Monsieur Girard's pleasant round face was now an interesting shade of scarlet. Madame Girard just became more and more hunched over, as if she was trying to shrink into herself.

Had I entered a war zone? All I wanted to do was lock myself in a room and weep. No, more than that, I wanted to pick up my bags and move back in with the Beaupres.

"That's enough, Bruno," Monsieur Girard barked. "Go to the cellar and wash the glasses for our six o'clock tasting."

Bruno got up with an exasperated sigh and shot his parents a parting dirty look.

"Tasting?" I asked.

"The building where you were during the harvest is my wife's family home. Her mother still lives there alone. Bruno will move in there eventually, of course, but for the time being we have a nice cellar here where we conduct our tastings and store most of our vintages. We have some clients coming by in fifteen minutes for a tasting."

"How interesting," I said.

"I don't want you to think we are being harsh with Bruno," Monsieur Girard continued. "But we're worried that if he leaves, he will never come back. He has a bit too much impulsiveness in his personality—always has."

"Couldn't Yves take over?" I asked.

Madame Girard wordlessly shook her head.

"No," Monsieur Girard said. "That could never happen. You see, we also have extensive farm holdings. Bruno, as the oldest, was groomed to take over the vineyards, and Yves has been groomed to take over the farming. He's been attending the agricultural college for the last year. Everything has been set up this way—"

"What about Élise?" I couldn't help asking.

"What do you mean?" Monsieur Girard asked, his features perplexed.

"Well...what is she being groomed to do? You know...what is she taking over?"

Madame Girard's eyes were huge. "Nothing, of course. We are sending her to an excellent school in Dijon, so she will perhaps work for a while. Then she will get married and have children."

I didn't say anything but just took a sip of my drink. *No wonder Élise doesn't strike me as the most satisfied of females.* I could even excuse her rudeness.

"Please," Monsieur Girard said, "don't encourage Bruno too much by talking about travel, or about life in Canada."

Madame Girard said nothing but cast me a beseeching look.

I wasn't sure how I was going to avoid talking about Canada, especially if Bruno asked me questions. Also, even though I loved France, I couldn't be disloyal about a country that, not only did I adore but which remained my birthplace. On the other hand, I saw that the Girards were desperate, though I thought their attempts at trying to hold their adult son hostage were futile. I debated how to respond.

"Would you like to come to the wine tasting with me for a bit?" Monsieur Girard said, changing the topic, thankfully. Even when things were bad in Burgundy, there was always wine.

"I need to make supper," Madame Girard unfolded her petite frame and got off the couch. "We are so glad to have you, Laura," she added. She sounded sincere, although with her two youngest children, who seemed to resent my presence, and the oldest, who could possibly attempt to flee because of it, I wouldn't have blamed her if she hadn't been.

Monsieur Girard led me out to the courtyard. The December wind was bitter, and the whole village—a few houses and a church huddled together on an empty plain—seemed exposed to the elements.

There was a round-topped, short wooden door inset into the side of the house. Monsieur Girard unlocked it and beckoned me down the steep, worn stone steps that descended into the darkness below. When he got to the bottom, he turned on the lights. Although they were dim, they revealed a beautiful stone cellar that was filled as far as the eye could see with barrels. Cobwebs festooned most of the corners, but I was beginning to learn that this was a treasured feature of any Burgundian cellar worth its salt. Cellars in Burgundy had a particular smell—a musty yet inviting scent of squished grapes, macerating wine, and mold.

Bruno was already down there, hunched over an ancient-looking stone sink in the corner, drying glasses with a linen dishtowel. He eyed his father with disfavor. "Do you have cellars like this in Canada?" he asked me.

"No. We don't really have any winemaking to speak of—not good wine anyway." I was hoping this would dampen Bruno's enthusiasm for the Great White North, but instead his eyes sparkled at the idea of "no winemaking to speak of."

"That's all anyone talks of here in Burgundy," he said. "Wine. Wine. Wine."

"I love the wine here," I said. "And I find everything about winemaking to be fascinating. I don't think you appreciate things until—" *Damn. That was not the right thing to say at all.*

"Until what?"

I was going to say "until you leave home," but of course that was not the right thing to say. God, it was a minefield.

"Until you realize how lucky you are," I finished, lamely.

"I don't think that's what you were going to say." Bruno was close to me now, putting the wine glasses on the barrel. His father had wandered into an adjacent cellar to select a few bottles of wine. "Maybe I'll break up with my girlfriend, and you can bring me back to Canada with you."

I turned to him in shock. What was that supposed to be? Flirting? A joke? I said the first thing that popped into my head. "Canada is very cold, you know."

"Maybe you could keep me warm," he said, giving me an appraising look that made me feel distinctly squirmy.

chapter eighteen

With a distinctly less comfortable home life, I became more and more invested with my friends at school. Sandrine was always loyal and friendly. She and Stéphanie commiserated with me over lunch at Le Square that the village where I had landed was indeed in the middle of nowhere.

"*Noiron*!" Stéphanie said with disgust. "I couldn't stand living in la Plaine."

"Why not?" I asked.

Sandrine shook her head. "When you are from the Hautes-Côtes, like we are, going to live in la Plaine is like..." She waved her *jambon beurre* in the air, clearly searching for the right words.

"It's like living in the enemy camp," Stéphanie said. "Plus, it's so *flat*. I had a great aunt who made my great uncle move to la Plaine and he never recovered." She tapped her temple. "He lost his mind. Never got better."

"Who could blame him?" Sandrine said.

"Well...for now I'm stuck in la Plaine at the Girards," I said. "The only saving grace is that I have my own room where I can hide."

"We were thinking of going shoe shopping next weekend to Chalon," Sandrine, who had just gotten her license, said. "Would you like to come?"

"Yes!" I said. "I would love that." I probably appeared overeager—desperate even, but...too bad. It was the truth.

But the next weekend, which was the week before Christmas, the temperature plunged below zero, and on Friday night, the whole region received an enormous dump of snow.

Sandrine called me on Saturday morning. "I can't come pick you up. *Désolée*," she said, "my dad won't let me drive the car in the snow." She broke off and said something biting to her mother. "It's ridiculous."

My heart sank. "I understand. What are you going to do instead?"

"We have a lot of snow up here in Villers—we're at a higher altitude, so we usually get tons. We're all stuck in the village, so I'll probably go over to Stéph's house. Franck made it home from Dijon last night just before the trains were stopped, so we'll all hang out. Olivier will probably come too."

"Olivier?"

"You don't know him. He's Franck's age, and they're really close. It's too bad you can't come up here and hang out with us. You really have to meet Franck. He's so great..."

I looked out the living room window, where the snow was piling up as I spoke. The weekend stuck in Noiron dragged out in front of me. "I wish I could too."

"What are you going to do?" Sandrine asked, concern in her voice.

"I think I'm going to go for a walk," I said. Élise had been giving me dirty looks since breakfast, Yves had been scuttling around in the dark corners and shadows trying to avoid me at all costs, and Bruno continued to interrogate me about life in North America despite his parents' strictures. Were the cars really as big as they were on the TV shows? Did people really drink that much Coke? I needed to escape the house, even for a little bit.

"It's cold out there," Sandrine said. "I'm not sure a walk is such a good idea."

"Sandrine. Please. I'm Canadian." I didn't need to mention that, in fact, where I lived in Canada was actually milder than Burgundy.

She laughed. "*D'accord.* We'll try to do it after Christmas, OK?"

I found Madame Girard, who was in the kitchen braising some sort of meat for lunch, and let her know that I was headed out for a walk around the village. I brandished my camera. "I want to take photos of the snow. So beautiful."

Her forehead creased. I could tell she wanted to clear up this bizarre behavior with her husband, who happened to be out doing something to frozen pipes with the other volunteer firefighters of the village.

"It's cold," she said.

"My jacket is warm," I said. "I'm Canadian." It had worked on Sandrine, after all.

She laughed too. "I suppose you are right. Don't be too long though!"

I headed out, deciding to go up the trail, which I knew was somewhere alongside the road underneath the snow. *Where should I go?* There were about twenty houses and then the church. My options were hardly overwhelming. The church was near the opposite end of the village, so I trudged that way through the snow. My legs were burning and my face freezing by the time I reached the graveyard.

It would be good to go and warm myself up on a pew. The churches of Nuits-Saint-Georges were always open, and I had gotten into the habit of venturing inside just to sit in peace for a few minutes and enjoy to the flickering candlelight of the offerings and the way the light shone through the stain glass windows.

I hadn't seen a soul since leaving the house, and Noiron's church looked similarly deserted. I trudged up to the large wooden door set in the stone edifice. I pulled down on the latch. It didn't open. I rattled the door some more. *Locked.* I had never come across a church that was locked before in France.

I walked around the church; maybe there was a second door. There was, but it was locked as well. I let slip an un-Christian word, then wandered out between the snow-capped gravestones and finally wiped the snow off a wide granite one and perched myself on top. All around me, big fluffy flakes of snow floated to the ground.

Without the crunch and squeak of my footsteps, the quiet reasserted itself. What was an eighteen-year-old supposed to do with all this silence? My thoughts wandered to Bruno and his flirtations. He was nice to look at—that was certain—but there was something about him that didn't appeal to me. He was too used to getting his own way, and he transformed into a petulant boy whenever his parents were around.

My ache was back, that longing for the person I could go for a walk with in the snow and then curl up with afterward in front of a blazing fire; somebody I could confide in about Élise's hatred of me and Madame Girard's shrinking demeanor and even Bruno's behavior; someone who I could laugh with about all of this and who, in doing so with me, would make it all seem lighter.

I was brought up to believe that no well-educated, ambitious woman needs a man. I should be enough all by myself. I *was* enough all by myself. Still, my soul felt as though it was missing a piece, and no amount of shaming myself or trying to rationalize my way out of it made any difference. Of course, I was far too young to think of committing to somebody long term, but still, I just wanted to find the person with whom that could be within the realm of possibility.

My problem, I concluded, was that I was a hopeless romantic. I had always been one, but this was a part of myself that I had never shared with anyone else. With boys back in Canada, and even boys in France like Thibaut, I played the role of a cynic. I acted as though I didn't care because I cared too much. It was a secret that I might have to keep locked away forever, I reflected, if I never met that elusive, perhaps non-existent person. The thought of never sharing my true self with anybody else was the final nail in my depression. I got up and trudged back to the house, thoroughly wretched.

I opened the door. Madame Girard must have been peering out the kitchen window, watching for me, because she was there before I had even been able to shut it behind me.

"I'm so relieved you're back." She wrung her hands. "I was worried you got lost."

I wanted to ask how it was possible to get lost around there, with the village visible in the flat plain for miles around. I took off my jacket. "No. It was just so pretty with the snow."

"Aren't you freezing?"

My hands and toes were feeling a little numb, but I didn't want to add any additional worry to her already-fretting mind. "Not at all. This is like a spring day back in Canada."

She smiled at that and hurried me into the dining room with the massive, dark table in the middle and sat me down at my seat. The table had already been set, and we all had wine glasses in front of us. I was discovering that generous consumption of wine at lunch and dinner is something that was par for the course with winemakers. She poured me a glass of their delicious white. There was much good in this family—I knew it—the proof was that their wine was truly excellent.

She called the rest of the family for lunch in her thin voice. First came Bruno, who eyed me up and down suggestively, as was his habit. Next came Yves, who took his seat and stared down at his plate without making any eye contact. Last came Élise, who had inherited her petite stature and thin face from her mother. Whereas Madame Girard's expression was sweetly strained, Élise's was sour. She didn't hesitate to make eye contact with me, but she made it abundantly clear through a series of eye rolls and dagger looks at me that she resented everything about my presence.

I was going to have to try to make friends with her. I wasn't quite sure how, but it was my job there to be conciliatory. I had no inkling why she hated me so much and was surprised to find it bothered me more than it should. I was used to being liked, or at least tolerated.

I realized that Élise and Yves were both wearing blue cotton shirts with badges on their sleeves and a kind of rolled up tie thing secured by a lanyard around their necks.

"Are those uniforms?" I asked, making polite conversation.

They were not very attractive uniforms, to be sure, but I thought of my pin-emblazoned navy Rotary blazer. *People in glass houses...*

Élise just glared at me, seemingly furious at my innocuous question. Yves continued to stare at his plate, as though waiting for food to magically materialize on it and for someone else to answer my question.

I took a few deep sips of my wine.

Bruno laughed. "Scouts," he said derisively. "Can you believe that at their age they are Scouts? Of all the stupid wastes of time—"

"Bruno," said Monsieur Girard warningly, as he refilled my wine glass with red this time.

Bruno snorted. "Yves should be out picking up girls instead of hanging out with a bunch of losers, and Élise should...I don't know...be doing girl stuff. Scouts! You wouldn't catch me dead at one of their meetings."

Yves looked up and snarled at his older brother. "We wouldn't have you anyway."

I almost jumped out of my seat in surprise. That, I realized, was the most I had ever heard Yves say in one go. He had already gone back to looking at his plate.

Bruno just rolled his eyes. Élise kept staring daggers at me, as if I was to blame for the altercation—in fact, as though I was to blame for every bad thing that had happened in the universe since the dawn of time. Maybe even before that.

Madame Girard served a delectable meat in mustard sauce. I wasn't sure exactly what it was, but it was good. I didn't want to ask more details, as I was beginning to think that talking was a minefield best to be avoided. Instead, I applied myself to eating and drinking my excellent wine. Monsieur Girard, bless him, always kept my glass full.

"What are you going to do this afternoon, Laura?" he asked me in a friendly tone.

I shrugged. "A friend and I were going to go to Chalon, but we can't because of the snow. I guess I'll read a bit and do some homework."

He nodded, but then a few seconds later looked up at me again. "I know! Yves and Élise can take you to their Scouts meeting with them. There are lots of young people there. Maybe you can even join!"

My fork froze midair. I had absolutely no desire to go to a Scouts meeting in Canada, France, or anywhere else. I had been unceremoniously asked to leave my Brownies troop when I was eight years old because I kept failing my domestic arts badge. I could never remember to set the table with the knife blades pointing inwards instead of outwards—or perhaps it had been a subversive act to thwart my old battle-axe of a Brown Owl. The day I was kicked out was a day of heady freedom. The last thing I wanted to do was join any kind of organization like that ever again. Then it dawned on me—as an Ursus exchange student, I currently *was* a member of exactly that type of organization. *Quelle horreur.*

"Papa! *Non*!" Élise cried. "I hate you!" She burst into tears and fled from the table.

Scratch that—the last thing I ever wanted to do was to go to a Scouts meeting with Élise and Yves.

That was the last thing I wanted to do. "I really don't need to—" I began.

"You will take Laura to the Scouts meeting with you," Monsieur Girard ordered Yves, his tone brooking no disagreement.

"There's no need. I am happy to stay here—"

"And you will introduce her to all the young people there," Monsieur Girard added. Nobody seemed to be at all interested in my opinion.

Yves ate for a few more minutes in stony silence, then threw his utensils down on his empty plate with a clatter and stormed upstairs.

"Would you like some more wine, Laura?" Madame Girard asked.

I held out my glass. "Yes please."

By the time Monsieur Girard handed Yves the car keys and told me to get my coat on, I was sloshed. I got up from my chair and swayed alarmingly. I admonished myself to act sober.

This was my first foray into over-imbibing alcoholic beverages...except for the time in Grade 10 when I ill-advisedly drank a Slurpee heavily dosed with Peppermint Schnapps and went to a school dance, only to throw it all up in Technicolor in front of the headmaster. Since then, I always drank in moderation. Even though I enjoyed wine, I knew my limits and stuck to them. At lunch, I had been thoroughly depressed about the prospect of the Scouts meeting, and the delicious wine seemed like such a blessed comfort in the midst of the Gaza Strip of the Girard children. My sisters and I grew up fighting, as all siblings do, but even at our worst, we were only a pale shadow of the strife contained within the Girards' walls. How much had I drunk? I had lost count of the glasses. Five, maybe. Or six?

Yves was waiting by the front door for me, as was Élise, who was now sporting a tear-stained face and puffy eyes, her little face screwed up into an almost comical expression of hatred.

"We're waiting for you," she said.

"Perhaps I should drive you," Monsieur Girard said to Yves. "They've cleared the roads, but it's still icy out there."

"Papa," Yves groaned, turning scarlet, "I can drive."

"Have you had your license for long?" I asked Yves.

He didn't answer me, but Monsieur Girard did. "He just got it last month, but he's been driving tractors for years. You don't need to be afraid."

"I'm not afraid," I said, although I wasn't sure that was exactly true. I wasn't so much afraid of his driving as of Yves and Élise conspiring to kill me and leave me in a snowy ditch somewhere between the village and Nuits-Saint-Georges.

As it turned out, my instincts were wrong. From the moment Yves spun the family car out of the gates of the property, he drove at an insane speed along roads that were basically sheets of ice. Silence reigned in the car, but I was already sweating with fear by the time we exited the village. The car slipped and slid all over the road, yet Yves did not slow down one iota.

When we were halfway to Nuits, I snapped. "Stop being such a fucking idiot!" I silently thanked Thibaut for teaching me the full lexicon of French swear words and how to employ them properly. "You've both made it abundantly clear that you want me dead, but unless you slow down, you're going to get all of us killed."

Yves did slow down, and almost stopped in fact. He and Élise turned to me in shock. "You just swore...," Élise said, sounding mystified. What did they think I was? A mute? A robot with no feelings? Just because I had been polite until then, despite their appalling behavior, didn't mean I had no backbone.

"Yes, I did," I said. "I get the message that neither of you like me or want me to be staying at your house. Trust me, the way you guys have been acting, I don't want to be staying at your house either. Still, your parents want me to stay, so I have no choice. We don't have to like each other. We don't even have to talk to each other more than absolutely necessary, but we do have to live in the same house for the next two months."

"We don't want you coming to Scouts with us," Élise said.

"Do you seriously think I want to be going to a Scouts meeting with you?" I asked. "For fuck's sake, I would rather pull out my own fingernails. Still, unlike you, I was well brought up, and while I am a fucking guest in your home, I will fucking well try to make your parents happy."

"Where did you learn to swear like that?" Yves asked, now completely stopped and staring over his shoulder at me. He sounded impressed, despite himself.

"A friend at school," I said. "A big, burly friend who is very protective of me. I have many of those. Also, I know how to shoot and I have excellent aim. I hunt moose back in Canada, you know."

All of that was either an exaggeration or an outright lie, but now that the gloves were off, I wasn't feeling particularly reasonable. Instilling a little bit of fear in them would be a good thing, I decided. Or perhaps that was the wine talking.

"My parents like you more than they like me!" Élise burst out.

"Can you blame them? All you do is walk around with that

sour look on your face, pouting and crying and being mad at everyone. Rest assured, though, I have two perfectly wonderful parents of my own. Your parents have been kind to me, but I'm not looking for any more. Two is *plenty.*"

Yves burst out in a strange honking sound that took me several seconds to recognize as laughter. "Isn't that the truth!" he gasped.

Élise didn't laugh, but I could see from her profile that she was fighting a smile. "*Oui*," she agreed, finally. "Two is plenty."

Nobody apologized, but I sat back in my seat and looked out the window to the white landscape outside, conscious of a perceptible lifting of the atmosphere. My head was still spinning and I felt slightly nauseous.

We pulled into the parking lot of a nondescript utilitarian building on the outskirts of Nuits-Saint-Georges. I briefly debated walking to the Beaupres to drop by and say *bonjour* in lieu of attending the Scouts meeting, but then I thought better of it. I was feeling on the verge of tears as it was. I didn't want to make them feel guilty about a situation that was mine alone to handle. They had done enough for me. I wanted them to think my stay at the Girards was trucking along happily.

We went into the room, which was cold enough for me to see my own breath. I opted to keep my coat on. About five other kids, all probably my age or a year or two younger, wearing identical blue shirts and lanyard-tied scarves, were milling around.

Élise made unenthusiastic introductions, but at least she was acknowledging my presence. That, I decided as I tried not to sway, was progress of a sort.

The kids came forward and gave me *les bises*, some more enthusiastically than others. The last boy had a friendly face and brown hair in messy loose curls. His kiss was a bit wet, but he was definitely the most welcoming of the bunch.

"How do you like Burgundy?" he asked.

"Wonderful," I said.

"And living with the Girards?"

The boy and I were now standing alone, as the others had

moved off to the far corner of the room where a table was set up with a bunch of photos laid on top.

"Interesting," I said.

"Élise has a personality that is not always easy," he said, cocking a brow.

"Really? I hadn't noticed."

He bit his lip to stop himself from laughing. "My name is Félix. Come, let's sit down and chat for a bit." He motioned to a beat-up, old couch that was positioned against the far wall of the room.

I shrugged. "All right."

"So, you must be used to all this snow," he began as we sat down. "This must be nothing compared to Canada."

I went on with the usual explanation about how the part of Canada I am from actually has a very temperate climate and how it is actually milder back home than in Burgundy. I swear, all French people think Canada is basically like Santa's village at the North Pole.

He nodded and smiled, but I wasn't sure if he actually believed me.

"Where do you live?" I asked. "Here in Nuits-Saint-Georges?"

He shook his head. "God no. I'm from a little village up in the hills. You've probably never heard of it."

"Try me."

"Villers-la-Faye."

I laughed. This reminded me of the almost identical exchange I'd had with Sandrine a couple of months earlier.

"What?" he asked.

"I've heard of it," I said, wrapping my coat tighter around myself. It wasn't getting any warmer in there. "In fact, I ate snails for the first time in Villers-la-Faye—at La Maison des Hautes-Côtes."

"*Non!*"

"Yes. They were delicious too. Also, one of my best friends at school is Sandrine Bissette. She lives in Villers-la-Faye. Do you know her?"

Félix guffawed. "Sort of...she's my cousin. Bissette is my last name too."

"Really?"

"Well, it's the last name of over half the people who live in Villers-la-Faye, so that's no big surprise."

"I have another friend from Villers," I said. "I don't think she's your cousin."

"Who?"

"Stéphanie Germain. Do you know her?"

"Of course! Our house is right across the lane from theirs. La Stéph and I go to school together. Do you know Franck?"

"Her brother? No. He's in Dijon, apparently, doing something for his military service. Stéphanie keeps saying I should meet him though." Why did everyone keep bringing up this Franck person?

"I don't know about that," Félix said, wiggling his eyebrows comically. "Franck is a good guy, but I think I'd rather keep you to myself."

I laughed. His flirting, unlike Bruno's, didn't feel as if it had any seriousness to it at all. Rather, it was as if Félix flirted simply as a way to be polite and to make me feel good.

"Did you know I'm having a New Year's party at my house?"

I shook my head. "Élise somehow managed to neglect mentioning that to me. *Quelle surprise*."

He reached over and squeezed my hand. "Well, you're invited. I will be mortally wounded if you don't come."

I had been holding out on a secret hope that maybe Sandrine would ask me to do something with her gang for New Year's, but that hadn't happened yet. Anyway, I liked Félix. He was warm and engaging and...what was there not to like? He was certainly no one I would ever be attracted to, but he would make a great friend.

"I'd be honored," I said. "Thank you."

"Maybe Sandrine and Stéph and Franck will come by too," he added.

"That would be fantastic," I said. I hoped they would. That would show Élise and Yves once and for all that I didn't need them and their stupid Scouts friends, except perhaps Félix.

chapter nineteen

It was my first Christmas away from home. I dreaded calling my family on Christmas Day, as I was certain hearing the cacophony as they prepared the family turkey dinner would make me feel homesick and teary. It was a good thing long distance phone calls were so expensive, because I knew drawing my call out would be torturous. The day before Christmas, I was invited to the Beaupres, where Mamy was staying over the holidays and Julien and his older brother, Antoine, were as well.

We had a proper French Christmas meal—*foie gras* and sauternes wine, a roasted goose with the most delectable stuffing made of chestnuts, an enormous cheese platter, *bûche de Noël*—which was a massive improvement on the dried fruit-filled fruitcake and plum pudding at home that I had always despised—clementine oranges, and brightly wrapped individual chocolates called *papillotes* with the *café*. All of that was washed down by Henri's fine wine purchased during our bicycle wine-tasting excursion to Vosne-Romanée in the fall.

We exchanged gifts, and I soaked up every last ounce of the family's uncomplicated warmth and affection.

It was odd how easy it was for me to choose gifts for the Beaupres compared to choosing them for the Girards. I had only stayed with the Beaupres for three months, but they felt like family. I picked out a leather key chain for Julien from a chic store he liked in Dijon, a book on Ferraris for Monsieur Beaupre, a blue silk scarf that would set off her lovely eyes for Madame Beaupre, and a set of floral linen tablemats and napkins for Mamy.

Madame Beaupre and I laughed as I opened my gift from her—a stunning Hermès scarf of my own—one that I had admired when we were in Paris. I was so relieved that I had forced myself to eat that pig's foot. That way, our memories of Paris remained unblemished.

The meal took about seven hours, and when I put on my jacket, Julien leaned over and whispered to me. "We wanted this to be your true Christmas," he said. "With us. That way, no matter what happens tomorrow, you will have had a true French Christmas with your true French family." All our eyes were swimming by the time I kissed them all once, then a second time, and finally climbed into the car beside Monsieur Beaupre to head back to Noiron.

In the car, my eyes filled with tears again at the thought of returning to Noiron, but at the same time I felt bad for the Girards. Monsieur and Madame Girard were not the Beaupres, to be sure, but they were truly kind and attentive. It was hardly their fault that their children were the way they were. Well, maybe it was a bit their fault, but the lottery of genetics was probably largely to blame.

In the end, Christmas at the Girards was much better than I had anticipated. I tried to phone my parents several times, but the circuits were always busy. Part of me was disappointed, but the other part of me was relieved to avoid a trigger that I knew would leave me feeling homesick. While Élise and Yves didn't seem to like me any better, they did appear to accept my presence in the house as a necessary evil.

Madame Girard's mother, the eagle-eyed octogenarian, sat beside me, and we had a delightful conversation about life during the Nazi occupation. "The worst was the curfews," she said. "I was young, like you are now. When you are that age, nature doesn't intend you to go to bed early. It wants you to dance and sing and talk and kiss boys..." She cocked a knowing eyebrow. "Like I found you doing during *les vendanges* with that Swiss boy."

I popped another one of her delicious homemade *escargots*

into my mouth. "About that—" I began.

She patted my hand with her claw-like hand and chuckled. "If you weren't doing that at your age, I would worry something was wrong. It is *la vie. C'est comme ça*! Do you like my *escargots*?"

"I love them," I said. "I never in my life thought that one of my favorite foods would be snails."

She smiled. "You know where we all met after curfew during the war?"

"Where?"

"The wine cellars. They were perfect. Deep underground—always the same temperature—and no light or sound made its way outside to the Nazis. Getting in and out without being noticed was another *paire de manches*, but I tell you that many couples met in the wine cellars during the war, and many babies were conceived there too."

I widened my eyes.

"What do you think about Élise?" she asked. I scrambled to keep up with her conversational pace. "Do you think she will ever find a man?"

My Canadian diplomacy asserted itself. "Of course. Perhaps when she is a bit older though—"

Madame Girard's mother made a sound of derision. "She'll have to wipe that scowl off her face before she does. I don't know where she got that personality from." She chewed thoughtfully on an *escargot*. "Probably from me, actually. I always had a bad *caractère* too, come to think of it. My mother, who was sweet like my daughter, despaired of me. I guess it skips a generation."

My maternal grandmother was also a bit of a rebel—marrying a man twenty years older despite her parents' vehement opposition and resolutely refusing to act ladylike, much to her mother's despair. Part of me wished that I could be as unconcerned with other people's opinions as she was, and that it had skipped a generation in my family too.

"I'm sure it will hold Élise in good stead later on in life," I said.

She shrugged, non-committal. "Perhaps."

The week between Christmas and New Year's passed slowly. Sandrine had gone skiing with her family, but I told her I would be at her cousin's house for New Year's.

"That's too bad," she said over the phone. "I was going to ask you to celebrate New Year's with us. Do you think you can get out of it?"

I bit my lip. I wanted to, but then I thought of Félix's kindness to me at that horrific Scouts meeting. "I promised your cousin I would go."

"Things like that are important to Félix," Sandrine said. "He's always been the sentimental sort. It's too bad, because Stéphanie's brother Franck overheard us talking about you, and he is dying to meet you."

I was getting sick of hearing Sandrine and everyone from Villers-la-Faye gush on about Stéphanie's brother. I got the distinct feeling that Sandrine and Stéphanie were trying to set me up with him, and it wounded my pride to think I was a sad enough case to necessitate a blind date. I had never had to resort to a blind date in my life and wasn't about to start. Also, hadn't they figured out that a surefire way to make me disinterested in this Franck was to tell me constantly that I needed to meet him?

"Maybe you and I can see each other at Félix's for New Year's," I said and extracted a promise from her to try to drop by.

New Year's rolled around and Madame Girard filled our arms with wine bottles to take to Félix's party. She also packed two bags full of *gougères* to heat up and about two hundred frozen *escargots*.

Félix's house was situated in a small alley just down from the gate where I had seen the young people hanging out on my way to La Maison des Hautes-Côtes. That warm summer evening seemed like years ago. Now, gusts of icy winds that felt as if they came straight off the Siberian tundra blew dry snow around. We all hunched over against the cold as we hurried toward the front door.

He welcomed us with delight, divested us of our coats, and before we had even caught our breath, he pressed glasses of kir in our hands. He was, I could tell immediately, the consummate host. The house was decorated in what I was beginning to think of as "Burgundian winemaker style"—a lot of dark stained wood, flashes of deep scarlet and mustard yellow, and a profusion of decorative items and furniture made from both gnarled old grapevines and wine barrels.

"Sandrine said she might drop by," I said to Félix.

"She told me," he said. "We had a family lunch yesterday." He rolled his eyes. "Nine hours long. She had to excuse herself for a lot of cigarettes, so I went with her to keep her company. We talked about you."

"Oh?"

"Good things." He pinched my cheek in the same manner as Sophie's Mamy had done so many times. "Only good things."

He ushered us downstairs into the *cuverie*. I had already deduced that Félix came from a winemaking family, but this confirmed it. The amount of food was incredible—pâtés and salads of every description, as well as bowls of chips and *gougères* and little cheese *feuilletés*. The wine flowed. I couldn't keep track of whether it was Félix's family's wine or the Girards' or indeed the wine of any of the thirty or so people milling around, many from winemaking families, but it didn't matter. By the time I drank two kirs and a glass of wine, I had warmed up nicely and was enjoying a lively conversation with a girl who was not a Scout either. She reassured me that, in fact, the majority of Félix's friends were not.

"We all tease him mercilessly about the Scouts thing," she said. "But he takes it in stride. He always does. He's the most good-humored person I've ever met in my life."

As the evening went on, several raclette machines were pulled out. Raclette was a favored winter dish in France, named somewhat unoriginally after the cheese that took center stage. I had already tasted this delicacy—loads of different *charcuterie*, boiled potatoes, and *cornichons*; and all of this with melted raclette cheese poured over it—at the Beaupres. It was the perfect meal for a cold night, and "*convivial*" as the French say, with everyone mixing up their little trays of cheese.

Félix sat beside me and, at one point, slung his arm across my shoulders. I didn't interpret this as anything more than friendly. It just seemed a normal part of his personality. After the raclette machines had been tidied up, Félix and his mother brought down a mind-blowing selection of tarts and cakes for a dessert buffet. Félix and I crossed paths as I was heading up to the bathroom and he was coming down with the last two fruit tarts.

"Have you had a nice time?" he asked. His eyes were bright, but he was certainly not drunk. Nor was I.

"It's a great party," I said. "*Merci.*"

I continued up the stairs, but Félix somehow managed to transfer both tarts into one hand and caught my arm with the other.

"Wait," he said. "I need to do something."

"What?" I asked, smiling and leaning closer. He looked as if he wanted to tell me a secret.

Instead, he planted his lips on mine and began kissing me. I didn't draw back immediately. I was worried he was going to drop the tarts, and also, I didn't want to hurt his feelings. He wasn't a great kisser—entirely too much saliva, like Florian—but it was nice to actually feel close to someone after feeling lonely for the past while. Despite that, I pulled away. I didn't like Félix in that way at all.

"*Pute*!" A voice shouted from the bottom of the stairs. I jerked back and saw Élise's little face, screwed up into misery. "I hate you, Laura!"

"*Eh merde*," Félix sighed.

Élise burst into tears and took off downstairs again.

"I think she has a crush on me," Félix said.

"That was nice, Félix," I said, needing to set the record straight. "But you know it didn't mean anything, right?"

Félix smiled at me. "I know. Sorry. You look sad sometimes,

and it was just a Happy New Year's kiss." He consulted his watch. "It's five minutes past midnight. *Bonne année*."

"*Bonne année*," I said to him. "Maybe you should go and reassure Élise."

"I will," he promised. "I don't want her to poison you or anything over this."

"Neither do I," I said. Félix headed back downstairs again. "Wait," I called out. "Would she?"

He turned around slightly and considered this. "With her, who knows?"

I walked up the last few steps, suddenly feeling as if all the energy had been sucked out of my cells.

After my trip to the bathroom, I collapsed on one of the leather couches in the living room, not yet feeling fit for company or to face Élise. A wave of despondency washed over me. I'd never loved New Year's. It always felt like too much pressure to have fun, but this year was worse than ever.

My year was almost half over. I still hadn't fallen in love. I didn't have a group of friends to hang out with on a regular basis. I lived with a family whose children seemed to want to either sleep with me or kill me. I *had* learned to speak French, I reminded myself. That was something. Still, if the rest of the year continued like this, I wouldn't fulfill the most important of my daydreams.

Where was he? Where was this great love of my life? Had it been ridiculous to even dream that I would meet him there in France? He probably didn't even exist, I thought, let alone have a path that was going to intersect with mine.

"*C'est quoi ça?*" A booming voice came from above my bowed head.

I turned around on the couch to see a hearty-looking Burgundian man with a red face and a rotund belly staring down at me. He had both his hands full of wine glasses, which he was holding by the stems. He was clearly perplexed. "What on earth is a pretty girl like you doing up here all by herself on New Year's Eve?" he demanded. "This is all wrong."

"I was at Félix's party downstairs." I jerked my thumb in

that direction.

"Is he not serving you enough wine down there?" he asked, suspiciously.

"*Non, non.* I just came up to use the bathroom and just needed some time to think..."

"Man trouble?"

That hit too close to home. "No. Not that."

"What is your accent?" he demanded.

"Canadian," I said. "I'm Canadian."

"*Québecois?*" He sounded dubious.

"No. I'm from English-speaking Canada. I just learned French when I came here in September."

"Do you like wine?" he asked.

"Adore it," I said.

"Well I am Félix's father, Gérard. You must do me the honor of coming down to my cellar for a tasting. I have one group just on their way out and another just arriving. Will you?"

I thought of Élise's face when she had seen Félix and me on the stairs. "I'd love to."

He didn't have a free hand but nodded at me to follow him. I put on my jacket, and we went out the front door and crunched across the gravel courtyard. It was pitch black out, and snow swirled around in the frigid air.

A group of youngish adults stumbled across the courtyard in the opposite direction, hunched over in the cold but laughing and singing some French song.

"*Salut,* Gérard!" they called out. "Thank you for the tasting! *Bonne année*! *Bonne santé*!"

As they passed me, one of the men—one whose face I couldn't make out in the dark but who seemed to have black hair—bumped into me. Our arms merely brushed, but I felt it like an electric shock, so much so that I stopped in my tracks.

"*Desolé*!" he called out to me, stopping too. He peered in my general direction and took a step toward me, but his friends doubled back. They grabbed him by each arm and pulled him inexorably forward. They began singing again.

"This way!" Gérard ushered me toward a little rectangle of

light in the far wall and down the stone steps of his cellar. I recognized the smell of a Burgundian wine cellar immediately, and it warmed my heart. "That was my previous group," he said once we were at the bottom of the steps. "Some boys from the village."

"Boys?" They didn't look like boys to me.

"Well…I suppose they're not really boys any longer, but I'll always think of them that way."

Four different men were already down there encircling the tasting barrel, expectant expressions on their faces. They were all pushing fifty or sixty, and for a moment I wished that the village "boys" from the courtyard were down in the cellar with me instead.

"What have you brought us?" one of them declared when he saw me behind Gérard.

"*Une petite Canadienne*!" Gérard declared, triumphantly. "I found her all alone on one of my couches, and I couldn't have that, *évidemment*. She clearly was in dire need of some proper Burgundian hospitality."

The next several hours became somewhat of a blur. Down in the coziness of Gérard's cellar, we tasted all kinds of different wines, some dating back to the early 1900s, or so Gérard thought. The men, friends of Gérard's—I now saw where Félix got his hospitable personality from—flirted with me and paid me lots of innocuous and gallant compliments on my charm and beauty that made me laugh.

When we stumbled out of the cellar, the dark sky was paling to gray.

"I think I might have missed my ride," I said, but couldn't find it in myself to be overly concerned.

"You can stay over here," Gérard said. "Plenty of beds! We usually have a few strays after our parties."

Just then, Félix made his way into the courtyard.

"Laura!" he said. "We were wondering where you were! Did my father kidnap you?"

"Yes," I chuckled. "And he forced me to drink wine."

Gérard squeezed my shoulder. "I like this one, Félix!" he

declared. "You should marry her."

"We're just friends," I said to Gérard.

"Alas, that is the story of my son's life." He shook his head in mock sadness.

"Do you want to come with us for breakfast?" Félix asked. I saw two of his non-Scouts friends were behind him.

"Where?"

"My grandparents' house just down the road."

"I think I need to find Élise and Yves, if they haven't left already."

"Oh, they haven't." Félix waved his hand. "They're asleep downstairs with pretty much everyone else."

"All right," I said. I found I was in no hurry to see Élise.

I thanked Gérard and gave him a kiss on each cheek, which made his skin turn an even deeper shade of red.

"Did you talk to Élise?" I asked Félix as we all crossed the courtyard and ventured into the snowy lane.

"Yes." There were puckers in his forehead. "She does hold on to grudges though. I think I may have made things even harder for you. Sorry about that."

I shrugged. "It was hardly great to begin with."

Félix waved at the tall stone wall that dominated the end of the lane. "That's Stéphanie's house," he said.

"Did she and Sandrine come in the end?"

He shook his head. "I don't remember seeing them."

We slipped and slid down the road—the same road across from the village bakery that we had slowed down on, on our way to La Maison des Hautes-Côtes.

"Won't we be waking up your grandparents?" I asked Félix.

Félix snorted. "Are you kidding? They're winemakers. They're incapable of sleeping past four o'clock in the morning."

Their house was a ramshackle stone affair at the bottom of the street. We climbed up a set of steep stone stairs, and Félix knocked on the door.

Almost immediately, it was opened by a white-haired old lady in a flowered housecoat.

"*Bonne année.*" Félix leaned forward and gave her a kiss.

"These are my friends." He introduced us all. "We're here to have breakfast."

Félix's grandmother did not seem to be at all surprised or put out by this announcement, and opened the door and ushered us in. She told us to take a seat at the table, which was covered with a red oilcloth. At the table sat a wrinkled old man. A cane leaned against his chair.

"Doudou," Félix said and gave him a kiss, then repeated the introductions again. He introduced his grandfather as le Doudou, which wasn't a word I was familiar with—but people in these villages had all kinds of strange nicknames. We all kissed each other in greeting before sitting down.

Félix's grandmother measured coffee into an aluminum stovetop coffee pot. She ordered her husband to the *boulangerie* to get things to eat. Le Doudou struggled to stand up with his cane.

"I can go," I whispered to Félix. "I don't want him to slip and fall."

"It's good for him," Félix whispered back. "He'll see some friends he knows, have a chat. There's nothing worse for him than sitting around all day at home."

Grand-mère set out glass *café au lait* bowls in front of all of us, then began heating up milk in an ancient casserole on an equally ancient stove. I admired the massive wooden buffet that stood like a sentinel and took up the whole back wall of the kitchen.

Le Doudou was taking quite a while to come back, long enough for me to start imagining him lying in the icy street with a broken leg. In the meantime, Félix entertained his grandmother with tales of the previous night's party. She appeared to be a dour woman at first glance, but she possessed a taste for the ribald, and Félix had her in stitches.

At last, le Doudou blew back in the door, snow sprinkled on the shoulders of his woolen jacket. "*Il fait un froid du canard* out there," he declared. Now that was an expression I wasn't yet familiar with—it is "duck cold" out there. I'd have to look that one up in my dictionary. He did look far cheerier than when he'd left.

"Who did you see?" Félix asked.

"Le Père Curie was talking to Olivier and Franck. Apparently, the boys were tasting at Gérard's last night. They haven't gone to sleep yet."

"You should have invited them here for breakfast," Grand-mère chastised.

"They were going back to Franck's house," le Doudou said. "La Michèle will take care of them."

"I think I might have crossed with them when I was going to the cellar last night," I said. "It was dark and cold though. Hard to see."

Le Doudou sat down again, his wrinkled cheeks rosy. "Gérard needs to replace his courtyard light," he said. "I keep telling him."

"I didn't see Sandrine or Stéph, though," I said to Félix. "Did they come?"

"I'll bet Sandrine was waylaid by a boy," Félix said.

His grandmother swatted him unceremoniously on the head. "Don't say such things about your cousin." Her eyes glinted. "Even if they are true."

Grand-mère filled our *café au lait* bowls, then followed that with the basket full of croissants and *pains au chocolat*, plus three fresh baguettes, a block of creamy butter, and several jars of homemade jam.

We all dug in. As far as a beginning to the new year, it was far better than I had hoped.

chapter twenty

When school started up again a few days later, Sandrine apologized for not meeting up with me on New Year's in Villers-la-Faye. Félix had been right—both she and Stéphanie met some new boys from a different village, and that had required a last-minute change in plans involving Mobylettes and a party in Beaune.

Thibaut pulled me aside before school to ask me how my holidays had been. I described some of the trials and tribulations of living with the Girard offspring, including the Scouts meeting in Nuits-Saint-Georges, and quickly had him in stitches.

"You know, Laura," he said. "I missed you over the break. I was surprised how much."

"Oh really?" I never knew when he was mocking me, and I didn't want to fall into yet another trap and expose myself. I rolled my eyes to underline that I didn't take him seriously.

"I did," he insisted. "The prof is showing us a film about Rousseau in Philosophy today. I'll save you a seat. *D'accord*?"

"Sure," I said. "Whatever."

He leaned over and gave me a kiss on each cheek, even though we had already had our *bises* greeting a few minutes before.

"We just did *les bises*. Did you forget?"

"I didn't forget." He turned and walked toward a group of other guys.

Philosophie was the last class of the day, and Sandrine didn't have it with me. It was basically Thibaut and a bunch of his friends, who were also becoming my friends. I walked in a bit on the late side, and most of the desks were filled up. Thibaut and his buddies were at the very back of the room, their desks pushed right up against the wall.

"Laura!" He waved at me. "Over here!"

I went over and took the one empty seat left that was pushed up against Thibaut's.

I stuck my bag underneath the chair. "Why do I get the impression you guys aren't planning on watching much of this movie?"

"Such an accusation!" said Maxime, a tall blond boy who was always joking. He reminded me of Big Bird from *Sesame Street*. "I'm offended."

The teacher came in then, looking distinctly disenchanted about school being back in session. "I have things to do while you are watching this," he said. "I will be in and out, but I expect you all to be on your best behavior."

We all exchanged smiles. Now *there* was a rule that was just begging to be broken.

He shut off the lights and began the movie on an old TV set that he'd rolled in on a metal cart. The voice of the narrator began banging on about Rousseau and his ideas of freedom and nature. After a few minutes, I shut my eyes and was just conjuring up a pleasant daydream when a hand moved across my desk and clasped my hand.

My eyes flew open.

"What are you doing?" I hissed at Thibaut.

He put a finger to his lips. "*Shhhhhhh.*"

He then murmured something else that I didn't hear, so I leaned closer and signaled him to repeat himself. Instead of whispering in my ear, he kissed me. I looked up at him. Surprise must have been written all over my face.

"Did you not like that?" he asked.

I thought about it. There was...something...there. I wasn't sure if I even liked Thibaut sometimes, but I was drawn to him. Besides, I was lonely.

"Maybe. I think we'll have to try again for me to know for sure."

He kissed me again, and I felt a flash of something. Not a lightning bolt, but a spark of lust. *Maybe we can fan that into something?*

I spent the rest of the class making out with Thibaut in the corner of the room.

The next morning, Sandrine caught me as soon as I got off the bus from Noiron. "Tell me it's not true," she said, her features frozen in a scowl of disapproval. "You and Thibaut."

I shrugged. That morning I had twisted my hair up in a barrette just as the French girls did, and the nonchalance of the style had rubbed off on me. "I was bored. It was just a bit of fun."

"You can do better," she said.

"It's nothing serious. Really. Don't worry."

She rolled her eyes but didn't say anything further.

Two weeks later, we were all together in PE class. Thibaut and I hadn't gone beyond kissing in dark corners and empty classrooms. That, though, we did at every opportunity.

We had begun a gymnastics unit. I had always been remarkably ungifted at that particular sport. I could barely execute a cartwheel.

Thibaut stood beside me as we watched our classmates scurry up a rope attached to the twenty-foot gymnasium ceiling. "God, I'm never going to be able to do that," I said.

"Me neither," he said. "I'm strong—good for ripping out old vines and such—but I don't seem to have a knack for vertical motion."

"Maybe if I keep going to the back of the line, the teacher won't realize that I haven't gone."

Thibaut smiled down at me. "Doubt it. She's got a list." He jutted his chin to indicate the clipboard our officious Gym teacher held in her hand.

"*Merde.*"

Thibaut laughed. I wondered again why Thibaut always insisted in keeping our assignations in the dark. He never acted at all like a boyfriend around me at school, except when we were alone. It made me feel angry, hurt, and a little embarrassed. Still, my pride wouldn't let me broach the topic with him.

I admonished myself to stop overworking my brain trying to figure out what this thing was between Thibaut and me. It was just fun, right? Why couldn't I just be the kind of person to just enjoy something for what it was? *My damned brain, always working overtime.*

Sandrine had her turn on the rope, and I was relieved to see she didn't get more than a meter off the ground, despite the jeers doled out by the gym teacher. They weren't that big on the idea of positive reinforcement at French high schools.

Sandrine came over and inserted herself between Thibaut and me. She turned her back on him. "Cigarettes," she wheezed. "I have to stop one of these days."

"I'm dreading my turn," I said.

"You can't possibly do worse than me."

"Want to bet?"

"Mademoiselle Bradbury!" The PE teacher's voice rang across the gymnasium. "On the rope! Or have you forgotten that this class is not just for fulfilling your socializing needs?"

I called the teacher a rude French word under my breath.

Sandrine burst out laughing, and the PE teacher was opening her mouth and gathering steam to yell at both of us when a man came in carrying two large square boxes, which, on closer inspection, were tied up with yellow ribbon and looked as if they had come from a *boulangerie*.

The PE teacher was distracted from giving me a bollocking. "You're late!" she said to the man, consulting her watch.

"They're fresh out of the oven," he said, ignoring her tone.

"Everyone!" she shouted, and blew the whistle that always hung around her neck. "Who would like to share some *galette*?"

My fellow students exploded with cheers and all rushed forwards.

She blew the whistle again. "Let me cut it first," she said, laughing. I was quickly revising my opinion of her.

"What is *galette*?" I asked Sandrine.

Thibaut was still lingering beside us. "You don't have

galettes in Canada?" he asked.

"No. At least I don't think so."

"No *galettes*? What a strange country Canada must be," he said. "Not very Catholic."

I thought of all the various churches in my hometown—Scientology right across from the Jehovah's Witnesses and kitty corner to the Church of England and the Church of Latter Day Saints. "It's not any one religion."

"Heathen," Thibaut observed, but with an engaging smile.

"It's a special dessert we have only during Epiphany," Sandrine said. "It's to commemorate the Three Kings or...something like that."

Thibaut snorted. "Who wasn't listening during her catechism classes, *n'est-ce pas*, Sandrine?"

"All right, Thibaut." Sandrine put her hands on her hips. "How about you tell us all about the history and religious meaning of the *galettes de rois*."

"Is it good?" I interrupted.

"Good?" Thibaut asked, his eyes round. "It's delicious! Layers of puff pastry filled with almond *crème*."

The teacher had cut up both *galettes*, and began to hand out pieces. "Thibaut," Sandrine said, "be gallant for once in your life and get Laura and me pieces."

"Why should...," he began, but stopped talking when he saw Sandrine's narrowed eyes.

He expelled a momentous sigh and pushed through the crowd toward the *galettes*. In Canada, we would have naturally formed an orderly line-up. There, it was an instant mob.

"Inside each *galette* is a tiny ceramic figurine called a *fève*," Sandrine continued. "The person who finds the *fève* in his or her piece is the queen or king, and then they have to choose a queen or king of the opposite gender. The royal couples have to wear those crowns," she said, pointing at a pile of flattened but golden things lying beside the *galette* boxes.

"That's not very republican," I said.

Sandrine shrugged. "Neither is being Catholic, but we all are." It also wasn't an equitable system for people who preferred people of the same gender, I reflected, but apparently the Catholic religion and the *boulangeries* hadn't spared much thought for that.

Thibaut eventually returned, looking put-upon but carrying three slices of *galette* on a napkin.

"*Merci*," said Sandrine, taking hers. "Maybe you're not all bad."

"Tell that to your friend here instead of warning her away from me." Thibaut nodded at me.

"She wasn't—"

"I was." Sandrine interrupted me. "And, just for the record, I still think I'm right."

A girl named Aude was whooping and hollering and holding up something in her hand.

"She found the first *fève*," Sandrine said.

Aude was going out with a boy named Pierre, so it was no big surprise that she chose him to be her king, and they both went up to the front to be ceremoniously crowned. They kissed each other once, then again. Then I started to see some flashes of tongue. The teacher blew her whistle again. They finally pulled apart.

I took a bite of my *galette*. I hoped I didn't have the *fève* in my piece. I would probably choose Thibaut, but that would be making a public declaration that I wasn't at all certain he was prepared to make. I peeked under the crust of my slice and was relieved to see no sign of a *fève*.

Now I could just concentrate on the taste. The crust was flaky and buttery and melted on my tongue, and inside was a creamy filling that tasted perfectly of almonds and vanilla. It was simple, but perfect. So perfect that it made me severely regret, for the first time in my existence, that I hadn't been brought up Catholic. To think, French kids got to eat these every January for their whole lives. *Lucky bastards.*

I was finishing up every last crumb when I noticed that Thibaut had gone still beside me. I glanced over and saw a ceramic figurine that looked like Baby Jesus in the manger between his fingers.

"Thibaut found *la fève*!" a boy beside us shouted for all to hear. I felt my face burn scarlet. Was he going to name me his queen? How I hated feeling so uncertain all the time. Why couldn't we just try having a normal relationship?

"What are you waiting for, my little man?" the prof said. "Come up here, get your crown, and name your queen."

Sandrine, I noticed, was watching Thibaut, intently. Thibaut made his way up to the front, cocky and self-assured. I sort of hated him at that moment. The prof put Thibaut's crown together and placed it on his head in mock ceremony. She did a little curtsey. "Your queen?" she prompted.

He surveyed the crowd. His eyes caught mine, then passed over me. I felt cold.

"Rose," he said.

I felt that other girl's name like a slap across the face. Rose was the prettiest girl in the class—out of every boy's league. She only dated men who were several years older. However, with her huge blue eyes, blond hair, dimples, and neat little figure always encased in tight jeans, she was the socially acceptable focus of all the boys' desires.

She twinkled up to the front to be crowned beside Thibaut. He pointed at his cheek for a kiss, and at first she declined but finally ended up giving him a peck. Thibaut played to the audience of his friends, giving a triumphant thumb's up and then high fiving his way back into the crowd again.

As for me, I felt like a royal fool. Of course, he wasn't going to claim me in front of everyone. He didn't even want me as his girlfriend. I forced myself to look at the facts—he was just biding his time until something better came along.

As we exited the gymnasium to go back to the school, Thibaut materialized beside Sandrine and me once again. "You're not mad, are you?" he whispered to me.

I shook my head. "Don't be stupid." My eyes were smarting with tears, but I would never let him see them. I wouldn't let anyone see them.

"I was right," Sandrine said to Thibaut.

"Right about what?" Thibaut asked.

"To warn Laura away from you. You have never known how to treat women, and you never will."

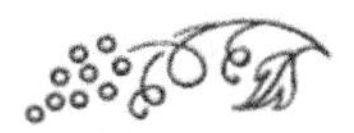

The next few days were a misery. It was cold, it was snowing, and it was late January. The only bright spot was that the Girards loved *galettes* as much as I did, and I had eaten two more since that fateful PE class.

My gut reaction was to act angry with Thibaut and give him the cold shoulder. The problem was this behavior would only show him I was hurt. My pride wouldn't let me do that. All I could do was act as if I didn't care or long for a relationship where I was secure enough to be able to show that I did, indeed, care very much.

Thibaut had been extra attentive to me, but I worked very hard to treat him just as I would any other friend.

On a Friday after school he said to me, "You're still mad at me, aren't you?"

"What are you talking about?" I answered off-handedly as I scanned the arriving buses for the one I needed to catch back to the Girards.

"About the *galette*. About me choosing Rose."

I snorted. "Get over yourself. I wouldn't have wanted you to say my name. Hardly anything happened between us and hardly anybody knows. It's for the best that way."

"You are acting different," he said.

I probably was. I was probably acting as if I didn't care, rather than feeding his ego with needless glances and attention paid in his direction. "You're imagining things."

He looked around us and furtively ducked to kiss me. I jerked backwards.

"See?" he said. "You didn't used to jerk away."

"We've always been alone. I don't want anybody to see."

With a screech, the school bus came to a stop in front of me, and the doors flipped open. The driver was there in the same filthy wool sweater he wore everyday, with a cigarette that was permanently hanging out of his mouth.

"*Allez*," he grunted, which I had learned meant "*Get on now, or I'm leaving without you.*"

"See you Monday," I said to Thibaut, and walked up the steps.

Out the window, as the bus pulled away from the curb and into the maw of the crazy French traffic, I could see Thibaut still watching.

chapter twenty-one

Saturday I was woken by the most horrible squealing sound. I ran downstairs, wondering if someone was being viciously attacked. Madame Girard met me in the hallway.

"We have a special treat for you today, Laura," she said. "We're making *boudin noir.*" I had no idea what *boudin noir* was, but if it had anything to do with the dreadful shrieking sound, I wanted no part of it. "You must come watch," she said. "It's happening at our neighbors' house. Hurry!"

I flung on some clothes and went back downstairs. All I really wanted to do was have a quiet *café au lait* and maybe some breakfast, but *non*, I had to trudge over to the neighbors' house in the cold.

The neighbors also had a farm, and the closer I got, the louder the squealing became. When I walked behind the courtyard to where the farming operations took place, I found its source—a large pig tied to a stake with a rope around its neck.

Dread filled me. The sound tapped right into my central nervous system and made me want to run away or hit somebody. I had forgotten my gloves and a toque, I realized, as my fingers began to go numb.

Bruno came over to me. "Come closer so you can get a good view." He put a hand on my back and steered me to a spot at the front of the crowd of assembled villagers. The neighbor came out of his house brandishing a fearsome knife and a plastic pail. I did not like where this was heading.

"I forgot my gloves," I mumbled and began to back up.

"You can't leave now!" Monsieur Girard caught my arm. "It's the most important part."

I heard a particularly piercing squeal, followed by the gush of something, which—I saw when I turned around—was the pig's blood pouring into the bucket.

"Oh God," I said in English, horrified.

"It's the blood for the *boudin noir*," Bruno said. "Nice and fresh. It's going to be delicious." I knew they made *coq au vin* sauce with blood, but that was something I tried hard not to dwell on. I had a strong foreboding that *boudin noir* was not going to be to my taste.

The ensuing silence was worse than the squealing beforehand. I am hardly a squeamish person. My father was a hunter and a fisherman. It wasn't uncommon for me to come home from school to find two flayed deer carcasses hanging up on the rafters of the garage or an entire moose being butchered on the kitchen table. I could gut a fish and chop a crab in half with an axe.

Still, there was something uniquely bloodthirsty about slitting the pig's throat with everyone standing around watching as if it was a public execution at the guillotine during the Revolution. I love a perfect slice of *saucisson sec* or a good pork cutlet, so I realized how hypocritical this was of me, yet something about seeing all that fresh pig's blood splattered on the white snow made me want to vomit.

"My hands are cold," I said to Bruno. "I'm heading back."

"All right," he said. "Tell my *maman* that I'll bring the blood soon."

I nodded, blinking back tears. I couldn't figure out what was wrong with me. Why did I feel like an exposed nerve? A deep sadness pervaded my bones. The ache was back, stronger than ever. My feet crunched in the snow as I walked to the Girards' house. Fat flakes began to fall, and I stopped and stood on the side of the road for a moment. The church bell rang out. Where was my missing piece? It clearly wasn't Thibaut.

I sometimes wondered if I had already loved the person I

was searching for in a previous existence and had vowed to find him in this one. Or maybe that was just my overactive imagination playing its tricks again...

I began walking again, and when I got home, I delivered Bruno's message to Madame Girard, who was busy in the kitchen with her mother, sautéing onions and spices. I retreated to my bedroom, where I wrote in my journal and cried, then lay on my bed and watched the snowflakes fall from the leaden sky until I fell into a disturbed sleep.

I was woken by Madame Girard calling my name up the stairs. I rarely napped, but when I did, I felt as if I was coming up from one thousand leagues under the sea when I emerged from my slumber.

I stumbled out of my room and down the stairs, still rubbing my eyes. I went into the dining room, where the table was set and the neighbors and the Girards had all taken a place. There was one empty seat left for me at the end of the table.

"I'm sorry." I pulled out my chair and sat down. "I fell asleep. I guess I was more tired than I realized."

Monsieur sweetly waved away my apology. "It is no matter," he said. "Are you ready to enjoy my wife's famous *boudin noir*? It is a true delicacy. Nobody in Burgundy makes it better."

I had forgotten about the *boudin noir*. I hoped it would be something akin to *coq au vin*, so delicious that I could forget about the fact it contained blood. I felt my heart trip with nerves but smiled and said *oui*, which seemed to gratify the assembled guests immensely. I got the impression that this special treat of *boudin noir* was partly being done in my honor.

"To think I had heard that Americans were unadventurous eaters," said the neighbor, a bearded, woodsy sort who liked to hunt wild boars on the weekends.

"Not Laura, here," said Monsieur Girard proudly. "She loves snails and pâté and well...everything." I had never mentioned the *pied de cochon* incident with Madame Beaupre and never would—as far as she knew I had loved every bite. "Unlike some French girls I know," he added and raised a pointed eyebrow at Élise, who glowered at me from across the table.

"*Voilà*!" Madame Girard came into the dining room, looking almost confident carrying a huge earthenware platter. She was strong for such a tiny thing. Piled on the platter were huge black sausages.

Oh my God. Was that *boudin noir*? If so, it was even worse than I had imagined.

She came to me first. "I've picked the biggest one for you," she said, and plucked the sausage from the top of the pile and placed it on my plate. It lay there, hanging over the edges of my large dinner plate by about an inch on either side. The thing was massive.

"*Merci*," I managed, but stared down at it in horror.

"So, have you had these before?" the neighbor asked.

I shook my head. "Never."

"You are in for a treat!" he declared. "*Bon appétit*!"

"I'll wait for everyone else," I demurred.

"*Non. Non.* Start while it's still hot," he insisted.

I took a large gulp of wine and then cut off a slice of the sausage. When I cut through the casing, the interior of the sausage popped out, as if contained under pressure. I stared at it in horror. It was deep brownish red, the color of congealed blood. I poked it with my fork. It *was* basically congealed blood. Congealed blood of that pig that they had killed that morning.

I forked a tiny bit and put it in my mouth. It had the metallic taste of blood, like a cut on the tongue or lip. I contemplated with horror the size of the thing on my plate. It was far worse than the *pied de cochon*. I looked up and saw that everyone around the table was watching me.

"Do you not like it?" Madame Girard asked in a tiny voice, sounding hurt.

I cut off a huge chunk and shoved it in my mouth. I was eating congealed blood, my brain kept chanting. I swallowed. *Please don't let me throw up. Please don't let me throw up...*

"Wonderful!" The table erupted in cheers, and everyone launched into "*Le Ban Bourguignon*," (or simply, a *Ban Bourguignon*, as the French refer to it) the traditional Burgundian eating, drinking, and celebration song with the "la la la laaaas"—all except Élise, who'd been given a piece of goat cheese quiche from the night before, which I glanced at with longing. She sent me a baleful look, but I felt like telling her that she wouldn't be nearly so angry with me if she knew how much I hated *boudin noir*.

It was the longest, most torturous meal of my life. The only thing that got me through it was being able to wash the revolting mouthfuls down with wine.

I made a getaway upstairs as quickly as I could and walked circles in my room trying to will myself not to barf. I was victorious, but as I lay awake at three o'clock in the morning with one of the worst stomach aches in my life, I started to question just how far I should go to be a good guest for my Ursus families. Maybe I had just pushed the limits of politeness beyond self-preservation.

The next day, I straggled downstairs at around ten o'clock. I looked for Madame Girard to see if I could help do anything around the house, but everything was quiet. Was it possible that I was alone?

I finally went into the TV room where Bruno was lying stomach down on the couch. I sat down in the armchair. "Where is everyone?" I asked.

"Maman and Papa and Yves have gone to look at a secondhand tractor, and Élise is over at my aunt's house."

"Oh." I sat back, then glanced at the TV screen. "What are you watching?" An ad for Prince biscuits filled the screen.

"Cartoons."

I had glimpsed at enough French cartoons to know that I was better off going to get my breakfast. I started to sit up from my chair.

"Wait!" Bruno said.

I sat back down again. "What?"

"I need to talk to you about something."

I wasn't scared of Bruno—I knew he wouldn't dare touch me or hurt me, but I did feel a little weird about being alone in the house with him.

"What about?"

"About my girlfriend."

"What about her?" I asked. Maybe he wanted some advice from a female perspective.

"I miss her a lot. Especially at times like this when I'm not busy working. Do you have a boyfriend back in Canada?"

"No. Not back in Canada."

"Do you have one here in France? At school?"

What would I call Thibaut exactly? Definitely not my boyfriend, especially not after the *galette* incident. He wasn't anything, really. "Maybe," I said. "Sort of." I had no idea why I lied, but suspected it had something to do with wanting Bruno to believe I wasn't available.

"Do you and he…?" Bruno thrust his hips into the couch a few times to indicate what he meant.

I drew back, disgusted. "That's none of your business."

"I really miss doing that." He thrust his hips into the couch a few more times just to underline his point. "Don't you?"

"No," I said curtly and stood up to leave.

"Wait!" he said again. "Do you…you know…want to do it with me right now?"

I was standing above him now, and crossed my arms across my chest. "Non!" I said. "Like so, so…*not*!"

"I was just asking," he said, petulant now, and went back to watching his *Astérix* cartoon while I stared at him in disbelief.

I went to the kitchen, my brain whirring as I heated up the milk and got myself a Petit Suisse out of the fridge. Is that all Bruno thought of me, as someone to have sex with when he was feeling bored and horny? I was certain that I had never given him any indication that I was interested in him, but then again, many guys, probably Bruno included, probably looked at most women that way. He clearly saw sex as merely a physical release completely separate from what I truly wanted—love and romance.

I felt completely despondent. How many men out there were such pigs that they would ask a houseguest for casual sex with no feelings involved? Thibaut was far from perfect—such as the part about not wanting any part of our relationship to be public or official—but he did seem to like me, and he was a pretty decent kisser. Bruno disgusted me so much that I began to doubt there were any good men out there in the world.

At that moment, Bruno wandered into the kitchen, a raging erection still evident in his jogging pants. He plucked a *pain au chocolat* from the counter. "*Scooby-Doo* is on, if you want to come watch it," he said, then wandered out, but not before reaching down the front of his pants to scratch his testicles. Nothing like a little French charm...

chapter twenty-two

By the time Monday rolled around and the hideous weekend was over, Thibaut's overtures had become quite overt in nature. Playing as though I didn't care fueled something in him. He pulled me aside after giving me the *bises* several seconds longer than necessary.

"Next weekend," he said, "are you free?"

I thought of the previous weekend of *boudin noir* and Bruno. I would make myself free. There was no way I was going to spend another weekend in Noiron. "Yes."

"Great," he said. "It's my birthday and I was thinking of having a party. I wasn't going to, but then...well...I thought it would be nice for us to be able to spend some time together outside of school. What do you think?"

I smiled back. "That would be nice. Where?"

"My father is going to rent the *salle des fêtes* in Puligny-Montrachet. I think I'll invite the whole class. We'll all stay overnight. Bring a sleeping bag." He wiggled his eyebrows suggestively. I laughed.

"An overnight, co-ed birthday party? Is that some sort of Burgundian tradition?"

"It's not uncommon."

"I'll have to ask the Girards for permission," I warned him.

"Can you tonight? I won't have it if you can't come."

I stared at him so long that he said, "*Quoi*?"

"That's really sweet," I said. "I had a rough weekend and...well...it's just a nice thing to hear. Don't tell me if it's not true. I don't want to know."

Monsieur Girard, as it turned out, vaguely knew Thibaut's parents from wine-tasting circles, and getting permission for the birthday sleepover was not nearly as arduous as I'd thought it would be. They talked on the phone and apparently were reassured this was a parent-sanctioned event. Apparently, these two-day-long parties were quite common among Burgundian teens. My parents were relatively trusting of my sisters and me, but I was certain a sleepover with boys would not be condoned.

I wasn't quite sure what to expect, but Madame Girard loaned me one of Yves's sleeping bags, and Sandrine came to pick me up on the way to Puligny-Montrachet. "You're not planning on getting together with Thibaut at the party, are you?" she asked without preamble when I got in the car. The snow had turned to sleet, which had washed away all the white fluffiness that had covered the village.

"I'm not planning anything," I said.

"I just don't...I just don't think that would be a great idea," she said. "I was relieved when I thought it was over after that thing with the *galette des rois*."

I turned to her. "Look Sandrine," I said, "I'm lonely. I'm bored. There is nobody else on the horizon."

"Join the club!" she snorted.

We drove out of the village, each lost in thought, until Sandrine turned onto la Nationale toward Beaune, and then on to Puligny.

"You need to meet Franck," she said.

"Who? Stéphanie's brother?"

"Yes."

"I'm not going to pin all my hopes on him," I grumbled. "Besides, I don't like being set up. I'm not that desperate."

Sandrine didn't say anything for a while after that. But by the time we got to Puligny-Montrachet, we were in stitches—Sandrine had recounted a story of how her father had, that morning, found a married woman from the village having sex with her lover in the back of a Citroën parked on a path that intersected the vineyards.

The *salle des fêtes* was a beautiful stone building across from the picturesque village church.

"This is where we're having the party?" I asked.

"Yes," she said. "Thibaut's parents are winemakers, you know, lots of Premier Crus and a few Grand Crus." Sandrine rubbed her thumb and her forefinger together. Very wealthy.

I had never bothered to think about that before. Then again, how else would they afford throwing a two-day birthday party including food and wine for their son's entire class?

"How old do you think this building is?" I asked, getting out of the car.

Sandrine looked at me strangely and shrugged. "I don't know," she said. "Old."

Several other cars were parked already, and a few parents, who were being shooed away by their offspring, lingered around the entrance to the building.

Sandrine slung her sleeping bag over her shoulder. "There was no way I was allowing my parents to drive me here."

We found Thibaut inside, being pestered by an elegantly officious-looking woman who shared his bulky build and dark eyes. She had to be his mother.

Sandrine and I went over and kissed Thibaut, and I had to work at acting nonchalant. My heart was beating too fast. Thibaut's face flushed, and he introduced us to his imposing mother.

"I know you," she said to Sandrine, then she lifted her chin in my direction. "So, you're the Canadian girl we've been hearing about?"

Thibaut had mentioned me at home? "I guess so," I said.

"Hmmmmmm," she said darkly and narrowed her eyes at me.

Sandrine tugged at my arm. "Come on, Laura. Let's go find a place to leave our sleeping bags."

"Why does Thibaut's mother seem to hate me?" I asked

when we were far enough away, mystified and a little hurt.

"She thinks you're going to steal her son, *bien sûr*, and whisk him off to Canada with you."

"That's ridiculous," I said. "I'm eighteen. I'm light years away from committing to a serious relationship."

Sandrine found a spot near the corner where all the other guests had started leaving their backpacks and sleeping stuff. "Maybe so, but all Burgundian *mamans* are going to be worried and protective of their sons. If my brother said he was going to leave the vineyards and take off to travel the world, my parents would have an apoplexy."

"Thibaut's mother doesn't need to worry." I nudged Sandrine. "Hey! What about you and Thibaut? You are both from winemaking stock. I bet your mothers would love that."

"They would," Sandrine gave her sleeping bag an unnecessary kick. "Trust me." Something in her voice made me twig.

"Wait a second. Have you dated Thibaut? That's why you are always warning me away from him. If you're still interested—"

She motioned at me to speak more quietly and shook her head. "We did date for a little while two years ago. Our parents were thrilled, especially mine—and his family's crus are more prestigious than mine. However, he dumped me unceremoniously and then pretended as if nothing had happened. I got over it, but he really hurt me. I don't want him to do the same thing to you."

I would much rather have lost Thibaut than have risked losing Sandrine, who had been such a good friend to me from the start. "If you still like him—"

Sandrine shook her brown curls. "I don't. That's the truth."

"OK," I said.

We all milled around for some time after that. Kirs were served, as well as a dizzying assortment of *petits fours*, mini quiches, *feuilletés*, and *canapés*. It was all extremely sophisticated for a teenage party where everyone was wearing jeans.

I thought back to our high school parties in Canada, where AC/ DC's "All Night Long" and "Back in Black" were played in a nonstop, deafening loop. Drinking beer via homemade bongs had been the main source of entertainment, especially after a Grade 12 boy stole a pink plastic flamingo from someone's garden and transformed it into what became known as "Bird the Bong." Beer and cheap wine coolers were spilled all over the floors. There was never any food offered. The party usually ended when the police came to break it up and poured out all of our alcohol. As a result, I didn't know quite what to make of my first French high school party. I wasn't used to anything this refined. The Canadian free-for-alls were much more relaxed.

Rose came up to me and gave me *les bises*. "Ah, Laura! I didn't see you, but of course you would be here. We all know how much you like Thibaut." She batted her eyelashes meaningfully.

"He's amusing," I said coolly. I didn't like Rose. She struck me as the type of girl who needed to push other girls down so she could be at the top of the pile. I had little time for that. Still, she persisted.

"Maybe tonight is the night, *n'est-ce pas*?" she asked.

Sandrine must have been behind us. "It wasn't so long ago that you were going out with Thibaut, Rose," she said. "Jealous?"

Rose looked momentarily rattled, but then laughed prettily. "Oh no. After I finished with Thibaut, I changed to older men, and I haven't looked back since! None of these young boys for me."

"Then what are you doing here?" asked Sandrine.

"Younger boys are fine for friends..."

Thibaut bellowed, "*À table*!" and everyone was ushered to find a place at the huge U-shaped tables that were covered by yellow paper tablecloths. *Jaune* tablecloths! I no longer had to search for the French word for "yellow."

I sat down, not really sure what to expect. A veritable parade of women—many of whom looked enough like Thibaut to be aunts and other family members—streamed through a sliding door at the far end of the room. They were bearing platter upon platter of *charcuterie*—salty, paper-thin slices of *jambon de parme*, sliced sausages of every shape and size imaginable, rolls of pink *jambon blanc*, and thick slabs of *jambon persillé* (another Burgundian specialty of salted ham mixed with parsley and garlic, which was in a terrine and served cold). All of it was delicious. Little ceramic bowls of *cornichons* were placed between each half dozen people.

I had just begun to wonder where Thibaut's father was in all these preparations, when he appeared through the doorway bearing the biggest bottle of wine I had ever seen.

"What the hell is that? I asked Maxime, who was sitting with me and Sandrine and a few of our other friends.

"Haven't you ever seen one of those before?"

"No! It's like...it's like a wine bottle for giants!"

"It's called a methuselah. It's the equivalent of eight bottles of wine. They're often served here in Burgundy for special occasions. Baptisms, birthdays, weddings—"

"Funerals?"

"*Non*. But they might as well be because there is always a lot of wine at those too."

Thibaut's father came over ceremoniously to Thibaut and presented him with the massive bottle to uncork.

"They're often tricky to uncork," Maxime whispered to me. "Very stressful moment, *tu sais*? If he breaks the cork and it falls in the bottle..."

"Not good?" I could tell I was witnessing a crucial Burgundian rite of passage.

"Nope. That could ruin all the wine in there. It's old wine too. Surely from the year of his birth. They must have put it away when he was born."

I thought I could make out some beads of sweat on Thibaut's brow as he carefully inserted the corkscrew and began to twist it gently out. A hush fell over the crowd. His father watched him.

"*Doucement*," he said to his son. Gently.

Finally, with a soft pop, the cork was out, and in one piece. The whole room erupted in a *Ban Bourguignon*. The meal became a bit of a blur after that. Wine after wine was served, most from Thibaut's family estate. The food was a delectable *boeuf bourguignon*, and the cake was a *pièce montée*—a tower of sweet puff pastries filled with vanilla-tinted pastry cream and webbed together with filament-thin strands of caramel.

Finally, the adults left and music was played, and we all starting dancing. Thibaut led me into a quiet corner behind a sort of makeshift screen to make out.

"I've been thinking about this all week," he said.

"Me too," I admitted. It was lovely to feel appreciated, especially after Bruno. Bruno had not mentioned the incident since, and I was pretty sure it was because, for him, it was forgotten instantaneously. It was an offer made to me simply because he wanted to have sex and I was the nearest non-family member of the female gender around. My disgust continued, unabated.

"You know, though," Thibaut continued between kisses, "we still can't act like boyfriend and girlfriend at school."

I froze. "Why not?"

"It's just that...I want this to be just for us. It's not like I'm with anyone else...I'm not. I don't want it to be everyone else's business. Do you understand?"

"Yeah," I said, distractedly, my mind trying to make sense of what he had just said. "I guess."

"Are you all right with that?" He kissed me again.

"Sure." I lied. "Whatever."

chapter twenty-three

A few weeks after Thibaut's party, I moved out of the Girards' house and into my next host family's house, right beside the huge cathedral in Nuits-Saint-Georges.

I was sorry to say good-bye to Monsieur and Madame Girard, who had never been anything but kind, even when serving me homemade *boudin noir*.

I couldn't say the same for the children. Bruno gave me a lingering *bises* that made my skin crawl, Yves still didn't look me in the eye, and Élise, that little cow, burst into tears and clung on to me, saying how much she would miss having a sister. Shock left me incapable of returning her emotional farewells, but I did feel a pang of compassion for her—eternally discontented little thing.

I was living back in town again with the Lacanches, although by then I had realized how small Nuits-Saint-Georges was compared to Beaune or Dijon. Still, anything was better than the isolation of Noiron. They prepared a fantastic room for me in an attic space right beside the bell tower. The first time the huge bell rang, I nearly jumped out of my skin. It reverberated throughout the entire room and made the glass panes on my windows shake. Still, I loved the privacy and quirkiness of my little nest beside the bell tower and far above the streets below.

As I headed down for my first dinner with the family, I was impressed with the stunning dining room, lit with stained glass windows and featuring a large, ancient oak table. Monsieur Lacanche sat at the head of the table. I had met him before at

Ursus meetings, and he struck me as a rigid man, in both appearance and demeanor. He made me feel as though I always needed to be on my best behavior, but I told myself he would loosen up when the family got used to me.

He waved me to the one empty seat that was not filled by his wife or two children—the athletic son and the adorable younger daughter, both as flaxen blond as Florian the Swiss grape harvester.

He was talking, I realized after a few seconds, about the difference between French northerners and southerners. "Here in Burgundy, I like to think we have more in common with our German neighbours," he explained to his children and me. "We are more orderly and law-abiding, and not as dirty as our southern brothers."

That wasn't really what I had seen so far—Burgundy had its fair share of anarchy—but I could just sense that Monsieur Lacanche would not take kindly to being interrupted or having his words questioned.

Madame Lacanche got up and disappeared in the direction of the kitchen.

"We Burgundians are much closer genetically to the Germans than to the Italians or the Spanish," he added. Monsieur Lacanche, it dawned on me, didn't so much chat as give speeches as though the table was a lectern.

Madame Lacanche arrived with a delicious first course of braised chicory wrapped in ham slices and covered with a cheesy béchamel, and served me some. She wore her white blond hair in a demure bob. I wasn't sure about Burgundians as a whole being genetically closer to Germans, but the Lacanche family certainly looked as if they were.

After serving everyone, Madame Lacanche served herself and sat down.

"So, Laura," Monsieur Lacanche said, "tell me about your friends. Have you become close with any of the children of the Ursus members?"

"No," I said. "None of them seem to go to my school. My best friend is probably la Sandrine. She was my first friend here, then she introduced me to la Stéph—"

The Lacanches' son Anton burst out laughing.

"What?" I asked, smiling.

"Don't say '*la*' in front of their names!" he said.

"Why?" Why indeed? It was the way that my group of friends at Le Square always referred to each other. It was a way of expressing affection, like saying that there was only one Sandrine—*the* Sandrine—and she was unique.

Anton made a derisive sound. "It's how *country* people talk. You know, people who aren't educated or cultured."

I bristled at that. Sandrine and Stéphanie were both educated and cultured, as well as unstintingly kind to foreigners like me. I was sure Monsieur Lacanche would jump in to defend me against his son's rudeness, but he just smiled at him, approving.

"He is quite right, you know," Monsieur Lacanche told me. "It will not do for you to speak like that. It would give us Ursus members a bad name."

I nodded and bent my head to eat my lunch. I mutinously vowed to never stop talking like my friends from Villers-la-Faye.

The week after I moved in with the Lacanches, they took me skiing in the Alps for a week during the school vacation at the end of February. Sandrine and I discovered that she was also going to be at Saint Gervais, the same ski station, where her parents owned an apartment. Better yet, she was bringing Stéphanie for the week.

We met up the first morning at the base of the gondola. Stéphanie, for the first time in her life, did not look confident.

"I haven't skied much before," she admitted. "This is only my second time."

Sandrine, on the other hand, came to the Alps several times every winter, and swooshed down the slopes with an elegance she didn't normally possess.

As for me, I skied in my usual kamikaze fashion, without style or grace but with a lot of speed and spectacular wipe-outs, which had Stéphanie and Sandrine in stitches.

We made frequent stops for mulled wine in the mountain-top chalets and took lots of photos.

At one of the chalets, Stéphanie bought a wad of postcards to send home. "That's one of the rules in our family," she said. "If you go somewhere nice, everyone expects a postcard. Will you guys help me write these? I can never think of what to say."

She picked out a picturesque mountain scene for her parents, one with a dog skiing for her little brother, one with a photo of the wooden chalet we were sitting in for her grandmother (who she called her Mémé), and a replica of a 1950s advertising poster for her brother Franck. Sandrine and I told her to write the sun was shining, her friends skied so well they could be in the Olympics, and she adopted a Saint Bernard that we had found near the ski lift. Stéphanie made us sign each of these epistles, and I signed all four "*Bisous*, Laura (*la Canadienne*)."

"They know Sandrine," I said as I signed the last one for Franck, "but they're going to think it's awfully strange that I've signed them—none of them has ever met me."

"We'll fix that when *les vacances* are over," Stéphanie said, then began to lick her stamps.

True to her word, two weeks after the ski trip in the middle of March, Stéphanie and Sandrine informed me one day over our *jambon beurres* at Le Square that I was coming to a *discothèque* with them the next Saturday night. Thibaut never asked to do things with me on the weekend, so my schedule was wide open. Still, my initial reaction was suspicion.

"Why?" I said.

Stéphanie shrugged. "To dance, *bien sûr*. Olivier from our village is coming as well our friends Martial and Isabelle and Franck."

"Franck?" Ah hah! There it was.

Stéphanie's eyes slid away from mine. "He'll be home from the air force base for the weekend. We can hardly leave him at home. He hates having to waste a year doing the military service as it is."

Sandrine swallowed her bite of sandwich. "Plus, he's been hounding Stéphanie to meet you even more since he saw the photos of us in Saint Gervais."

I could feel Stéphanie kick Sandrine under the table. "I told you. I don't want you to set me up on a blind date with your brother," I said to Stéph." I'm sure he's perfectly nice, but I'm going out with Thibaut."

Sandrine choked on her baguette. When she had cleared her airway, she glared at me. "You are going out with Thibaut, are you? Is that what you call it?"

I crossed my arms over my chest and glared back. "I don't know. It's...something."

Sandrine rolled her eyes.

"Besides," I said, "I have my tap dancing performance that evening."

"Wait," Stéph grabbed my arm. "What? Tap dancing?"

I exchanged glances with Sandrine. Up to then, she was the only one who'd known.

"I've always wanted to tap dance, and I saw that there was a mini course being put on in Nuits-Saint-Georges the past two weekends." I could feel my face heat up with embarrassment. "I've been learning how to tap dance, and this Saturday night is our performance. We're doing it on the stage at the movie theatre."

"Did you tap dance growing up?" Stéph asked.

"I always wanted to, but my mom never let me. She said it was too noisy and vulgar. I had to do ballet instead, which I hated."

I braced myself for mockery, but Stéph just shrugged. "That sounds like fun...if you like tap dancing."

"As it turns out, I love it," I confessed. "It's really fun, actually."

"What time is your performance?"

"Six o'clock."

"How long is it?"

"About forty minutes. You can't learn that much in two weekends, you know."

"We'll pick you up just under *le beffroi* at eight."

"But—"

"Look," Stéphanie said, "it's just a group of friends going to hang out and dance for a bit. Franck will be there, but we're not trying to set you guys up."

Sandrine snorted.

"Shut up, Sandrine!" Stéph said, and then dissolved into laughter.

I realized after school that Friday that I couldn't possibly make the blind date. I wouldn't have time to get back to the Lacanches' to drop off my tap shoes. Also, I was coming down with a cold. My nose was pouring, and the last thing I felt like being was polite to some guy all evening just so as not to offend my friends.

I called Sandrine. "Salut, Sandrine," I said. "I can't come tonight. I won't have time to drop off my stuff after the performance. Besides, I think I'm coming down with something."

"We'll pick you up at eight underneath the *beffroi*," she said in a tone that brooked no argument. "I won't talk to you anymore if you don't come. Trust me, I'm good at sulking." Her family was right: she *was* as stubborn as a donkey.

"Sandrine!"

"Be there!" she said. "*Bisous*." She hung up the phone.

As the day wore on and I prepared myself for my performance, I actually did feel a thrill at tying on my tap shoes. I loved tap dancing, as it turned out, just as I had always thought I would. My mom had been wrong.

I shoved some extra clothes into my backpack so I could get changed out of the shiny, red silk shirt I had to don for the performance before meeting up with Sandrine and Stéph's gang. I purposely didn't take much care in choosing nice clothes, as I had no intention of playing along with this whole blind date thing. I was with Thibaut...well, not exactly *with* him, but something beyond mere friendship was still percolating there. Besides, I just didn't know if I had it in me to risk being disappointed yet again.

The tap performance was surprisingly nerve-wracking. The entire theatre was full of friends and family, and all the Lacanches had come to see me perform, even Anton who, at fourteen years old, looked distinctly exasperated with the family outing.

I took a deep breath, concentrated on my steps, and did my best not to think of the blind date afterward. *Clickety-clack, clickety-clack*... Tap dancing was loud, but so noisily satisfying. Also, I could tell from their congratulations after the performance, the Lacanches approved of what they felt was a most wholesome activity for an Ursus exchange student. They didn't consider it vulgar at all. They also knew I was going out with my friends from school and, perhaps because I had only mentioned the girls, gave me permission to stay over at Sandrine's house.

I checked my watch after I had bid them good-bye. It was already five minutes to eight. I quickly changed in the bathroom in the theatre, not even checking my face before running outside. I had no room in my backpack for my tap shoes, so I carried them slung over my shoulder by their red, silk ribbons.

Just then, I sneezed. Maybe I could just say a quick *bonjour* and then make my escape. As I hurried toward the *beffroi*, I fantasized about spending the evening in my cozy room beside the bell tower with a warm duvet and a hot lemon drink.

Just as I neared the bell tower, a snazzy, black French sportscar screeched to a stop beside me. Stéphanie leapt out of the car with her habitual verve, cigarette in hand. When she swung her shiny black hair out of her face and kissed me, I couldn't mistake the mischievous expression on her face.

Her brother followed closely on her heels. It had to be Franck. His cheeky smile struck me first, as though he knew that I would have preferred to stay at home but was having none of such spiritless behavior. He hadn't uttered a word, yet his eyes dared me to join them.

I gave him the traditional *bises* on each cheek. There was something electric when my skin touched his, something that made me hold my breath. He was clean-shaven, and his olive skin smelled vaguely of apples and wood chips. I hadn't expected Stéphanie's brother to be so handsome. *Devilishly* handsome. The cliché popped into my head out of nowhere, but I had to admit that, with his lean muscles, chiseled cheekbones, and those flashing, almond-shaped eyes, it was accurate. My pride bolstered me even as my heart sank. Men like Franck were invariably bad news, as well as not interested in the likes of me.

I stepped back—mainly because I couldn't think straight in his vicinity—and cocked an appraising eyebrow. "I've heard a lot about you," I said.

Franck's brows flew up for a split, but gratifying, second. He laughed. "*Bon*. I guess I have a lot to live up to."

"I guess you do."

He took my hand and pulled me down into the back seat of the car beside him. Somehow, I forgot all about backing out of the evening.

We were going to Buisson first, to pick up their other friends Martial and Isabelle. They were a couple and were already living together, Stéph told me. Nobody seemed at all shocked by this. I was pressed up against Franck's side in the car, and my heart, as a result, seemed determined to pound out of my chest. There was chemistry here, but I told myself that it was probably one-sided and only felt by little old *moi*.

"I almost didn't come tonight," I said to Franck. He turned to me, and I had the strangest feeling that at that moment we were the only people in the car. "I'm coming down with a cold, and I was tired from my tap-dancing. Sandrine didn't give me a choice."

"That doesn't surprise me," he said, and then picked up my tap shoes from my lap. "These are pretty with the ribbons and everything..." His hands ran over the lengths of red silk, and I repressed a shiver, wondering how those same hands would feel running over my skin.

"They're noisy too," I said. "They clickety-clack. It's awesome."

"You like making noise?" Franck kept the tap shoes in his hands.

"I'm starting to realize that I do sometimes, yes." I then broke this intense moment by sneezing three times.

"A cold. Poor you." Franck reached down and squeezed my forearm. "Do you know what I would do for you?"

"What?" I couldn't tear my eyes away from his face.

"I would have you take off most of your clothes and then wrap you up very tightly in a warm feather duvet. Then I would make you one of my special hot toddies and make sure you drink it all. You would get so warm in there that you would sweat it out, and I would wipe your forehead with a cool cloth. Then I would stay with you until your fever broke—which it would—and then maybe lie down and stay beside you until you fell asleep."

Franck's plan sounded appealing in such a myriad of ways. "Oh," I said simply, my imagination spinning too wildly to allow me to say anything more coherent.

"I almost canceled too," Franck admitted, smiling at me.

"Really?" Had he not wanted to be set up with me, either?

"My father and I spent the day moving huge pieces of stone from the floor of the barn to make an outside eating area under the wisteria." He rubbed his lower back. "I'm a little sore."

"What changed your mind?" I asked.

"You," he said. "I've been wanting to meet you for months, ever since Stéph started talking about you."

I stared at him. *And now? What does he think now?* If only I were a mind reader.

Olivier pulled up in front of a small stone house in a picturesque little village just down from Aloxe-Corton. Everyone leapt out except Franck and me.

"Laura's got a cold and I have a sore back. We'll wait here for you." Franck waved his friends on. "Is that OK?" he asked me, once we were alone in the back seat.

I nodded, not trusting my voice. I wanted to kiss him. I had no idea why, but all I could think of was *getting closer*.

"I am sort of going out with someone at school," I blurted out, then cursed myself. I was such an ass. Franck hadn't even said he was interested in me…

"Is it serious?" he asked.

"Not really. No."

"Then I don't see that as an insurmountable problem."

"An insurmountable problem for what?" I asked, confused.

"For this." Franck leaned toward me and, trailing his thumb along the line of my jaw, set a gentle kiss on my lips. This was so much gentler than Florian or Thibaut, yet a million times more electric. It left me wanting so much more. I moved closer and kissed him back. Franck's way of kissing me made me feel as though I had never been kissed before. The air between and around us was charged with desire, pushing us closer together and then closer still.

"I think I'm glad I came, after all," I murmured at one point.

"*Moi aussi.*"

The kisses became deeper and longer and more intriguing, until we were interrupted by a pounding on the car window. Olivier and Sandrine and Stéphanie were all peering in with huge grins on their faces, and a tall blond man and a much shorter blond girl—who had to be Martial and Isabelle—stood behind them, trying to get in a good look as well.

Stéph got in the car first, bubbling with laughter. "*That* didn't take long."

I felt my face burning. Had that really been me, making out with a guy I had met literally minutes before? Still, snuggled under Franck's arm, I couldn't regret anything.

"No, it didn't," Franck answered, able to maintain a certain dignity. "Some things, I guess, are just meant to be."

chapter twenty-four

Sandrine and I were woken up by her mother and the sound of a few insistent roosters in her garden.

"Come now, sleepyheads!" Madame Bissette burst into the bedroom with her usual energy. "It's almost ten o'clock. I've been up since dawn."

Sandrine buried her head deeper in her duvet. I opened my eyes, and it all came back to me in a rush—Franck and I making out shamelessly on the dance floor, and then on those couch things along the sides of the room... My heart skipped several beats. When Olivier had dropped us off the night before, he and Sandrine had arranged for us all to meet at Franck and Stéphanie's house at ten thirty to go for a *café* in Savigny. I hadn't been paying much attention, as I had been tangled in Franck's arms at the time.

I wasn't sure how he would act when he saw me. Would Franck be like Thibaut and pretend as though nothing happened? The mere idea of that felt like a lead weight in my gut. I wasn't sure I could bear that after the lightning bolt of the night before—the one I had been waiting to feel all my life. I knew, instinctively, that with Franck, the hurt would go deeper than mere wounded pride.

Madame Bissette came in again and yelled, "Sandrine!" in shrill tones, then ordered us to hurry down to eat our breakfast.

Sandrine groaned and turned over so she faced me. "*Alors*? You and Franck last night...?"

It was definitely a question. I considered lying but decided to be brave instead. "He's amazing."

Sandrine grinned at me. "Franck is handsome. He's smart, he's nice, he's funny…we don't get many of those around here."

I wondered briefly if Sandrine didn't have a little crush on him herself, then dismissed the idea. They had grown up together. "We don't get many of those in Canada either."

Sandrine stood up and began to get dressed. I followed her lead but found it a challenge to find my clothes among the piles of stuff that carpeted Sandrine's floor. "Franck and you…that was a real *coup de foudre*," Sandrine said as we walked down the stairs.

A lightning bolt. So, she had seen it too. That was exactly what I had felt. I had daydreamed about feeling that with a guy for years, but some part of me didn't believe it would ever really happen. Yet it did. I hoped it was mutual.

"How do you think he's going to act when I see him?" I ask Sandrine.

She cocked her head. "I don't know." Sometimes I wished the French weren't so incurably honest. "He's nice, though, so I'm sure it will be fine."

Nice. I didn't want nice. I wanted what we'd had the night before. More of that.

In the kitchen, Sandrine's father was preparing to go out and prune the vines. I gave him a kiss hello, and he patted my head and said he was happy to see the "*petite Canadienne*" again.

Sandrine's mother placed a steaming bowl of *café au lait* in front of each of us, and then two fresh baguettes, a plate of salted butter from Brittany, and three jars of homemade jam. "Try the Reine Claude," she instructed me. "My plum jam is my best."

The meeting with Franck loomed in my mind to the point where I was about to say I wasn't hungry enough to eat anything. Then Sandrine passed me a slice of baguette, and I began to spread the beautiful butter on it. I inhaled the smell of freshly baked bread. Maybe I could eat after all.

Sandrine dipped her baguette in her *café au lait.* "What about Thibaut?" she asked.

"To be honest, I've never known exactly what I'm doing with him. Anyway, I told Franck about him last night."

Sandrine's baguette halted mid air. "That was…honest…of you. Unnecessary, in my opinion, but honest. What did he say?"

"He said it didn't matter."

When I considered Franck's reaction to my confession about Thibaut, doubt washed over me again. Did Franck say Thibaut didn't matter because he never planned on us being together more than one night? I put my baguette down.

I was an independent woman. There was nothing wrong with getting together with a guy just for fun. It didn't have to mean anything. Except that, in the case with Franck, I wanted it to… I wouldn't show Franck that though. I would pretend as though we were just friends. That would be the best way to waylay the possibility of rejection. I just had to lock away the longing in my heart.

Forty minutes later, Sandrine and I were walking up the road from her house to Stéphanie's house. There was a stream of people coming in and out the door of a bistro that a red painted sign announced as Chez Jacky. Many of them waved at Sandrine, but they just stared at me.

"Don't mind them." Sandrine stopped walking for a second to cup her hands around her cigarette and light it. "They stare at anyone who's not from the village."

"They don't like strangers?"

Sandrine sucked in a deep drag of nicotine and then blew it out. "Not much. We Burgundians are always suspicious of outsiders. The thing to do is just stare right back at them."

I wished for a second that I smoked. I couldn't seem to figure out what to do with my hands. My fingers were trembling, I realized. I buried them deep in the pockets of my jacket.

"Do Stéph and Franck live far away?" I asked.

"Nothing in this village is far away. It's just past the mayor's office and across from the bakery. You remember—across the lane from my cousin Félix's house where you had New Year's."

I remembered the man I had bumped into in the dark that night in Félix's courtyard. Something in me was sure that had been Franck. "Right. Of course."

"We'll be there in a minute."

I tried to school my face into a blasé expression. Sandrine took a few more puffs of her cigarette then turned her shrewd blue eyes on me. "Nervous?"

I shook my head, then grimaced. "A bit."

Sandrine shrugged. "I've grown up with Franck, and whatever he does, it won't be mean. He's...how do you say in English? A gentleman."

The way she said "gentleman" with a crazy mix of her French and a mock upper-class British accent made me laugh. We turned the corner just after the village church and walked down the street that had the village bakery just to the right—the street I had driven up that night when I'd first tasted *escargots* with the Beaupres, and that I had slid down with Félix on my way to breakfast at his grandparents' house. All that time, Franck had been so close...

There, in front of the *boulangerie*, was a familiar, tousled head.

"Félix!" Sandrine called over to her cousin.

Félix, with four baguettes firmly anchored under his arm and a bag of pastries in his hand, was talking to an extremely elderly man wearing a voluminous black cape and leaning on a gnarled cane.

We greeted them. Félix kissed me with his usual uncomplicated warmth and introduced me to his friend, le Père Curie, the village priest.

The priest gave me a sweet smile and, on learning I was from Canada, launched into a detailed explanation of an old friend of his who had spent years up in the Northwest Territories researching a deceased French explorer from the 1800s.

Félix must have sensed I was having a difficult time following this rambling discourse and leapt in during one of the priest's rare pauses. "So, to what do we owe this pleasure?" he asked. "Why is our favorite *Canadienne* bestowing her presence on Villers-la-Faye this weekend?"

"I went out with Sandrine last night," I said, not sure how

much I should tell Félix given our brief—very brief—romantic interlude months before.

"She and Franck..." Sandrine wiggled her eyebrows, making her meaning clear. "They got along *extremely* well."

Félix rolled his eyes. "I knew I was right not to introduce you two. Now I'll have to share you!"

"Franck Germain?" *Père* Curie interjected. "He was one of my altar boys, you know. Terrible for stealing wine, but a charming lad."

Sandrine glanced at her watch. "We need to go. We're already late."

We kissed Félix good-bye, and he gave my arm a soulful squeeze. "It was lovely seeing you again, Laura. You deserve something good after putting up with Élise for three months."

"I do," I said, and laughed.

"Did you finally get it, you think?" he asked, a searching look in his eyes.

"You mean Franck?"

He nodded.

I wished I knew what the answer to that was. I would know in the next few minutes. I shrugged. "I'll keep you informed," I promised.

"*D'accord,*" he said, and waved us on our way.

Sandrine pointed to a wooden gate across the street. "That's their house."

She stopped in front of the gate and arched her thin eyebrows in question. "Are you ready?"

My heart was jumping around erratically in my chest. I could feel a flush heat up my face. God. This feigning nonchalance wasn't going so well. Sandrine rang the doorbell mounted on the stone pillar beside the gate.

I heard a low babble of voices and then the crunch of pea gravel under someone's feet. The gate opened. I couldn't breathe. Then I caught a telltale flash of long black hair and realized it was Stéphanie. She was also smoking a cigarette. She gave both Sandrine and I *les bises* and then beckoned us to come in.

"Did you have fun last night, Laura?" she smiled mischievously.

"Yes," I said simply. I wasn't sure how long my knees would hold me up. Franck had to be close by somewhere.

"Franck's just getting changed." She answered my unspoken question. "He'll be out in a second."

Sandrine made goggle eyes at me.

"Stop it, you two," I growled, smacking Sandrine on the shoulder. "You're terrible."

Stéph grinned. "OK. OK. But didn't I say that you and Franck would get along?"

"You did," I admitted.

"I just wanted everyone to acknowledge that this was my idea."

"It was my idea too!" Sandrine protested.

"Stop!" My gaze kept flitting toward the door that led from the kitchen out to the courtyard. As much as I loved Sandrine and Stéph, I wished more than anything that Franck and I didn't have an audience. It made things one hundred times more nerve-wracking.

I bit my lip, steeling myself for the inevitable disappointment. In the cold light of the morning, I realized that the idea of an older, gorgeous Frenchman falling in love with me was a tad far-fetched.

The door opened and Franck stepped out, wearing a faded pair of jeans, a white T-shirt, and the worn jacket I had found so soft the night before. His eyes met mine with a glint of mischief and—was I really seeing it or did the set of his mouth hint that he too was nervous?

I was sure my pupils dilated. I felt his nearness with every cell in my body.

"*Bonjour*," he said. He gave Sandrine, who was standing closest to the door, *les bises*.

Meanwhile, I stood rooted to my spot, just staring at him. *So much for being cool and collected.*

He stepped in front of me and looked down into my face. I caught a whiff of savon de Marseille and apples. I was right at eye level with that delectable bit of skin just under his earlobe that I had tasted extensively just hours before. How was I supposed to act as though nothing had happened? All I wanted to do was grab him by the collar and kiss him.

He took one step closer. My heart pounded. I felt a crazy dip in my stomach. He reached out and ran a finger down my jawline. "*Bonjour, toi,*" he murmured, low enough that I knew it was just for me.

"*Bonjour,*" I managed to get out.

He leaned down and planted the softest but most thorough kiss. My arms found their way around his back, and I sank into the rightness of our embrace.

I forgot about Sandrine and Stéphanie standing right beside us as Franck's hand reached up behind the weight of my hair and caressed the nape of my neck. I sighed against his chest. He gave me a gentle kiss, and then another, before wrapping an arm around my shoulders and pulling me close to him.

Sandrine and Stéphanie were watching us with identical bemused expressions. "Like I said last night," Sandrine said to Stéphanie, as though continuing a conversation, "*un vrai coup de foudre.*"

As I stood there, still reeling from Franck's unequivocal greeting, I did feel exactly like I had been hit by a lightning bolt. Shocked. Electrified. Glowing. Every molecule in my body alight.

Franck just smiled and bent down to plant a kiss on the top of my head.

"Where are your parents?" Sandrine asked him.

"They went to Dijon to get groceries," he said. "Olivier should be here any minute. He'll drive us."

"Which café?" Sandrine asked.

"Not the one on the main square," Stéphanie said. "The one across from the good *boulangerie.*"

I was glad that all the attention was no longer on us. I could just enjoy the feeling of Franck's arm around my shoulders and revel in our greeting without thinking of anything else.

There was a knock at the gate, and Stéphanie went to open it to let in Olivier. He didn't seem to be particularly surprised to see Franck's arm around my shoulders and greeted us all with *les bises*. He seemed impatient to get going. "Ladies and Gentleman." He ushered us out the gate, and Franck detached himself from me long enough to lock it behind us.

"We'll be a seat short," Sandrine said.

"Excellent," Franck said. "Laura can sit on my lap...if she doesn't mind."

"I don't mind," I assured him. We all laughed and piled into Olivier's black Citroën sports car. I settled on Franck's thighs, and he pulled me back so I was nestled against him. He tracked scrumptious little kisses down my collarbone.

"I guess I don't have a seat belt," I said.

Franck tightened his arms around me. "Don't worry. I'm not going to let you go."

chapter twenty-five

Olivier drove at breakneck speed down through the vineyards toward Beaune. We whipped past a stunning village built on a hillside that looked like something out of a storybook, although I couldn't quite pay one hundred percent attention to the landscape with Franck nibbling on my neck.

"Mmmmm," I said, "what was that village we just went through?"

"Pernand-Vergelesses," he murmured in the whorl of my ear, so that I shivered with pleasure. "I'll bring you back here."

Part of me felt self-conscious sitting on his lap and intermittingly making out while Sandrine and Stéphanie sat beside us. Neither of them seemed remotely uncomfortable. In fact, the only time they acknowledged us at all was when they flashed us satisfied grins.

I was not this kind of person. I was not the girl sitting on a boy's lap, kissing him, in the light of day… I had always been the friend sitting nearby, trying hard to act as though I was perfectly fine with it never being my turn to fall in love. Yet this felt right. Being with Franck was the strangest dichotomy of excitement and calm. His mere proximity gave me the most incredible feeling of comfort, but it also unleashed a million new sensations in my body and mind.

I was still wondering at this unexpected turn of events when Olivier parked his car in front of a huge stone fountain. Franck had wound my hair around his wrist and was peppering my mouth with gentle, teasing kisses.

Sandrine poked my side. "*Eh, les amoureux*. We're here."

I surfaced briefly. "Where?" I could stay exactly where I was—and happily—for much longer.

Franck laughed. "Savigny-les-Beaune. You can't mistake it for any other village around here. Just look at the castle."

He gently repositioned me so that out our window I could see the huge castle that looked as though it had been plucked directly from a Grimm's fairy tale. It was built of glowing, cream stone, anchored by four chubby, medieval turrets on its four corners.

"Wow," I murmured in English.

Franck kissed me once more. "Wow," he repeated with his heavy French accent. "I like that. Did I pronounce it right?"

I gave him one last kiss before sliding off his lap and opening our door. "We can work on it." A corner of Franck's mouth lifted in a lopsided smile, and he got out after me. He interlaced his fingers in mine.

Sandrine, Stéphanie, and Olivier all lit cigarettes, which they began to puff on as we walked across the square in the shadow of the looming castle. I knew from the previous night that Franck smoked too, but he held firm onto my hand instead of fishing in his pocket for his package of Gitanes.

"Can we go visit the castle?" I asked.

They all, including Franck, looked at me with an amused expression on their faces.

Stéphanie laughed, not unkindly. "We don't really visit castles. That's for tourists. For us, they're just...there."

"Besides," Olivier added, "that one is owned by a crazy count who collects old sport cars and airplanes and motorcycles, so the castle is full of them."

As Franck led me by the hand into the café, I marveled at being blasé at the proximity of such an incredible and ancient building. Despite having a French *amoureux*—boyfriend still sounded too official for something so brand new—I didn't think I would ever be blasé enough about such things to be truly French.

Inside the café, Martial and Isabelle were waiting for us, nursing tiny cups of espresso. They shared a look with Sandrine and Stéphanie when they saw Franck pull me close to him, give me a kiss, and whisper, "Would you like a *café* or something else?" in my ear.

"*Un café*," I murmured back, giving his hand a squeeze. He nodded and headed off to the zinc café counter to order.

I sat down beside Isabelle.

"*Alors?*" She widened her eyes at me. "You like our Franck?"

I could feel a blush warming my cheeks, but I nodded and said, "*Oui.*"

Isabelle sat back and smiled at me. "The feeling looks mutual. I haven't seen him this happy in a long time. I'm glad for you."

"How long have you and Martial—"

She hooted with laughter. "It feels like forever! Since I was fifteen, I think...or sixteen. Young. But when you've found your *âme soeur*, why bother looking any further?"

"*Âme soeur*—I haven't heard that expression before."

She tapped her cigarette against the ashtray and leaned back in her chair. "*L'âme soeur*...let me try to explain. It means the person whose soul matches yours. The person you are meant to be with. Martial and I figured that out right away. Who knows? Maybe you and our Franck—"

"We just met last night," I reminded her, thinking it was perhaps a bit premature to declare us soul mates already. Part of me—that crazy romantic part of me that I had always had to squash down in the past—did think I certainly didn't want to jinx anything.

"When it's right, it's right," Isabelle shrugged. "That's just the way it is. You'll know."

Franck set an espresso in front of me and sat across from me at the table. He reached over and took my hand in his. "I thought I might leave you one hand free to drink your *café*."

"That's thoughtful of you."

"Yes. If I wasn't as gallant as I am, we wouldn't be here at all," Franck said.

"Where would we be instead?"

"Probably still in the back seat of Olivier's car."

"And what would we be doing in there?" I teased him.

"Many things." Franck caressed the palm of my hand with his thumb. "Many, *many* things."

We shared a long look.

"But since we *are* here, I suppose I should initiate some stimulating conversation." Franck's eyes glinted. "Who is your favorite French philosopher?"

I had certainly never gotten together with a guy and then had him ask me about philosophy.

"Sartre," I said. "Rousseau is a bit extreme—you know the bit about sending your kids out in the woods to bring themselves up. In Canada, you see, the problem with that is that we have bears and cougars in the woods."

"Really?" Franck was riveted. "That sounds intriguing."

"Not if you encounter them in the wild. They get hungry, and small children move and sound like forest animals."

Franck's lips twitched. "That would be a problem."

"Yes. So, I would have to say I prefer Sartre to Rousseau."

"You know about French philosophers," Franck looked impressed.

"Yes. I suppose you do too?"

"Oh yes. I studied at the Sorbonne for two years. I did my first two years in Dijon, but then a friend and I went up to Paris."

"What did you study?"

"My degree was in communications, but I did a lot of philosophy courses."

I narrowed my eyes at him, skeptical. This was exactly one of those instances I had experienced so many times since arriving in France when people tried to make me believe stuff and then, as soon as I bit the hook, teased me for being so gullible. Thibaut was one of the worst for this. The Sorbonne is one of the most prestigious schools in the world. Was Franck just teasing me about having gone there?

"You went to *the* Sorbonne?" I clarified. "The one in Paris?"

"Is there another?"

"I don't know but...that's the one you attended?"

"I just told you I did." He leaned back in his chair, looking amused rather than offended. "You don't believe me?"

Now I was really uncertain. Was his amusement because he was lying and I believed him, or was it because he was telling the truth and I didn't believe him?

"Stéphanie," I called down the table to her, "did Franck really go to the Sorbonne?"

Stéphanie exchanged glances with Sandrine and started laughing. Now I was even more confused. Were they all playing a joke on me?

"Tell me." I said. "Please."

"Why would you think he hadn't?" Sandrine asked.

I shrugged. "I don't know. It's just such a prestigious school—"

"I'm not stupid." Franck laughed. "Some teachers actually thought I was quite smart."

"That's not what I meant." I lowered my head to the table in exasperation.

Franck squeezed my hand. "Not that it matters in the grand scheme of things, but I really did go to the Sorbonne. But you don't have to believe me yet. Are you finished your coffee?"

I looked down at my empty cup. "Yes."

"Will you come for a drive with me?" Franck asked.

I hesitated a moment. Franck is almost five years older than me, and even though I had become an expert at playing as though I was far worldlier than I actually was, I did not suffer from a surfeit of actual experience with boys, or more accurately in the case of Franck, men. I didn't know him that well. Besides, what about that "No Dating" Ursus rule? With Thibaut, I was always secure with the knowledge that I could put forward a convincing argument that whatever weird thing we had going on between us, it couldn't be called "dating." With Franck, though, things already felt much more...unambiguous.

Franck was waiting for my answer.

The desire to be alone with him pulsed within me. I was teetering on the top of something very tall and I wanted to jump. "Yes," I said.

"Can I borrow your car?" Franck asked Olivier, his hand already out for the keys.

Olivier passed them over without blinking an eye. "Don't be so hard on the clutch this time," he said.

"We'll be back in about an hour," Franck said. "Then we can all head back to Villers. I have to catch a train back to Dijon by four o'clock."

Olivier raised an eyebrow at me. "I'm trusting you to keep an eye on the time, Laura," he said. "That has never been one of Franck's talents."

I got up from the table, my legs a bit unsteady. "It does happen to be one of my talents." I brandished my wristwatch.

Franck took me outside, holding my hand and casting me a complicit look that I couldn't help but share.

"Where are you taking me?"

"You'll see," he said.

Nerves battled with curiosity in my gut. "Can I trust you?" I got in the car and Franck shut the door behind me before walking over to his side.

"That's a good question. I'm not sure what to answer."

"You should answer yes."

Franck studied me as he turned the key and revved up the motor. "To be honest I don't even know myself if I can trust myself around you. You are extremely *séduisante*."

I stared at him as he busied himself with backing the car out without hitting any of the other insane drivers whipping through the streets or running over a villager. No man had ever called me seductive before, certainly not in that way that made it sound as though he was merely stating the obvious.

He drove quickly out of the village and back up to the beautiful village perched on the hillside. "What did you say this village was called again?" I asked.

"Pernand-Vergelesses," he answered. "There's a special spot here I want to show you."

So, at least he wasn't dragging me to a hotel room or something. That reassured me...a bit.

Franck drove beyond the village on a steep road that dropped off vertiginously on one side as a slope of vineyards. Finally, he spun into a clearing.

I bit my lip. Where *was* he taking me?

He pulled up the parking brake and looked over at me. He reached over and took my hand, studying my face. "Are you scared of me?" Already the solid, warm feel of his hand was anchoring me.

"A bit," I admitted. "I mean, we just met. I don't know you."

He reached over to brush some stray strands of hair behind my ear "I'm not so sure about that. I feel like we do know each other somehow."

"Part of me feels like that too," I said. "Still..."

"You never need to be afraid of me. Will you remember that?"

I nodded.

He led me across a field of grass that still smelled like earth and spring rain. In the distance I saw something large and carved out of gray stone.

"Is that a statue?" I couldn't help feeling a bit amused. It was not at all what I had been imagining.

"Yes," he glanced at me sideways. "Well, that and the view. I just wanted to bring you here. It's always been a special place for me. Maybe you'll think it's silly."

"I don't," I said.

We walked around the front of the statue, and I realized that the hill we were on provided a bird's-eye view down the valley that led from Pernand-Vergelesses all the way over to Beaune and the row upon row and slope upon slope of vineyards, now bright green with the budding leaves of spring.

I looked up and saw the unmistakable form of the Virgin Mary holding Jesus in her arms towering over us.

"You brought me to a statue of Virgin Mary?" I asked in disbelief. Sneaking away for wild sex had obviously not been in Franck's plans.

Franck glanced up at Mary's serene stone face. It was an exceptionally beautiful statue. The carving was exquisite. Nevertheless... "*Oui.*" Obviously, he didn't see anything odd in this at all.

Above the stone figures the words "*Priez pour Nous*" were etched into the stone above the Virgin's head. *Pray for us. Indeed.* Whatever Franck ended up being, he was radically different from any other guy I had been with before.

I turned back to admire the stunning view. "It's beautiful."

Franck took my hand and led me over to the foot of the statue, which had a base made up of three stone stairs. He pulled me down on his knee. "It's beautiful down here too." He took my face in his hands. We fell into a deep, long kiss.

I finally broke away to catch my breath. "I wonder what the Virgin Mary thinks of that." I glanced up at her serene countenance.

"I'm sure she approves," Franck assured me, easily. "She's all about love, *après tout*."

I hoped she did approve, because Franck and I couldn't stop kissing. It was as though we had invented kissing. Our mouths fit together in so many endless ways and permutations, and I soaked up every second of feeling so safe yet alive in his arms. Finally, I said faintly, "What time is it?"

"I don't know," Franck said between kisses. He was caressing the trail of my vertebra. His hands had mysteriously made their way up the back of my sweater. "To be perfectly honest, I don't really care."

"We promised Olivier..."

"Olivier's a good friend. He'd understand."

"Not that I want this to end because, believe me, I don't, but didn't you have to take the train back to Dijon?"

Franck moaned. "You're right. The French military is, sadly, not as understanding as Olivier. The punishment for reporting back late is restricting future leaves."

"I have to get back too," I said, doubt descending upon me again. "The Lacanches will be wondering where I am."

Will I see Franck again? I knew I wanted to, and he didn't talk as though he was only interested in this weekend, but then again, he had never brought up Thibaut again either. Was that because he didn't remember, didn't want to bring it up, or didn't care? That last possibility pierced my heart.

"So..." I began to get up. "It was nice meeting you." I cursed myself. That came out in French sounding so awkward and formal—so *not* what I wanted to say—despite the fact that we'd been kissing a few seconds previously. Still, I thought of Thibaut and how many times I had misjudged his intentions.

"You say that like you are saying good-bye," Franck said, pulling back to examine my face. "Do you not want to see me again?"

"I do! I just didn't know...you know...if you had a lot of time, with your military service and everything."

"I'll make the time." Franck fixed me with his hazel eyes. "Even if it means having to be on time for the first time in my life. Can I see you next weekend?"

"Yes." I was still feeling at a loss for words, so I leaned down and began kissing him again. He responded in kind, and it was several more minutes until we surfaced. Why was this kind of communication so easy, and the verbal kind so difficult?

"What about that other guy?" Franck asked.

Relief washed over me. So, he hadn't forgotten about Thibaut and he did care. "It's over. I just need to tell him."

Franck's lips were making their way down my neck, making my breath come short and quick. "I'm glad to hear that."

I could only conjure up a vague impression of Thibaut in my mind. What Franck was doing seemed to obliterate all thought.

Franck picked up one of my hands and turned it over, giving me a gentle kiss on the tender skin on the inside of my wrist before examining the time on my watch. "*Merde*! I am going to miss my train if we don't hurry."

I hopped up, and hand in hand we ran back to the car and sped back to Savigny, stealing kisses whenever possible. I felt as though I was flying, amazed and a bit terrified to think that I may have met someone who filled that vacant place in my soul.

chapter twenty-six

The next day at school, I didn't see Thibaut until lunchtime in the cafeteria. Sandrine had already sat down beside me, determined not to miss the show.

"Has Franck called you yet?" she asked.

"Not yet," I said, "but he warned me he wouldn't be able to until later in the week. The base has crazy rules about phone calls."

"Stéphanie said that on the way back down to the train station, he stopped talking about you only long enough to take the odd breath. Complete *coup de foudre*."

I was so engrossed in pleasant memories that I didn't realize Thibaut had come to sit down beside us. "What's this about a *coup de foudre*?" he asked. "You, Sandrine?"

Sandrine shook her head, mischief written on every feature. "Laura," she clarified with no small amount of satisfaction.

"What?" Thibaut demanded, confused. I knew he was thinking of how we had been making out in the Philosophy class on Friday during a film on Voltaire in our usual covert fashion. "Laura? *Un coup de foudre?* That's impossible. Unless you mean with me."

"No," I said, in measured tones. "Don't you remember what we learned about Pascal in Philosophy class? *Le coeur a ses raisons que la raison ne connaît pas.*" The heart has reasons that reason does not recognize.

"What's his name?" Thibaut demanded.

I answered with a perfectly gauged French shrug.

"I don't believe it," Thibaut declared. "I think you and Sandrine have just concocted this story to tease me."

"Believe what you like," I said.

Sandrine started laughing with delight. "This is too good! I can't wait to tell Stéphanie."

"Laura, I'm warning you," Thibaut said, and now the entire table of our friends was paying attention. What had happened to him being so secretive about us? "If there is another guy, there will be no more kisses from me."

I took a spoonful of my *crème brûlée* dessert and gave him a sweet smile. "Don't worry yourself about that, Thibaut," I said. "It just so happens that I'm not in need of your kisses anymore."

Later on that day, Thibaut seemed to be getting desperate and, as I was standing beside Sandrine waiting for the bus back to Nuits-Saint-Georges, sent over Maxime as an emissary.

"What you said to Thibaut at lunch wasn't very kind." Maxime chided me, but at the same time fidgeted with the strap on his backpack, not looking entirely confident in his role.

"Are you serious?" I said. "What about Thibaut's behavior?"

"What do you mean?" Maxime's eyes were like those of a trapped animal.

"I mean," I said, "making out with me in secret but then wanting to hide it so as to keep his options open for several months. *That* wasn't very kind of Thibaut."

Maxime scuffed one of his long sneaker-shod feet on the ground. "I never understood why he was doing that. We all knew anyway."

"It was hardly flattering."

Sandrine smoked her cigarette, nodding.

"What happens if things don't work out with this new guy?"

Maxime asked.

The question was a valid one. This thing with Franck was so brand new—what if he didn't call me, and all I would ever have was last weekend?

I knew the answer. Just that weekend, even if nothing more came of it, gave me hope that what I yearned for in the depths of my romantic heart might truly exist. I could never go back to the paltry compromise I accepted with Thibaut. I wanted more. I wanted it all.

I couldn't help but listen for the phone over the next few days. There were only two in the Lacanches' house—one in their bedroom, and one for the family, which sat in a place of honor on the shiny, black piano in the living room, which Monsieur Lacanche was wont to play when he had had a few too many glasses of wine. Because my bedroom was upstairs beside the massive church bell, I was always the last one to hear the phone ring, and the last one to get to it as well. How was I going to explain that a man was calling me? Every time the phone rang when I was downstairs in the main part of the house, my heart leapt to my throat, and I became paralyzed until I overheard the conversation long enough to know it wasn't Franck on the other end.

Finally, on Thursday night at around nine o'clock, just when I was about to go upstairs to my church bell hideaway, the phone rang. Goose bumps prickled all over my skin. It was him. I *knew* it.

Madame Lacanche glided over and picked up the phone. "*Bonjour, j'écoute*!" she said in her usual chipper voice.

She listened for a few seconds and then turned to me slowly, her thin, blond eyebrows raised almost to her hairline. "Laura, it's for you," she said. "It's a person named Franck. A man."

"*Ah bon*?" I tried to look surprised. "*Merci.*" I scuttled over and took the receiver, my palms sweaty and my heart pounding.

The entire family was sitting on the two couches watching a French variety show featuring a woman with a pet monkey who could dance the can-can. Anyone who labored under the misconception that the French are all unrelentingly highbrow just needed to watch a few minutes of the enormously popular variety shows.

"*Bonjour*," I said into the receiver, eyeing the family, who were now all watching me instead of the television. *Watch the monkey!* I felt like yelling at them. *It's a monkey in a can-can dress for goodness sakes!*

"Laura"—Franck's voice warmed me to my toes and brought back a wash of memories—"it is wonderful to hear your voice."

"Ah...it's the same for me," I said, aware of five sets of eyes on me.

"You sound strange," Franck observed.

"*Ahhhh...non*," I said. "*Tout va bien*."

"Are you alone?" he asked.

"*Non*," I answered, emphatic. "Not at all. Like, really...no. Definitely not."

"Ah. I see."

"*Oui*. That's it."

"This weekend? Can we see each—"

"Yes. I'd like that."

Franck laughed. "Good. Can I pick you up in Nuits-Saint-Georges on Saturday morning when I get in from Dijon?"

"What time?"

"Ten o'clock. Is that too early?"

"*Non, non.*"

The Lacanches' nine-year-old daughter, Alix, began tugging at the phone cord. "Is he asking you out on a *date*, Laura? Who is it? Is it your *amoureux*?"

"Alix!" Madame Lacanche beckoned her back, but Alix wasn't listening. For an angelically fair little girl, she could certainly act like the very devil.

"Do you know something?" Franck had lowered his voice.

"What?" I asked, my heart flipping in my chest and my face on fire.

"I've been thinking about you all the time."

"You have?"

"What is he saying? What is he saying?" Alix demanded. I shook my head at her.

"Yes. And I've been thinking about how I am going to kiss you when I see you again."

"Really?" I tried not to sound as breathless as I felt.

"Really. Hundreds of kisses. Everywhere."

"Oh," I said faintly.

"I can hear you have an attentive audience on your end. Now say *au revoir* and put the phone down. I'll see you in two days."

"*Au revoir.*" I hung up.

"Who is Franck?" Monsieur Lacanche asked, motioning me down to the sole empty armchair, a place where I had seen him position his children when they were being interrogated.

"He is my friend Stéphanie's brother," I supplied. "He's doing his military service in Dijon."

"He sounds quite old," Madame Lacanche observed, frowning. "Not a boy."

"He's a few years older than me," I admitted. "He did his degree at the Sorbonne before his military service."

This seemed to mollify them a bit.

"Nothing too serious, I hope," added Monsieur Lacanche. "You know the Ursus rule against dating."

"Of course," I said. "We just basically hang out with a big group of friends."

Monsieur Lacanche nodded. "All right, but if he is picking you up, I would like to meet him first."

"That would be nice," I said, although I was secretly horrified at the idea of such a summit. How on earth was I going to spring that on Franck?

"Nothing too serious, right, Laura?" Madame Lacanche reminded me in a sweet but slightly menacing voice.

If I examined the bare facts of the previous weekend, so far nothing too serious had happened. Still, in my heart, it felt like something very serious indeed.

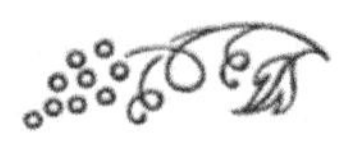

Saturday rolled around far too slowly. To think that only a week before I had been sitting up in my attic room, debating whether or not to cancel on the evening at the *discothèque* and forgo meeting Franck. I was sure that, like most of the other boys I had known, he would disappoint. So far, I couldn't have been more wrong.

When Franck called from the train station in Dijon, I warned him that the Lacanches wanted to meet him.

"An interview?" he divined.

"That's more or less what it's going to be," I admitted. "I'm sorry."

"It's fine," he assured me. "I'll be on my best behavior."

"I know it's a pain—"

"Laura, I'm happy to do it. If it means we can see each other more easily, it's worth it. I can be quite charming when I want, you know."

"I'm quite aware of that," I assured him.

An hour and a half later, Franck was being ushered into the Lacanches' living room and pressed to accept an *apéritif.* "A kir," he said, taking a seat on the couch. "Thank you."

I sat down beside him but quickly regretted that decision. I could feel his proximity like an electric charge in the air between us. I wanted to touch him so badly that I was having a hard time concentrating on the conversation.

Monsieur Lacanche was playing a cello concerto on his stereo system. "Bach's *Cello Suite No. 1*?" Franck asked. "Most people say that the best interpretation is Yo-Yo Ma's, but I don't agree. I have always thought Rostropovich puts far more emotion into his playing."

Monsieur Lacanche's face lit up. "You know classical music?"

His tone was so shocked that I wouldn't have blamed Franck for sending back a flinty answer, but instead he was charm personified. "Oh yes. I grew up listening to it. My mother plays nothing else. The first trip I ever took was when I was four, and we drove to Austria to follow in Mozart's footsteps."

"*Vraiment*?" Monsieur Lacanche answered. "What do you think of organ music?"

"I love it," Franck said. "Have you ever heard the organ at the Saint Sylvestre church in Ladoix-Serrigny? It is such a shame that church is closed now most of the time. There is no sound like it."

Monsieur Lacanche gasped. "As a matter of fact, that organ is my special little '*projet du coeur*' I am working on. I and a few other music lovers in the region have been fundraising to have the organ restored to its original glory and to put on a special series of recitals where we'll bring in master organists from all over the world."

"What a wonderful idea," Franck said. "Will you be bringing in Jean Guillou?"

"That would be a dream!" Monsieur Lacanche declared, clapping his hands together at the idea.

I stared at Franck in stupefaction. Who was this cultured man on the couch beside me? What other surprises was he hiding up his sleeve? And to think Julien told me long ago that villagers from the Hautes-Côtes were rougher around the edges than their counterparts on the lower *côtes*...

The conversation remained mainly between Franck and Monsieur Lacanche. They discussed the many classical performances Franck had attended in Paris while he was at the Sorbonne. This went on for a good forty minutes, until Franck took my wrist and consulted my watch in a gesture that seemed oddly intimate. I shivered at his touch.

"I'm afraid I have to cut short this fascinating conversation," he said, smiling at Monsieur Lacanche. "My family is waiting for us in Villers-la-Faye."

"So, you will be staying with Sandrine tonight again?" Madame Lacanche asked, giving me a pointed look.

"Yes," I said. "I left her home phone number on the chalkboard in the kitchen in case you need to reach me." This seemed to reassure Madame Lacanche a bit.

"I will bring Laura back tomorrow on my way to the train station, if that is acceptable to you," Franck said.

"Wonderful! Wonderful!" Monsieur Lacanche patted Franck on the back when he got up. "I do hope you will be able to dine with us one weekend soon when you are home from Dijon. We haven't even begun to talk about what you do on the military base!"

"Even though I am part of the Air Force, they unfortunately haven't seen fit to let me fly the Mirage 2000 jets," Franck said as we made our way down the stairs. "To be honest, I'm not much more than a glorified secretary."

Monsieur and Madame Lacanche laughed appreciatively at this piece of wit.

They waved us into the car, and Franck waved back as we pulled away from the curb. I felt nervous being alone with him again, as well as excited, but I was also expiring of curiosity.

At the end of the street, I began to clap. "Bravo! Well played, *monsieur*!"

Franck's lips twitched into a smile.

"How on earth did you know all that stuff about the cello concertos and the organ musicians?"

Franck was concentrating on another car that was coming at us quickly in the tiny cobblestoned street only wide enough for one car to pass. "I love classical music and I was brought up listening to it," he said. "That was the truth. It was a lucky coincidence, though, I'll give you that."

Franck drove two streets further until, without warning, he swerved over and parked the car haphazardly in the shadow of one of Nuits-Saint-George's many imposing wine domaines.

"What—" Before I could get another word out Franck unbuckled my seat belt and pulled me toward him in one urgent movement.

"I think this is far enough away to be safe," he said. "Anyway, it's as long as I can last without doing this." His hands found the sides of my face and his lips found mine.

The kiss, or kisses, lasted for a long time. By the time I came up for air, I couldn't string together a coherent thought.

"I've been wanting to do that from the moment I saw you waiting for me, all nervous, on the curb," Franck said. "Sitting so close to you on the couch was torture."

"I know," I tried in vain to marshal my senses. I leaned forward and kissed him again, and we didn't say another word for several more minutes.

"We're never going to get to Villers-la-Faye this way," I murmured against his mouth.

"*Non*," Franck said, interspersing his words with kisses, not seeming particularly bothered by this fact. "They must be waiting for us by now." His fingers were doing something magical at the nape of my neck and down my spine.

I sighed against him. Just then an irate man wearing a beret, who apparently wanted to turn his giant Mercedes into the gate we were blocking with the car, started honking at us. Franck gave me one last kiss and a burning look promising more before he revved the engine again and took off up through the vineyards toward Villers-la-Faye.

The road was steep, windy, and narrow, with a wicked drop-off on the side. It was the same one where Monsieur Beaupre had detached his rearview mirror on the way up to La Maison des Hautes-Côtes. Franck kept looking over at me.

"You should maybe watch the road," I said, as much as I liked the way he devoured me with his eyes.

"I love how you're so practical."

Me? Practical? I was known in my family as the space cadet always lost in daydreams. "Not always," I assured him.

"I know this road like the back of my hand," he said. "I could drive it blindfolded...actually...*non*, it's probably too soon to tell you that story. I've been going up and down it my whole life. Your face, on the other hand...I'm still discovering that."

His face was something I was discovering too. As he drove, I sat back and drank in his profile—his full lips, his square jaw, and his absolutely straight, perfect nose...the way his eyes kindled and his mouth quirked to one side as if having a hard time containing a smile...

The only problem was that in four months I was returning to Canada and Franck would be staying there in France. For the first time, my thrill over Franck was tinged with panic. Should I let myself fall this hard and fast for someone who I could only be with for such a short period of time? I didn't know the answer to that, so I just sat back in the seat and watched Franck, with my hand under his as he shifted gears.

chapter twenty-seven

Many hours later, we were sitting in the café in Savigny, sharing delicious thin-crust pizzas and washing them down with the house red that was exceedingly tolerable, probably because it *was* Savigny-les-Beaune, after all.

Franck and I sat side by side and laughed and talked with Olivier, Stéphanie, and Sandrine, who regaled us with stories. His arm rested on my shoulders, and we rarely made it past a minute without pausing for a kiss.

Olivier was drinking more than the rest of us, and as the evening wore on, he became increasingly maudlin. He began talking about a girl named Louise.

"*Eh merde.*" Sandrine took a deep drag of her cigarette. "He's on to Louise."

"Who is Louise?" I asked Sandrine.

"His ex-girlfriend," she said with a grimace.

Sandrine clearly knew Olivier well, because within half an hour, Olivier had ordered and downed several glasses of calvados—apple brandy from Normandy—and was weeping openly over Louise.

I turned to Franck. "I think I need a bit of background here," I said, indicating Olivier with my head.

"He went out with Louise last year," he whispered in my ear. I had to concentrate on what he was saying instead of just reveling in how good it felt. "They only went out for three months or so, but Olivier was hopelessly in love. She broke up with him, and he's never gotten over her, especially not when he gets into a bottle of calvados."

Olivier climbed up onto the tabletop and began singing an off-key song about a girl named Louise, pausing every few seconds to cry.

"I think it's time we take him home," Franck said, studying his friend.

"*Non*!" Olivier yelled down to Franck. "I'm not going anywhere. I'm staying right here. Louise is going to come here tonight. I feel it."

"Do you think you're going to need some help?" Sandrine asked. She had brought her car and was sober enough to drive it.

"*Non*!" Without warning, Olivier leapt off the table and ran outside the café door into the main square.

"Yes, I'll need help." Franck sighed. "I need to go after him," he said to us. "He's going to get hit by a car. Can you go and see if Martial is home?" he asked Sandrine.

"*D'accord*," Sandrine agreed and hurried out into the night.

"Sorry," he said to me as he got up and then gave me a kiss before putting on his jacket.

"I waved him off. "Go. Hurry. You're right. It's not safe for him out there in the state he's in."

"Has Olivier done this before?" I asked Stéphanie after Franck had left.

"He's never taken off before, but every three months or so we have to take him home because he goes a bit crazy about Louise. The taking off is a bit of a problem, though," Stéphanie mused. "Olivier is small but surprisingly speedy."

I peered outside, hoping that Franck would catch Olivier quickly. "It's dark out there."

"Franck is crazy about you," Stéphanie said, changing the topic. "You are all he talks about."

"I like him too," I said.

Stéphanie fiddled with the paper wrapped around the sugar cube that came with her espresso. "I just wanted to say...I haven't seen him this happy since he broke up with his ex-girlfriend last summer. There were some very hard months after that. We were all worried about him."

"He hasn't mentioned her," I said, a sick feeling in my stomach. So, he *had* been in love, and recently too....

"That doesn't surprise me," Stéphanie said. "He never went crazy about her like Olivier gets about Louise. Instead, he holed himself up in his bedroom and barely came out. All he did was read philosophy books and take notes...in a way, it would have been simpler if he had acted like Olivier."

I didn't want to put into words the first question that leapt into my mind, let alone pose it to Stéphanie, but I was driven by a sort of morbid curiosity. "Was Franck...was he very much in love with his ex-girlfriend?"

It took Stéphanie a while to answer. "I believe he thought he was, but none of us liked her much. She was jealous and possessive."

"What was her name?"

"Juliette."

There were so many other questions I wanted to ask. Where was she from? How old was she? Was she pretty? How long had they been going out? Why had they broken up? Instead, I just said, "Oh," my voice hollow. I hoped I wasn't a simple rebound relationship.

"The military service has been good for him," Stéphanie continued. "Given him some structure, and now, of course, there's you."

"I have to go back to Canada in July," I reminded her.

Stéphanie nodded. "We're all trying not to think about that. I know that makes things difficult. I guess what I'm trying to say is...don't hurt him. Not more than you have to by leaving, in any case."

What about me? I wanted to ask. Who is protecting me?

"I won't," I said. It was the truth. Whatever happened, I couldn't imagine Franck willfully hurting me or me wanting to willfully hurt him.

Just then, Franck ran inside the café. "Has he come back?" he gasped, out of breath.

"No," I said. "Can't you find him?"

Franck shook his head. "Is Martial here yet?"

"No," Stéph said. "But if Olivier comes back in here, Laura and I will tackle him to the ground. *Promets.*"

I nodded in agreement. Franck's mouth curved up and he ran over, gave me a solid kiss, then ran back outside again.

"You're blushing," Stéphanie observed as she twisted her long black hair around one finger. "I was right to set you two up, wasn't I?"

"You were," I admitted, just as Sandrine and Martial rushed in.

"What's the situation?" Martial demanded. He was wearing a frontal headlamp like a cave spelunker's and carried another sophisticated-looking flashlight in his hand. "Where is he?"

"Somewhere outside," Stéphanie said. "Franck's not having much luck finding him in the dark."

Martial's eyes took on a determined gleam and he ran back out.

"*Oh là,*" Sandrine shook her head, sitting down again. "What a mess. I knew it wasn't going to be good when he started singing about Louise."

"It's never been this bad before, though," Stéphanie noted. "I wonder why? He should be getting over her."

"I think he's lonely," Sandrine said. "Especially now that he sees Franck with Laura."

Stéph nodded.

"I think you two remind him of what he doesn't have," Sandrine said. She looked at Stéph, who also happened to be between boyfriends, although this wasn't from a lack of potential male suitors. "It reminds us all of what we don't have at the moment," she added and lit a cigarette. "Luckily, we can still smoke."

Just then Martial, with his headlamp set to full glare, and a tired-looking Franck dragged a protesting Olivier back into the café.

"Can you come with us, Laura?" Franck asked. "I think we may need a bit of assistance."

We dragged Olivier outside. "You *will* find the perfect

woman," I whispered to him. "She's out there waiting for you. It's just a matter of time."

"*Non!* All I want is Louise. LOUIIIISSSSSE," Olivier howled.

"Let's get him into his bed," Martial said.

I followed them out to Martial's car. Martial got behind the wheel, and Franck inserted Olivier's wiry body into the back seat. Franck wound down Olivier's window. "I think some fresh air would do him good."

I slid in beside Franck. "What can I do?"

"Nothing yet," Franck said. "But we'll see how it goes. I know this is ridiculous, but I wanted to spend more time with you, even if it's doing this."

My heart melted just a bit more. "It's not ridiculous," I said. "Unexpected, but not ridiculous."

Martial was barely out of the parking lot when Olivier shouted, "Martial! You're going too fast! I'm going to be sick!"

Martial turned around to Franck and me. "Please don't let him puke in my car. I'm still paying for it. You can never get that smell out of the upholstery."

I sniffed. I had never paid that much attention to cars, but come to think of it, this one did still have that new car smell.

"You're not really going to be sick, Olivier." Franck patted his shoulder and talked to him in soothing tones. "Right? Or at least you'll wait until we get you home."

Martial had turned onto the road through the vineyards and was gaining speed.

"Too fast!" Olivier shouted. "You're going too fast! Slow down!"

"*Mon Dieu*," Martial muttered but obligingly lowered his speed. "I could walk faster than this."

"I'm going to be sick." Olivier declared in penetrating tones. He performed a dry heave that left none of us in doubt as to the seriousness of his assertion.

Martial stopped the car. Franck, with lightening speed, opened the car door and pushed the top half of Olivier's body out so that his head was hanging over the road. Olivier upchucked several times.

"Poor guy," I murmured.

"Can you hold him here?" Franck asked me, indicating the belt loop on Olivier's jeans. I grabbed on and held him so that he didn't topple out of the car into his own vomit.

Franck leapt out and knelt down in front of him, to the side of the spray. We gave him time to finish.

"You feel better now, *mon vieux*?" Franck asked, patting his back.

"*Noooooooooon*," Olivier groaned.

"You must," Franck said. "You can't have anything left in your stomach. It's all here beside me on the road. The winemaker who owns these vines is going to be thrilled tomorrow morning when he sees the present you left him."

"At least he chose le Corton-Charlemagne," said Martial from the front seat. "No mere *appellation controlée* for Olivier's vomit. He only vomits in Grand Cru vineyards. Now that's class."

We all started to laugh, even Olivier.

Franck righted his friend again, got back in the car, and closed the door behind him.

"We're good?" Martial asked.

"Drive on, chauffeur!" Franck tapped the back of Martial's seat. "Homeward!"

Martial had not even been driving for a minute when Olivier began groaning again. "Tooooooo fast...slow down! I'm going to be sick again."

We repeated the scenario, all of us marveling that Olivier had anything left to throw up.

Every time we started driving again, Olivier would begin to gag and yell at Martial for driving too fast. Franck and Martial conferred.

"I don't know what to do. We're never going to get him home this way," Martial said. "And it's not exactly like one of us can carry him on our backs over the vineyards."

Franck rubbed his chin. "I may have an idea."

"I'm listening," said Martial.

"What if Laura and I hold him in the back seat so that his head is out of the car. You will have to drive very slowly. I'll hold his door slightly ajar for his head to fit through, and Laura will hang on to his belt so that he doesn't fall out.

Martial glanced back at Olivier skeptically, but then shrugged. "I can't think of anything better."

We set ourselves up with Olivier in the back seat exactly as Franck had described. I clung to Olivier's worn leather belt with an iron grip. I was *not* going to let him fall out.

Franck had the trickier job of holding the door open just enough so that it didn't hit the vineyards on the side of the road, but also wide enough so that Olivier's head could be outside and not be slammed between the door and the side of the car.

It seemed to take forever to get to Olivier's house in Villers-la-Faye with Martial driving roughly the same pace as an *escargot de Bourgogne*. If we tried to speed up at all, Olivier would begin shouting again.

I stayed in the car while Martial and Franck helped Olivier into his parents' house and handed him off to his mother—who I could see in the yellow porch light was an imposing Burgundian countrywoman in a spangled, floral dressing gown. There was a decidedly resigned expression on her broad countenance.

Martial and Franck walked back to the car, laughing.

"Can I drive you home?" Martial asked us.

"I have to go back to Sandrine's," I said. Franck and I would have only a few hours left together the next day before he'd leave for Dijon for another week. Time seemed so fleeting, and so precious. Dammit. Why had we not met earlier? But then, we could have so easily not met at all.

"Why don't you stay at my house?" Franck asked.

The suggestion gave me the equivalent of an electric shock. "I can't. Sandrine and her parents would be worried."

"No, they wouldn't," Martial said. "They've known Franck and his family forever. They know who you're with and where you are. They're not expecting you back tonight. Trust me."

"If the Lacanches found out, they would...well, I don't know what they would do, but it wouldn't be pretty." Staying over at Franck's house would definitely constitute breaking the "No Dating" rule, and in a rather spectacular fashion too. If the Lacanches found out, the entire Ursus Club would find out. That could spell disaster.

"What happens in Villers, stays in Villers," Martial assured me.

"It's true." Franck took my hand. He gestured to Olivier's house, where the porch light flickered off. "That wasn't exactly how I planned on spending this evening with you. Let me make up for it."

We did have only four months together. Still, I was scared. Franck was older and more experienced. I wasn't ready for things to move too fast. What did twenty-three-year old men expect? I had no clue.

Franck caressed my palm with his thumb. "I have to go back to Dijon tomorrow. Please. You'll be safe with me, I promise."

"OK," I said, listening to my heart and ignoring my head.

"Let's walk back to my place," Franck said. "It's only five minutes from here."

I gave Martial *les bises*, and Franck did as well.

"Thanks for your help, Laura," Martial said. "That was quite the initiation into our little tribe. I'm surprised you didn't run away screaming."

"There are compensations." My eyes slid over to Franck, and the corner of his mouth twitched. "Besides, it's going to make a funny story. Think of how much you can tease Olivier about it in the years to come."

"Now there is a happy thought." Martial ducked back in his car, waved, and drove off.

Franck interlaced his fingers in mine. We began walking through the village, which was lit only by the soft light of the street lamps. The air was mild but fresh. It smelled of new beginnings.

"You really didn't mind that whole thing with Olivier?" Franck asked.

"When a friend is in trouble, what else can you do but help them?"

Franck studied my face. "Do you mean that?"

"Of course. Why?"

"It's just that...my old girlfriend wouldn't have agreed. She would have gotten angry with me about it and sulked for days."

Ah. So here it is. The infamous ex-girlfriend. "Stéphanie mentioned her to me. She said you went through a hard time after you broke up."

"Stéphanie shouldn't talk so much," Franck said mildly. He didn't say anything for a few seconds. "Yes, I did have a hard time, but I think it was more about other things I needed to work through. The fact that Juliette and I broke up...that was just the catalyst."

"Apparently you shut yourself in your bedroom and tried to overdose on philosophy."

Franck looked slightly abashed, but amused. "That's a good way to put it. I was young and naïve."

"Less than a year ago?"

"Yes."

"Somehow, I just can't picture you ever being that naïve."

He gave me a wolfish look that made me doubt the wisdom of agreeing to spend the night with him. "You may be right about that."

We were walking in front of the church, which I knew was at the top of his street. I felt as if I was teetering at the apex of a steep roller coaster.

"Do you miss Canada?" Franck asked, as though sensing my need for distraction.

"Not as much as I thought I would. I miss the ocean though. I was born and brought up on the tip of an island. We vacationed on a different island. Not being able to go down to the beach when the urge strikes me still feels unnatural—as if I've had an arm chopped off."

In front of the bakery, which had its curtains drawn for the night, Franck stopped and pulled me toward him. He leaned down and gave me a gentle kiss. "Are you nervous?" he asked.

I hesitated a moment. "*Oui.*"

"Why?" he sounded truly surprised.

"I didn't really have many serious boyfriends before. I've never stayed over at anyone's house."

"*Vraiment*? That makes me wonder what is wrong with all the men in Canada."

I was flattered and a bit shocked at this revolutionary perspective. What if my dearth of boyfriends in high school hadn't been my fault, after all, but rather because the boys back home were lacking?

"You must have had boys back to your house in Canada," Franck said.

I chuckled. "My father is a hunter. Any boy who crossed the threshold of our house got a tour of my dad's extensive gun collection within the first five minutes of being under our roof. That cooled their jets pretty effectively."

Franck grinned. "*Vraiment?*"

"Really. I wasn't allowed to have any boys up in my room at all. That was the house rule, and after seeing my dad's rifles, no guys were keen to test it."

"Poor-spirited of them," Franck murmured in my ear. "Still, I'm not going to take advantage of you. I promise." He thought for a moment more. "I have an idea. Can you wait here a second?"

A fat, gray cat was our only company in the deserted street. Still, I didn't think there were many bandits or murderers roving the streets of Villers-la-Faye. Waiting there, I decided, was not as scary as going up to Franck's room with him. "OK."

Franck gave me a kiss and jogged down the street. I watched as he scaled the stone pillar on one side of his parents' gate and disappeared over the other side.

It hit me out of the blue that Franck's gate was the one where I had seen the young people on my way up to that dinner at La Maison des Hautes-Côtes with the Beaupres in late August—which felt like a lifetime ago. It must have been Stéphanie and Olivier and Franck I saw, and that man following me with his eyes...that had been Franck. Something powerful ran through me just then, some sense that, unbeknownst to me, fate had turned its focus on Franck and me some time ago, all the way back to that Rotary meeting in Victoria when I chose

France over Belgium. Suddenly everything took on a cosmic significance that shook me down to my soul.

What was I doing standing out in the silent street of a Burgundian village at—what time was it anyway?

Just then the village church began ringing—a resonant *clang* marking each hour. The bell beside my room in Nuits-Saint-Georges did this too but, by some miracle, I had learned to sleep through it. I counted out the twelve rings of the bell. The last slow chime shimmered through me and beyond to the vineyards that surrounded Villers like a magic carpet. *Midnight.* I shivered, and it wasn't from the evening chill.

There was a scraping noise and then, stealthy as a cat, Franck re-appeared over the stone pillar. He leapt down onto the road, landing far more gracefully than I ever could. I stared at him in the moonlight. Was this where life meant to bring me all along? To him?

He brandished a set of car keys. "I'm going to take you somewhere for a surprise."

"It's midnight." I forced myself to sound normal. "Are things still open?"

"The place I'm taking you is always open." He beckoned me behind the house, where his father's car was parked beside the tall stone wall of the barn that was covered in ivy, just across from Félix's house.

"Where are we going?" I asked as we climbed in. "I think I should warn you that I'm an extremely curious person."

"You're just going to have to wait, *ma belle.*" Franck smiled at me as he backed up the car. "Otherwise it wouldn't be a surprise."

As we whipped through the vineyards, an almost full moon emerged from behind some puffy clouds and illuminated the rolling vineyards.

"Are you glad you were sent to Burgundy?" Franck asked. "Stéphanie told me you could have been sent to Belgium."

Could he read my mind? The idea sped up my pulse. No. Be rational, Laura. Your imagination is running away with you as usual.

"I'm definitely glad," I said, reaching over and putting my

hand atop his on the gearshift. "Especially now."

Franck smiled at me between changing gears. A smile that almost stopped my heart. "So am I."

We went through one stone village, then another, until finally Franck turned the car onto a dirt track that ran under what looked like a tunnel of trees, where the shafts of silver moonlight barely penetrated. I couldn't decide if it was peaceful or ghostly. It was certainly beautiful. I wanted to ask more questions, of course. Or I could just trust him.

We drove until the road ended. Franck parked the car and got out of his side and came around to open my door.

"How gallant," I said.

He pulled me to him. "I try."

"Where—"

"Just let me lead you. Close your eyes."

I did and tried not to trip over my feet as Franck gently led me to what felt like a large, flat stone surface to sit on. The chill from the stone seeped through my jeans, but I could feel Franck's warmth as he sat down beside me.

"You can open them now."

In the moonlight—here the trees were behind us, so did not obscure the sky—a burbling river eddied and whorled in front of us. I looked down to where we were sitting on a monolithic slab of rough-cut stone set on two upright slabs of stones. This place was magical.

"Imagine it's the ocean," Franck said softly, his arm stealing around my waist. "It's the closest thing I could think of on short notice anyway—Burgundy is incredibly landlocked—but I thought maybe this would make you miss home a little less."

My fear vanished and was replaced by awe at the sweetness of Franck's gesture and the amazement of discovering him. Time seemed suspended by our kisses, but eventually the rock beneath us started to seem cold and hard.

"I think my bed might be more comfortable," Franck murmured. "Although I do love being here with you."

I laughed softly. "Let's go home." I still didn't know what was going to happen, but how could I not trust a man who had brought the ocean to Burgundy just for me?

chapter twenty-eight

We seemed to be passing through different villages on the way back to Villers-la-Faye; though, with the tricks of the moonlight, it was hard to know for sure.

"I'm just taking a little detour." Franck looked over and explained. "Are you hungry?"

It had been a long time since those few slices of pizza in Savigny. "Yes."

"Très bien."

Franck pulled the car up to the back of a non-descript stone building in the middle of the village. The only remarkable feature was that the back door was slightly ajar and a light was on inside.

"Who's up at this time?" I wondered out loud.

Franck winked at me. "You'll see." He got out of the car and disappeared inside.

When he re-emerged, he was carrying a small brown paper bag.

"What the—" The moment he opened his door, the heavenly smell that preceded him answered the question for me. I couldn't mistake the scent of freshly baked *pains au chocolat*. He passed me two.

"I hope you like *pains au chocolat*," he said.

"Who doesn't?"

"Exactly. The baker just took them out of the oven."

I took a bite. The pastry was flaky and piping hot, and the chocolate inside was melted and gooey. I let out a half groan, half moan of pleasure. I looked up after I had swallowed to see that Franck was watching me with an intent expression.

"What?" I said.

"I'm just wondering if I could make you make that sound with something else. Something that doesn't involve food."

I took another bite. "You could try." I sent him a mischievous look. "But there are few things better than a good *pain au chocolat.*"

"I've never really gotten along with anyone who doesn't love food."

"Me neither."

"I hope that you love other things as well."

I thought of our time spent at Franck's Burgundian "ocean." "I would say chances are good."

"So would I." Franck watched me with a glint in his eyes.

I waited a few minutes after Franck had started to drive while still managing to finish his *pain au chocolat.* "How did you know the *boulangerie* would be open?" I asked.

"That's the hours they keep. My grandmother used to be the *boulangère* in Villers."

"Really? At the bakery across the street from your house?"

Franck nodded. "The house we live in now was my grandfather's house. That's how my grandparents met." He twitched a shoulder. "He liked her bread."

I chuckled. These past several hours were unlike any evening that I had spent with a man before in my life. The amazing thing was, even though I was reeling from the novelty of Franck, part of me felt comfortable in a way that I had never felt before with anyone—as if all I had to be was myself, and that was enough. I yawned.

"Do you need your bed, *princesse*?"

Princesse. "I guess I do," I said to him. "What should I call you? *Mon prince*?"

"No. I have too much anarchist in me for that. I've always preferred pirates."

"OK then, *mon pirate.*"

Franck parked the car on the street where we had taken it from, and he informed me that we would have to climb up the stone pillar into the courtyard.

"I have never been gifted at moving my body vertically," I warned him, studying the pillar doubtfully.

Franck took my hand. "I won't let you fall."

He showed me some handholds in the stone and, with him pushing me up from behind, I somehow managed to scramble up and over the top. I waited for him there. The view was pretty fascinating in the moonlight.

"It's nice up here," I said when Franck joined me.

"I spent a lot of my childhood perched up here," Franck said. "When my grandparents lived in this house and I came to visit them, my grandmother would serve me my breakfast up here."

"What was your breakfast?"

"An entire baguette cut in half, with butter and her homemade jam."

I liked imagining little Franck up there, munching on his morning bread. I thought of myself when I was little, lying in the sand at Willows Beach, looking up at the clouds in the sky.

Franck jumped down to the pebble gravel in the courtyard below.

"How do you do that?" I hissed. "It's too high."

"I'll catch you!" he assured me.

"Right." I snorted.

I began to climb down but lost my grip about halfway and did end up toppling into Franck's arms.

"You see?" he whispered, squeezing me tight. "I told you." He put a finger to his lips. "We have to try to be as quiet as we can. We don't want to wake up my little brother."

I remembered that both Stéph and Franck had talked about their little brother, Emmanuel-Marie, who was sixteen years younger than Stéphanie and a full twenty years younger than Franck. Franck pushed open the front door, which led directly into the kitchen. It creaked a bit, but softly.

"My bedroom is at the very top of the house," he said, taking my hand. "There are a lot of stairs."

"Oh," I said, my breath coming up short, but not because of the thought of stairs.

"Hold my hand," Franck said. "I'll lead you."

We crept up the wooden stairs, which didn't feel at all straight—I wasn't sure if that was an effect of the dark or my nerves, or if the stairs were truly crooked.

At the top of the third flight of stairs, I heard the sound of somebody snoring softly.

"Stéph," Franck whispered. "This is her bedroom. We have to walk through it to get to mine. That's the way it is in these old houses. This space used to be the attic."

We skirted the far side of her bedroom, and then I felt Franck's hand pushing down my head. "My doorway is low," he explained. "I don't want you to give yourself a concussion."

"That would put a damper on things," I whispered.

"It would, but I'd take care of you."

Franck led me underneath a wooden beam that was, indeed, only set about four feet above the floor. There was no door, only a thick curtain, which felt as though it was made out of the same heavy canvas as a ship's sail.

Franck drew me back up to full height again, and I was surprised to see that his tiny little attic room was bathed by the light of the moon. It shone through a skylight set into the sloping ceiling.

It was a simple space, furnished with a double bed, several bookshelves bursting with books, and a small wine barrel that had been turned on its end and fashioned into a bedside table.

"It's luxurious compared to my bed in the military barracks in Dijon."

"I love it," I said. "A perfect pirate hideaway."

Franck wrapped his arms around me and began to kiss me gently. *Where is this going to lead?*

Franck must have sensed something, as he pulled back after a while and peered deeply into my eyes. "You don't need to worry. I'm not going to rush you. I was actually planning on sleeping a bit tonight."

"Really?"

"You could easily change my mind, however."

The next morning, I woke to breaths warming the back of my neck. It took several seconds to remember where I was. A toasty body was wrapped around me.

"*Bonjour*," Franck murmured.

Before long, Stéphanie's voice came through the curtain. "What do you want from the *boulangerie*? Papa is going now."

Franck looked at me and arched a brow. "*Croissant? Pain au chocolat? Baguette?*" he asked.

"*Croissant*," I said. "Just to mix things up a bit."

"*Deux croissants*," Franck called back. "*Merci, Stéph.*"

"Ah! *Salut*, Laura. I figured you'd be here," Stéph said. "*Ça va?*"

"Très bien," I answered, pulling a funny face at Franck. He smiled. "I guess we'd better get up," I said.

"I guess." He gave me a final kiss. "I could get used to waking up with you though."

"*Moi aussi.*"

I descended the stairs behind Franck with no small amount of trepidation. His parents were surely down there. What would they think of me spending the night? This was something absolutely forbidden in my household. I had no idea which way the winds blew in Franck's house. Franck was certainly old enough to be conducting his own relationships, but I was still only Stéph's age, and it was their home.

Franck opened the door at the bottom of the stairs that led into the kitchen. Around the table sat a youngish woman wearing overalls. Her hennaed hair was in a pixie cut. Beside her was a man with the lightest blue eyes I had ever seen. Stéph was talking to a chubby-cheeked, blond toddler in a high chair, who was occupied with gnawing on the end of a baguette.

"Maman, Papa, Manu." Franck went around and kissed all the members of his family. "*Je vous presente Laura.*"

"*Bonjour*," I said. I wasn't sure about the protocol, but I followed Franck's example and kissed everyone too.

I sat down in the chair beside Stéphanie, steeling myself for the inquisition to begin.

"Franck, you've been teaching Emmanuel-Marie swear words again." Franck's mother raised her eyebrows at him. Franck's dad, André, poured me a bowl of coffee, and Stéphanie passed me a croissant. Nobody seemed at all surprised by my presence. Was this because of the lack of French prudishness or because Franck brought strange girls to the breakfast table often?

"Never," Franck protested, but he did have a telltale glint in his eye.

"*Ah bon*? Listen to this." Franck's mother sat up and adjusted one of her overall straps. "Emmanuel-Marie," she addressed the two-year-old in the highchair, "how does your bread taste?"

"*Comme de la merde*!" he yelled, triumphant. He cast us each an exultant look, especially Franck.

"What do you have to say for yourself now?" Franck's mother demanded, but she was also fighting a smile.

"I'm sorry," Franck said. He reached out and ruffled his brother's blond hair. "Don't say those bad words I taught you, Emmanuel-Marie."

Emmanuel-Marie paused in his gnawing of the baguette again. "*Ta gueule*!" he exclaimed. I gasped. That was one of the rudest French expressions I had learned so far.

Then, we all burst out laughing. I choked on my *café au lait*, and Stéphanie had to whack me on the back.

"Rascal," Franck's mother said to him, without heat. "What will happen when your little brother goes to school and talks like that? Besides, I'm sure he shocked Laura."

I shook my head. "No. The words that Franck taught Emmanuel-Marie were the first ones I'd learned at Saint Coeur."

"Maybe you can teach Emmanuel-Marie to swear in English too!" Franck declared, passing me the jar of what looked like homemade jam. "Wouldn't that be wonderful?"

"It would *not*," his mother said.

"But Maman, it's a foreign language!" Franck protested. "It would be educational."

"Eat your croissant," she ordered. She meant Franck, but I tore open my croissant too and slathered it with the pale yellow butter that was studded with salt crystals. On top of that, I spooned on the dark red jam—berry of some kind. I took a bite. Flaky, salty, sweet, and buttery, all mixed together to create a truly perfect start to what was turning out to be one of the best weekends of my life.

"This jam is delicious," I said.

I could tell I had said the right thing, as a proud smile lit up her face. "André and I make it ourselves. From the black currants we pick at a neighbor's house."

"I love it."

Michèle, Franck's mother, pushed the jam jar even closer to me.

"Franck told me that his grandmother used to run the bakery across the street," I said. I had been brought up to make conversation like a polite guest, and I wasn't about to slack off.

Michèle nodded. "She did do that for about ten years. It was very hard work, but the villagers always say that no bread has ever even come close to hers."

"She must be an amazing cook."

"She is," Franck assured me, dipping his baguette into his coffee and gesturing at me to do the same. "The best."

Stéph rolled her eyes. "Of course he would say that. Franck

is her favorite."

"That's not true," Franck said.

Both Stéph and her mother snorted. André concentrated on eating his *tartine* of baguette and jam.

Franck's father was a fascinating anomaly in the midst of the rest of his family, who were olive skinned and dark eyed. André, in contrast, looked as though he had jumped off a boat sailing directly from Norway. His eyes were the palest translucent blue and his skin was pale. His hair had obviously never been anything but the whitest blond. It was as if he had been kidnapped by a band of Mediterranean gypsies and decided to stay.

When I finished my croissant, Franck asked if he could butter me a slice of baguette as well. I nodded. Apparently romance made me hungry. When he passed it over, I added another few spoonfuls of the delicious jam. He leaned across the table and kissed me. I was flustered. There was not a lot of public kissing in my house, especially not with boyfriends. When I looked up, however, I saw that his family didn't seem to consider it unusual at all. In fact, they didn't even appear to notice.

"What time is your train?" André asked Franck.

"Eleven forty-five," he said. "I don't know why we have to go back and waste the entire Sunday afternoon at the base. It's not like they ask us to do anything. He squeezed my knee under the table. "I'd much rather be spending my whole Sunday with Laura."

"When I was your age, the military service was eighteen months long, not twelve," André reminded Franck. "You've got it easy."

"And I don't have to do it at all," Stéph chortled with satisfaction. "It's a lucky thing being a girl."

"I'll remind you of that when you're nine months pregnant," Michèle said.

Stéph waved a hand. "Pfffffffff, that's nothing."

Michèle raised a skeptical eyebrow.

Two hours later, Franck was dropping me off in Nuits-Saint-Georges, just around the corner from the Lacanches' street, so we could say good-bye without being interrupted. He parked the car and reached for me. "I'm going to miss you this week. In fact, I'm going to miss you the minute I drive away from you."

"It went too fast," I said, between kisses.

A wave of fear washed over me. It was all going fast...and so well. It was wonderful, but I worried I might be missing something crucial. Already, I couldn't imagine breaking up with Franck, so how would it be four months from then? Experiencing something so wonderful made me so much more vulnerable than I had been before. With Thibaut, I had never invested much of my heart. I couldn't say the same for Franck already.

"Wait a second." Franck's hand was still behind my neck. "Do you have school on Wednesday afternoon?"

"No. I get out at lunch and then catch the bus to Nuits-Saint-Georges."

"There's a bus just across the street from Saint Coeur that goes to Dijon. I'm going to try and arrange to get leave on Wednesday afternoon. If I can, do you think maybe we can meet and spend the afternoon together in Dijon?"

"That would be nice," I said, imagining us whiling away the afternoon in Dijon's numerous wonderful cafés. It would be more than nice, but my nerves made me play it cooler than I felt.

"I'll call you Monday or Tuesday night, as soon as I hear anything, *d'accord*?"

"*Oui,*" I said. "If that works for you. Whatever."

Franck pulled back. "What's wrong? Why are you acting all of a sudden like you don't care?"

I considered making up a flippant lie, but when I looked into his face, which had already somehow become imprinted on my soul, I couldn't muster up the duplicity. "I've been with so many people who don't care." I fiddled with the clasp on my backpack. “I’m scared to...or I can’t help but care, but I’m frightened to show you that I do.”

Franck studied me for a long while.

“That probably makes no sense,” I said, looking up again. “Does it?”

“I told you when we met that you don’t need to be scared of me,” he said. “I meant that. I want to be with you, Laura. For me, it’s that simple.”

“No games?” I clarified.

He looked at me mystified. “I’m not even sure what you mean by playing games. Why would I play games with another person’s heart, or my own?”

chapter twenty-nine

That Wednesday, I tapped my pen on my textbook in English class as I waited for the final bell to ring before we'd all be let out at noon. Thibaut, who shared my desk, eyed me.

"Impatient?" he asked. He had acted hurt for a few days after learning about Franck, but we were starting to strike up a tentative friendship again.

"I'm heading to Dijon this afternoon," I said.

"To meet Franck?" he guessed.

I smiled. "Yeah."

"How is that going?" he asked, trying to sound nonchalant but not completely succeeding.

"*Fantastique.*" I couldn't seem to wipe the smile off my face as I thought of Franck's "ocean" and the *pains au chocolat.*

Thibaut studied me. "I was a terrible boyfriend, wasn't I?"

I chewed my pen. "*Oui,*" I said finally. "But I think that one day when you meet a girl you really fall in love with, you'll do better. You and me...we are better off being just friends."

Thibaut nodded, thoughtfully. "You broke my heart," he said.

I knew this wasn't true but rather his well-ingrained habit of flirting. "Maybe your pride," I said, "but not your heart."

Just then the bell rang, and I gave Thibaut a farewell wink and headed outside.

My progress was stopped in its tracks by the still-closed wooden doors. Where was le Dragon? Although she couldn't stop me from leaving the school now that I had permission, her favorite thing to do was ignore me until every single other student went through and only then deign to check my card and let me pass. As if she still needed to check my card. It hadn't changed since I bested her in September—exactly like her grudge against me.

The crowd of students at the door grew, and still no Dragon. Did she somehow *know* I had a romantic rendezvous in Dijon that very afternoon and I was about to miss my bus? It was impossible, but a little part of me still wondered.

Five minutes later, she trudged up the walkway with her enormous circle of keys clanging in her fist, scowling at all of us. She offered no excuses, apologies, or explanations for her tardiness.

I was near the front of the crowd, but as usual she ignored my card and me as she ushered all the other students past me, one by one. I checked my watch. The bus to Dijon—the *only* bus to Dijon for the next three hours—was leaving in five minutes.

More than anything I wanted to just push past le Dragon and walk out, but I knew this would just provide her with a pretext to rescind my right to leave campus. If I waited patiently and didn't let on that I was in a hurry, I would probably miss the bus, but if I showed that I was desperate to leave, she would probably detain me even longer to exact her revenge. I wouldn't even have put it past her to figure out some unscrupulous way of curtailing any future afternoons in Dijon.

I thought of Franck and how badly I wanted to see his smile and feel his arms around me and… I couldn't miss this bus. I schooled my face into an impassive expression and continued to wait, feigning boredom. I hated le Dragon. I hated rules. I hated tyrants who lived for enforcing stupid rules.

Finally, I was the last student left. I held out my card, which she took slowly and then proceeded to examine with exaggerated interest. I clamped my lips shut. I so wanted to tell her off, not to mention my bus to Dijon was probably leaving that very second—without me.

At long last she gave a grudging nod, and I sprinted off toward the bus line-up that formed in front of the *tabac*.

I needed to see Franck. Every minute I got to have with him now was to be treasured—the idea of missing out on an entire afternoon left me robbed.

The bus was still there! I gave a whoop of relief and leapt on. I heard laboured breathing beside me and turned to see the driver climbing up the stairs.

"I thought I wasn't going to make it!" I said to him.

"You wouldn't have," he said, flashing me two boxes of Gitanes, "except that there was a line-up for me to buy these."

I collapsed in my seat—a grin from ear to ear. Le Dragon had almost won that battle. The mere fact she hadn't succeeded would make these next few hours even sweeter.

As promised, Franck was waiting for me at the bus stop on rue de la Liberté, the main street in Dijon. It was located right in front of the beautiful old storefront that housed the Maille Mustard boutique, all polished wood and shiny black, with gold lettering and row upon row of glass jars of mustard.

Franck's face, with that smile of his—lopsided and roguish—tilted up to the tinted windows of the bus. Best of all, his smile was meant just for me.

I bounded out of the bus directly into his arms. He swung me around, narrowly missing a few pedestrians, before setting me down on the sidewalk.

"This was *such* a good idea," I said.

He kissed me. "It was, *n'est-ce pas*? Have you had lunch?"

"*Non*. In fact, I almost missed the bus. They let us out of school late."

"That would have been terrible." Franck took my hand, and we began walking along the sidewalk.

"Awful," I agreed.

"Ghastly."

"Appalling."

Franck led me through what looked like no more than a crack between two buildings but which widened into a cobblestoned lane. "But you made it," he said. "So let me feed you."

We ended up in a *brasserie* on the rue de Bourg—a pedestrian street that seemed to house mainly cafés and chic boutiques. We decided on the *menu du jour*, which was a *frisée* salad with *lardons* (thickly sliced bacon), then rabbit in mustard sauce, then a cheese platter, then little caramel puddings. I wasn't sure how I felt about the rabbit, but Franck persuaded me to try it. It turned out to be delicious—flavorful, lean meat in a spicy Dijon mustard sauce. Somehow it seemed like the fitting thing to be eating on my first romantic outing in Dijon. It was all washed down with a pitcher of house red that was powerful enough not to be overshadowed by the delectable dishes.

The spring sun shone through the *brasserie* window. Franck and I were nestled side by side on the leather bench against the wall, rather than across from each other. The impeccably dressed waiter in his black suit, long white apron, and black bow tie set a cup of espresso in front of each of us. I let go of Franck's hand long enough to unwrap my tiny chocolate, dip it in my coffee, and pop it into my mouth.

"What should we do next?" I asked.

Franck stirred a sugar cube into his cup. "There is so much to see in Dijon," he said. "Have you been to the museum?"

"No."

"It is worth the trip. There are some wonderful Titians and Rubens and Manets in the collection."

I kissed Franck's collarbone. "That sounds interesting."

"We could climb up the Phillippe le Bon tower. It's from the fifteenth century and, on a day like today, the view is stunning. Are you afraid of heights?"

"Not at all," I said. I was distracted, though, by Franck's hands at the small of my back.

"I almost forgot the cathedral," Franck added. "It is beautiful inside and has the most amazing gargoyles on the outside."

"I love gargoyles," I said. Franck's hand had moved up between my shoulder blades now and was working its way up the trail of my spine so that I could barely concentrate on his descriptions of Dijon's myriad wonders.

"You love gargoyles?"

"Yes. I don't know why. I just always have...ahhhhhh, that feels lovely...sounds like there are a lot of choices."

"There's one more." Something in Franck's voice made me meet his eyes.

"Oh?"

"The choice is completely yours, but my friend Nathanael, who is doing his military service with me, has an apartment here in Dijon. Right above this *brasserie* as a matter of fact. He gave me the keys." Franck removed a set of huge, old, iron keys from his back pocket and dangled them over his espresso cup to illustrate.

My heart started beating faster. "You mean we wouldn't see the museum, or the tower, or the cathedral?"

Franck blinked. "We could do all that if you'd like. As long as I'm with you, I'm happy. Honestly."

"But if we went up to Nathanael's apartment, we could be alone for a while?"

"Yes." Franck's eyes blazed with something I wanted to investigate further.

"Completely alone?"

"Yes."

"There's no chance your friend Nathanael will come back to his apartment?"

Franck shook his head. "None. He has to stay on the base all day."

I reached out and took the keys from his hand. They were satisfyingly heavy, as well as obviously ancient. "What are we waiting for?"

chapter thirty

A month and three Wednesday afternoons with Franck in Dijon later, I still hadn't seen the gargoyles on the cathedral, but Franck and I had spent a lot of time in Nathanael's apartment above the *brasserie.*

At the end of the month, I moved out of the Lacanches' house beside the church and into the palatial estate of my fourth host family, the Forestiers, in a small village five minutes from Beaune. Most of the time, I had the entire house and swimming pool to myself, as both Monsieur and Madame Forestier were notaries and, from what I could tell, worked from around seven o'clock in the morning until eleven o'clock at night in their offices in Beaune. Their work ethic mystified me and—from the snippets of conversations I'd overheard at the monthly meetings—many of the other Ursus members, apparently. Working so hard was viewed with distrust. It was not viewed as very "French" of the Forestiers to be slaving at their jobs from dawn till well past dusk.

As a result, the Forestiers were hands-off host parents, which suited me perfectly. I wanted, of course, to spend all of my free time with Franck in Villers-la-Faye.

As for Franck's family, all they had been talking about for weeks was Mémé's huge, family eightieth birthday party at the country house of Franck's aunt Jacqueline. I got the gist that it was going to be a massive event. Franck had asked me early on to go with him.

I asked the Forestiers when I finally was able to catch them at home. They shrugged and said, "*Pourquoi pas?*" This family definitely held me with the loosest of reins.

Madame Forestier actually looked relieved. "Can you stay the whole weekend?"

"Yes," I said.

"That might be for the best because I was thinking of going down to Monaco to visit my sister for a few days."

"No problem," I said. I wondered again why the Forestiers had bothered volunteering to host me in the first place. There was no payment involved in Ursus exchanges—not that they seemed to need money. They both had older children from previous marriages who had left home and seemed more than delighted when I made my own plans and stayed out of their hair.

The next Saturday morning found me in Olivier's car with Sandrine, Stéph, and Franck, driving through the Burgundian vineyards until they gave way to fields that were bright yellow with canola flowers. At Germain family parties, I learned, close friends like Sandrine and Olivier were always welcome. Martial and Isabelle had been invited too, but they had some other family event that required their attendance in Buisson.

We listened to Francis Cabrel's new album on repeat and sang along to the songs. I nestled close to Franck and wondered if I would ever be this happy again in my life.

"I can't wait to introduce you to la Mémé," Franck said.

I remembered that postcard Stéphanie had me sign when we were skiing. To think that now I was being brought to meet her as Franck's girlfriend... She played a huge role, I could tell, in Franck's life. I sent up a prayer to the Powers that Be that Mémé like me.

"I haven't seen her in a few months," Sandrine said, tapping her cigarette outside the car window. "*Sacrée Mémé.*"

"Do you know she made all the food for the party?" Franck said, pride in his voice.

"Really?" I was amazed. "How many people will be there?"

Franck shrugged. "Nobody ever knows for sure at our family parties. Strays always turn up, but probably seventy or eighty at least."

"Wow." I couldn't imagine cooking for two people, let alone eighty. Our window was slightly ajar, and the scent of freshly mowed grass and blossoming trees flowed into the car.

"My uncle from Provence is coming up and bringing most of the wine," Franck said. "He's my godfather too."

"Where does he get the wine from?" I asked.

"He's a winemaker. A few years ago, he created his own domaine in Provence from scratch. He's the hardest worker I've ever seen. When I was still in *lycée*, I went down to his domaine in the Luberon for a couple of weeks and helped him plant the vines.

"So, we'll be tasting wine from vines you actually helped plant?"

Franck gave me a kiss on my earlobe. "I've never thought about it before, but I guess so."

Franck was wearing a white T-shirt and a pair of his well-worn jeans. I loved pressing up against his solid chest and drinking in the masculine smell of his aftershave mixed with his scent of apples. I snuck a kiss on that soft spot of neck under his ear. He reached down and traced the line of my cheekbone with his finger.

Franck already felt like home to me. How was I ever going to leave him? I took his hand, turned it over, and pressed a kiss in the center of his palm. He brushed the hair off my forehead and kissed me there.

"Who else will be there?" I asked, pushing the thought of my approaching departure to the corner of my mind.

"There will also be my uncle Marcel. He's an *oenologue*. He always brings incredible wine from his unbelievable cellar with him. Then again, so does my uncle Jean. It is his country house we're going to—"

"How am I ever going to keep everyone straight?"

"I'll be there to help you." Franck pulled me tighter against him and whispered in my ear. "I am so happy to have you with me."

It was with a bubbling mix of excitement and trepidation

that I climbed out of the car just outside a set of massive white gates in a tiny village in Northern Burgundy.

Cars clogged up the narrow village street as far as the eye could see. A gaggle of children were hanging off the gates, some almost all the way at the top, forming an informal welcoming committee. "*Salut*!" They waved down at us and began to scrabble down. I almost shouted at them to be careful not to fall, but then thought the better of it. Hardy French children were used to looking after themselves.

Franck and Stéph seemed to know all of their names. The kids leapt down and greeted each of us with a wet kiss on each cheek. They then climbed back up again to wait for the next group of arrivals.

Franck took my hand and led me through the gardens of a magnificent, whitewashed country house. Actually, it was debatable whether his aunt and uncle's house could be more accurately referred to as a small château. In any case, it was massive and majestic. The shutters that hung on every window were nine or ten feet tall. Standing on the porch, flanked by elegant wrought iron railings moulded into elaborate curlicues, were a few men smoking cigarettes. We walked up the steps, and Franck greeted them all with a kiss. He introduced me to them. There were two direct cousins, a few cousins-in-law, and one man who Franck introduced as his quarter cousin.

"Quarter cousin?" I asked, confused.

Franck waved his hand, laughing. "It's a long story. I'll explain when we have more time."

He opened the door, and we entered into the front hallway of the house, which was highlighted by a swooping staircase with a polished wooden bannister that rose above us. The air carried the whiff of slightly damp plaster and over a hundred years of living that somehow reinforced the house's majesty. The ceiling height was at least twenty feet. To the right, I caught a glimpse of what looked like a study, with shelves lined with taxidermy animals and very old-looking books. I was dying to go in there—old books had always been a particular fetish of mine—but Franck was dragging me toward the back of the house.

We swung right and found ourselves in a kitchen that also had ridiculously high ceilings, high glass windows, and—placed in the heart of the room—the oldest and most massive stove I had ever seen. In front of it, with a white, linen dishtowel slung over her forearm and wearing a chic pair of navy slacks and white top with a lovely scarf swung over her shoulders, was a woman that could only be la Mémé. She was peering inside a huge copper pot.

"*Joyeux anniversaire,* Mémé!" Franck went up to her and swung her into a huge hug. She clung on to him, laughing a delicious, throaty laugh.

"*Mon Franck*!" She grasped his hands and did an impromptu jig with him across the wooden floor. "How good it is to see you! I've been very busy. I've cooked everything for this party—everything! I guarantee you that I will be the last one to sleep tonight. We are going to have such a *belle fête*!"

"There is someone special I'd like you to meet, Mémé," Franck beckoned me over to his side. "This is *mon amie*, Laura."

"Bonjour." I thought about sticking out my hand, but before I could do anything, I was swept up in a floury-smelling hug and kissed soundly on each cheek.

"*Enfin*!" she said, holding me at arm's length and examining me. "We get to meet Franck's Laura. He hasn't stopped talking about you. You aren't going to take him back to Canada with you, are you?"

I wasn't sure what to say. The truth dawned on me just then. If I could, I would.

She laughed again. "Don't worry. I won't pester you with that this weekend. We're here to celebrate, after all, and what is more a cause for celebration than *l'amour*? Except turning eighty, of course, and still being able to make all the food for my own party!"

Stéphanie came in then with Sandrine and Olivier. Mémé greeted all of them as if they were her own grandchildren. "What is this?" Mémé clapped her hands.

"Your hands are empty! A travesty! Jean! Jean! Where are you hiding?"

A deep voice answered from the general vicinity of the study with the taxidermy animals in it. "Yes, my lady?" A man materialized in the kitchen doorway. He was small in stature and wore a wry smile on his face. His aura of placidity could not have been more different than Mémé's electric energy.

"Jean!" Mémé said. "Look here! My guests' hands are empty. It is my party, and I decree that everyone must have a kir in their hands."

Jean cocked an eyebrow, and I got the distinct impression he was a man who did things on his own timetable.

"First," he turned to me, "here is a face I don't recognize."

Franck introduced me to his uncle Jean. "This is Jean's family home," he said.

"Thank you for having me." I leaned in to give him *les bises.* "Your house is stunning."

He nodded, serene. "Would you like kir?"

"Yes. I love kir."

"That's fortuitous if you are going to throw your lot in with this family." Jean motioned us into a room across the hall that contained a massive monastery table and an equally impressive buffet.

On the starched, white tablecloth sat a plethora of bottles and several trays of clean wine glasses sparkling in the sunlight.

Jean opened the bottles one by one, sniffing at them occasionally, and finally began pouring one with movements so slow that they made me wonder if he hadn't in fact been dipped in a vat of invisible honey.

"Are there lots of people here already?" Stéph asked.

Jean thought about this question for several moments, until I began to wonder if he had heard her at all. "It seems that way," he said, finally. "Most of them have disappeared outside or downstairs. We've fixed it up, you know, for the party...the cellars."

He began handing out the glasses filled with garnet kir. He was methodical and, as a consequence, had not spilled a drop.

He served the women first, starting with me, and then moving to Franck and Olivier.

"Now you are equipped to go and mingle. Take it from me. Stay away from the kitchen. Mémé gives jobs to anyone who is underfoot. *Au revoir*. I am going back to hide in the study." He turned and sauntered out of the room.

We wandered out the back door of the house and into a beautiful garden that was far too extensive to be called a garden at all. It was an actual enclosed "park," I realized, like the ones in the country houses and châteaus I had read about in Jane Austen's novels.

There were several groups of people milling around in the sunshine, and Franck took me over to each one, to introduce me and say hello. He kissed most of the people, including the men, meaning that he was related or close to the majority of our fellow party-goers. We moved slowly toward an area of the park that was farther away from the house, where a spirited match of *pétanque* was underway.

"*Ça alors*! It's our Franck!" A portly man with a glass of kir in his hand greeted us. "With his beautiful *Canadienne* who we've been hearing so much about, no less. Come and play with us. I'm Franck's uncle Roland." He gave me a kiss on each cheek. "And, just for the record, I am infinitely more charming than my nephew."

I was introduced to the other team—a ridiculously handsome young man with stunning blue eyes who was yet another of Franck's second cousins and several other young bucks who were either distantly related or offspring of close family friends. I was the only female.

"Do you want to play?" Franck asked.

"If you show me how."

"You've never played *pétanque* before?" He couldn't quite keep the astonishment from his voice.

"We play ice hockey in Canada. It can't be that different."

Franck's eyes widened. "I think it is quite different, actually."

"I'm a quick learner."

"I'm aware of that," he said, the corner of his mouth twitching. "It gets a bit competitive sometimes."

"I can handle it."

They split us into teams, and Franck and I landed on opposite sides. Roland noticed that our glasses were empty before the play began and insisted we wait to start until he went inside the house and got us something more to drink. Despite his impressive girth, he moved quickly on his mission and reappeared with two bottles of artisan-made cassis and two bottles of white aligoté under his arm.

"This will do for at least one or two games," he said. "It is against the rules to play *pétanque* with an empty glass in your hand," he explained while filling mine.

My head was spinning and my ears were burning with heat after just one kir. It went down like Kool-Aid but packed the wallop of hard alcohol. I was already feeling astonishingly confident in my non-existent *pétanque* skills.

Roland launched into a detailed explanation of the rules, but he kept getting mixed up, probably because he had most likely already consumed several of his own potently mixed kirs by the time Franck and I arrived. Finally, he waved his hand to sweep away all his preceding instructions.

"Forget everything I just said. The only crucial thing to remember is that you must be holding a drink while you play."

"That," I said, taking a drink of my kir, "I can do."

Shortly after the game began, I realized that, while the players seemed to take *pétanque* seriously, between the shots, there was a lot of ribbing and teasing that occurred. My kir and a half allowed me to take part in this, giving my French extra fluency and removing any inhibitions I had about grammar mistakes and my constant mixing up of the masculine and feminine modifiers.

Franck shot a lovely ball that landed right beside the diminutive lead *cochonnet*. Apparently, we all were trying to get our ball as close to the *cochonne*t (which inexplicably translates as "piglet"—I would have to ask Franck about that later) as possible, even if it meant knocking another person's ball out of range.

After Franck's turn, it was mine. I leaned forward and enjoyed the cool, solid weight of the *pétanque* ball in my hand. It reminded me of the fishing weights I used to make in the basement with my dad. I eyed Franck's ball and took my throw. Mine arced beautifully and then clanked against his, knocking his several feet away.

Franck stared. *"Traitor!"* He pointed an accusing finger at me.

"All's fair in love and *pétanque,*" I reminded him.

Franck gasped at my betrayal. I just laughed.

We all got pretty serious after that. Well, as serious as you can get when you are holding and drinking kirs as you play, which meant, of course, not all that serious.

My team had just won by a few points when we heard a distant shouting in French and the unmistakable sound of a cowbell. Roland consulted his watch. "It must be the hour for *l'apéritif.*"

I peered into the dregs of my third glass of kir, my head spinning. "Didn't we already start that?" I asked.

"*Non, non,*" Roland answered. "That was just hydration for our athletic endeavors."

chapter thirty-one

Franck took my arm, and we made our way back to the house. We were almost there when he pushed me suddenly behind the trunk of a large tree that had a large wooden swing tied to one of its lower branches.

"Wha—"

He cut me off with a feverish kiss.

"Nothing heats my blood like a woman who has the gall to beat me at *pétanque*."

Time became elastic, and I was so intoxicated with Franck that I forgot where we were and that everyone else had headed down into the cellar and might be wondering where we'd gotten off to.

"Franck! Franck!" Someone was calling him from the porch.

We broke apart, gasping. "Oh my God," I said. "We almost—"

"I know." He was breathing as hard as I was.

"Maybe the kir—"

Franck buttoned up my shirt for me and I tried to straighten his. Both of our hands were shaking.

"Franck! Where are you?"

"That's one of my aunts," Franck said, trying to smooth down my hair. "We should go in."

I laughed shakily. "Are we presentable?"

Franck looked me up and down. "Not really, but it will have to do."

I was struggling to clip my silver barrette in my hair.

"*Tiens*, let me do that." Franck took it from my hand. He gathered my hair into a ponytail and then clipped the barrette. His movements were awkward, and I could tell there were a lot of lumps and bumps and loose hair but...it was perfect. He lifted my ponytail and planted three soft kisses on the nape of my neck.

"If you keep doing that," I said, "we're going to miss lunch and I'm not even going to care."

"It's your fault for making me want you so badly." I gave him one final kiss...and then another, and then I turned and was in his arms again.

"Franck!" This time, it was la Mémé's unmistakable voice. "I need your help."

Franck broke away. "This time, I truly have to go."

"OK." I backed up, putting several feet of electric air between us. "Should we go together?"

Franck reached out and took my hand. "Yes. Come on."

Mémé caught sight of us as soon as we emerged from behind the tree. Instead of being mad or embarrassed, as I'd imagined she would be, she seemed delighted. "You naughty children. Far be it from me to discourage young love, but I can't have you missing all the food I made, can I?"

"*Non,* Mémé," Franck said. Mémé patted him fondly on the head.

"*C'est beau l'amour*," she commented wistfully, then shooed me down into the cellar and took Franck's arm in hers. "I'm going to borrow your *amoureux* for a few minutes," she said as she led him inside. "I need his strong arms."

The thought of his strong arms made me blush again as I hurried down the stone steps into the cool cellar to join the rest of the party. I found myself in a large room with a vaulted ceiling and freshly whitewashed stone walls. Long trestle tables were set up surrounded by an assortment of chairs, most of them looking like antiques. Here and there, barrels turned on their ends dotted the room for people to set down their glasses. Roland seemed to have taken up a new role as bartender behind a makeshift bar that was filled with bottles and glasses of every imaginable shape and size.

It was Roland who saw me first. "There she is, *la Canadienne*!" he shouted in a penetrating voice. He raised his hands and began to sing a raucous version of "*Le Ban Bourguignon.*" I felt my face burn as the entire room full of people joined in.

Franck had appeared by my side by the time the song was finished. "Sorry," he whispered in my ear, "I needed to move that huge pot for her."

Mémé came over to us, dancing and still clapping even though the song was finished. "Now the party can begin!"

Roland filled up both of our glasses, and we raised them as everyone cheered on Mémé as she continued her jig of joy. For an eighty-year-old, she was sprightly.

Jean and André appeared with huge baskets filled with airy *gougères* to go with the kir and little *feuilletés* of flaky pastry with layers of melted Emmenthal cheese.

Mémé grasped my shoulder and looked into my eyes. "Do you like cooking?" she asked.

I sensed this was an important question, but at the same time, I couldn't lie about my culinary expertise, or lack thereof. "I love eating," I said. This, as least, was true.

"That's good enough for me!" Mémé said, and kissed both Franck and me on our cheeks and then danced away in the direction of another gaggle of people, who greeted her with open arms.

"She's amazing," I said, watching her go.

"*Sacrée* Mémé," Franck said, watching her with pride. "There's no one like her."

During the *apéritif*, I met yet more people. The introductions didn't let up until Jean gave an impressive wolf whistle and commanded everyone to sit down.

Franck led me to a chair beside his, roughly in the middle of one of the two long tables. I gratefully collapsed in it. It seemed a little wobbly, and I looked down to see that the wood shone with a deep patina and was exquisitely carved. Franck glanced at it. "It's probably from the seventeenth century or something," he said, off-handedly. "Jean has a lot of stuff of that era in the attics. I would offer to switch yours with mine, but I think mine is even more wobbly."

"It's fine." I lay my hand on his arm. "I won't be sitting on any seventeenth-century chairs back in Canada."

A shadow fell over Franck's features. "Sorry," I said, wishing my words unsaid.

"You don't need to apologize. I just can't imagine you not being here anymore."

There were so many things I wanted to say, but they all stayed tangled in a knot in my throat. "Let's just enjoy Mémé's party."

Each of us had a china plate and a paper napkin beautifully folded into the shape of a swan. I picked mine up.

Mémé made those too," Franck said. There seemed no end to this woman's talents.

I surveyed the various glasses set in front of my place—a Champagne flute, two chubby kir glasses, a red wine glass, and a smaller glass suitable for a *digestif* or some other kind of hard alcohol. I was examining these when I heard the sound of scraping wood behind me. Mémé had thrown open two sliding barn-like doors to another room that I hadn't realized even existed. "*Servez-vous et bon appétit*!" She waved us all in.

We were carried by the chattering crowd into the next room where an L-shaped table groaned with food. There was a myriad of beautifully presented bowls of different kinds of cold salads, a mind-numbing array of *charcuterie* presented on massive platters and decorated with *cornichons* and radishes cut up into little flowers, terrines, and pâtés of every description. Huge baskets of bread bookended the table.

"She prepared all of this herself?" I asked Franck.

He nodded. "She even baked the bread. You'll see. It's delicious."

The problem was that my plate simply wasn't big enough. I wanted to taste everything. I was almost to the end of the table when Mémé came up beside me.

"Ah, Laura!" she said. "You have to taste some of this." She dug a spoon deep into a bowl that contained a gelatinous-looking meat mixture—one of the few dishes I hadn't selected. She served me several spoonfuls, and I didn't have the heart to tell her to stop. I had grabbed a few slices of her delectable-looking bread and followed Franck back to the table.

Once we were seated, Franck happened to glance at my plate. It was piled twice as high as his. "You're going to be able to eat all that?" he asked me dubiously. "This is only the entrée you know. The main course comes afterward."

"What?" I couldn't believe I had fallen for this French trick again. Yet there was so much food, I just assumed it was the main course… I looked down at my plate now, dismayed. "Oh God. What have I done?"

"I'll help you," Franck assured me.

I certainly did honor to Mémé in the end. I tried everything, and much to my surprise, even the gelatinous meat thing tasted delicious. It was flavored with parsley and had a deep, dense meaty taste that appealed to my inner cavewoman.

Franck pointed to the tiny bit of it left on my plate and asked, "Did you like that?"

"Loved it. What is it? Some kind of pâté?"

Franck shook his head. "*Fromage de tête*. One of Mémé's specialties."

I recoiled from my plate. Literally that translates as "head cheese." "Why didn't you tell me?"

Franck looked at me, surprised. "Tell you what?"

"What it was made of!"

"A pig's head? What's wrong with that? It's one of my favorite dishes, and nobody makes it like Mémé."

"How does she make it?"

Franck became animated in that way Burgundians do when describing food and its preparation. "You take a pig's head"—I could feel the blood draining out of my face—"and you boil all of the meat off it. And then, when all you have left is the skull," my boyfriend continued, "you pick the tender little bits of meat left over and season them with fresh parsley and garlic and several other secret things that Mémé has told no one, and then…well, I'm not exactly sure what she does next, but she mixes the whole thing with just the right amount of gelatin so that the consistency is right."

Franck watched me for a moment. He plucked a bottle of chilled white wine off the table and poured me a glass. "Here, it looks as though you may need this."

I took a deep swallow and felt a bit more settled, although very, very full. "It's just that I didn't grow up eating that kind of thing," I explained. "You know...innards."

"*Fromage de tête* isn't technically offal."

"If we're getting technical, I'm not used to eating animals' *heads*."

"What did you grow up eating then?" he asked.

I took another sip of wine. God, it was delicious. "Sandwiches, smoked salmon..." My voice trailed off. Memories of what I ate in Canada were foggy. Everything back home paled in comparison to the taste explosion that was France. "Moose. Deer..."

"Really?" Franck leaned forward, fascinated. "I've never tasted either of those."

"My dad hunts, so I grew up eating those more often than beef."

Franck reached out and caressed my cheek. "*Ma petite* moose-fed *Canadienne*, do you want to go outside for a walk? It helps the digestion during these Burgundian family meals."

I gladly went outside with him, blinking in the bright afternoon light.

"I am going to resist leading you behind that tree"—he nodded over to the tree with the swing—"as I got an early taste of the *coq au vin* Mémé has bubbling on the stove, and it would be a crime for you to miss that."

"We'll be good," I vowed. "Besides, I feel like an anaconda after all that food."

Franck laughed and interlaced my fingers in his. He led me all around the garden, which was massive and completely enclosed with rock walls several meters high. In some of the natural indentations formed by the roughly hewn stones, little white statues of the Virgin Mary were placed.

"How old is this place?" I asked.

"Maybe three hundred years?" Franck guessed. "I think it's been in Jean's family since the time of his great grandparents at least."

I took a moment to marvel at that. Three hundred years ago, the Europeans hadn't even discovered the city where I lived on the West Coast.

"The house was occupied by the Nazis during the Second World War as their headquarters in this area."

"Really?"

Franck nodded. "It's a miracle anything in the house is preserved at all, that they didn't rip out everything and send it to Germany."

"That must have been terrible."

"What's worse is that Jean and his mother had to stay here alone with the Nazis. Jean's father had already died before the war. It was the only way of protecting—or trying to anyway—the house and their possessions."

"I can't imagine..." In Canada, especially on the extreme West Coast where I am from, the Second World War hadn't impacted its residents nearly as much as in Europe. Even the idea of it is distant, something I read about in a history book or saw in a movie. In France, the memories are immediate, and many people at the party had lived through the Nazi occupation as children or young adults.

"What breaks all of our hearts is the wine cellar," Franck added.

"Did the Germans steal all the wine?"

"Of course, and Jean said it was a spectacular collection. Burgundies, Bordeaux, Champagne...what the soldiers staying at the house didn't drink themselves, they sent off to Germany. I think they probably drank the huge majority themselves. There were a lot of them living here, and even more who reported here for work every day."

"None of it was saved?"

"Jean and his mother did manage to sneak away a few of the oldest, most precious bottles to a secret cellar. The Nazis never found that."

Franck and I had been walking for quite some time and found ourselves in an orchard that was still within the garden walls. It was full of fruit trees covered in blossoms.

"This whole area of Burgundy was a hotbed of resistance activity." Franck waved his hand around. "The separation between occupied and unoccupied France was in Chalon, just south of us, so there were all kinds of people being ferried back and forth, and all kinds of sabotage taking place."

Under a blossoming apple tree, I turned around and took in the site of the huge white house in the distance. It was difficult to imagine it full of Nazis. They would have seemed so out of place in this place of bucolic splendor.

We began to walk toward the house again, stopping at the tree with the swing hanging from the branch.

"Do you want to try?" Franck asked me, motioning to the swing.

I settled on the wooden swing, and Franck pushed me gently from behind. I realized that it had been years since I'd been on a swing. Why had I stopped? The sensation of the rushing leaves above me and the *whoosh* of the air against my face was delicious.

"I think this seat is big enough for two," I said. Franck grabbed the ropes to stop me and then climbed on beside me. We swung and kissed.

"*Hé! Les amoureux*!" Olivier appeared through the cellar door and sauntered up to us. "I've heard rumors the *coq au vin* is incoming. You might want to get back down to the table."

"First, we'll go check if Mémé needs any help in the kitchen," Franck said.

"I'll come with you." Olivier took a deep drag on a barely smoked cigarette and flicked it into one of the ashtrays that were strategically placed all over the garden.

In the kitchen, Mémé was busy stirring the contents of the huge copper pot with the largest wooden spoon I had ever seen in my life. She tasted the sauce. "Come here, Laura!" she called over to me. "What do you think of this sauce?"

I tasted it from the spoon. It was delicious. Rich and savory with the depth of sublime wine and garlic. "It's delicious."

Mémé still didn't seem convinced, so she called Franck over, and he tasted it too and told her it needed perhaps a pinch more salt. She nodded briskly.

"I thought so." She took a pinch of gray sea salt from the old wooden cellar beside the stove and stirred it in.

"Shoo, you three!" she said. "You need to be sitting downstairs when I present my dish."

"Can't we help you down with it?" Franck asked.

"I have all the help I need," Mémé said, nodding to indicate her three daughters rushing around the kitchen, following her orders. "*Allez*!"

We did as we were told. Did anyone dare not do what they were told where Mémé was concerned?

We chatted with Olivier and Sandrine and Stéphanie and the other family members around us for about ten minutes, until the sound of laughter heralded Mémé's arrival. She was holding a massive earthenware dish full of her *coq au vin*. I marvelled at the strength contained in her two biceps. Behind her, Michèle, Jacqueline, and Renée carried further dishes, plus potatoes, plus several more baskets of bread. Mémé's arrival prompted another *Ban Bourguignon* that went on several rounds as she jigged around the table with her dish.

They served our plates at the head of the table, and as everyone dug in, the room was full of exclamations of Mémé's prodigious culinary skills.

"This is amazing," Sandrine said as she dug in. "I think this is even better than my own grandmother's *coq au vin*." Her eyes shifted guiltily "Don't ever tell her I said that."

Olivier smiled like the cat that caught the canary. "I am *so* going to use that to blackmail you."

"Have you forgotten about the 'Louise' evening in Savigny not so long ago?" Sandrine reminded him.

"*D'accord, d'accord*, we're even," Olivier said, grudgingly.

I chuckled, reveling in the feeling of being so completely included in this group of friends. I understood most of their in-jokes now and shared some of the same memories.

The Universe snapped into focus for a moment, as it had the weekend after I met Franck as I waited for him in the deserted street outside his gate. All of those random moments I'd thought meant nothing at the time—the man, who must have been Franck, following the Beaupres' car with his gaze; the man who bumped into me on my way out of Sandrine's uncle's cellar on New Year's Eve; the fact that things with Thibaut and I had never gotten off the ground—all of those seemingly meaningless events slotted into place to bring me where I was right then. Never before had I had such an intense certainty that, at that exact moment, I was exactly where the Universe conspired to put me. It was, quite simply, where I was meant to be.

How was I going to leave all this behind? I felt as though I had finally found the life I was meant to live, but I had to fly an ocean and a continent away to start a *different* life at university in Montreal. It seemed unimaginable.

These thoughts warred in my mind as seconds of the divine *coq au vin* were served. Afterward, we all helped take things back up to the kitchen, and once we were all shooed away, we went outside, where everybody but me smoked. Franck and I watched as Sandrine flirted with a cute guy from Paris, who was Franck's third or maybe fourth cousin. Then Franck gestured with his head over to the swing again.

Once ensconced there, we swung back and forth gently while chatting with everyone. The sky was beginning to darken slightly, but no stars were visible. Still, I could sense them up there, aligning for me after eighteen years on this earth. I had to venture halfway across the world and learn a new language for that to happen, but it *had* happened. There was only one question—how could I perform the impossible and preserve this new life of mine?

chapter thirty-two

The cheese course was, of course, one of the most spectacular I'd ever seen. It included cheeses of every texture and variety, from gooey Brie to crumbly Comté and everything in between. There were all my favorite Burgundian cheeses—the stinky l'Ami du Chambertin, its even stinkier cousin Époisses, Cîteaux, le Délice de Pommard studded with mustard grains—how was I going to revert to eating either yellow cheese or orange cheese in Canada? I'd never known these types of sublime cheeses existed, but now that I did, I couldn't imagine living without them. I served myself an extra slice of l'Ami du Chambertin. I needed to begin hoarding the pleasures of life in France to get me through the inevitable deprivation to come.

There was more of Mémé's fresh bread, studded this time with dried figs and nuts. Before we could dig in, though, Jean appeared downstairs, staggering under the weight of the biggest bottle of wine that I had ever seen, at least twice the size of the one served at Thibaut's birthday party.

"What the—?"

"That's a Balthazar," said Franck. "It's the equivalent of sixteen bottles of wine."

Of course, Jean's arrival caused the eruption of another *Ban Bourguignon*. Jean came around to all of us, showing off the label of the bottle—an Aloxe-Corton Grand Cru from 1966. It had been bottled six years before I had been born.

"I'm not certain it's still going to be good," Franck said to me, *sotto voce*. "It's always a dicey business with these big bottles, especially ones *that* old."

Mémé kissed Jean and danced around some more. Franck's uncle Jean-Marie from Provence helped Jean with the tricky business of extracting the enormous cork from the neck of the bottle. Jean tilted the bottle slightly and held it as Jean-Marie proceeded to insert a corkscrew with all the care and delicacy of a brain surgeon operating on the frontal lobe. A hushed silence, reverent and suspenseful at once, fell around the table.

"I almost can't watch," I said, but at the same time, I also couldn't tear my eyes away.

After what seemed like a very long time, Jean-Marie slowly extracted a blackened, but completely intact, cork. A *Ban Bourguignon* erupted yet again.

Jean-Marie and Jean quickly made their way around the table and poured the wine into everyone's glass. I lifted up mine once it was full and gazed in wonder at the ruby-and-rust-tinted wine. 1966. Hippies were swarming the streets of San Francisco. The Beatles were still together. My mom and dad got married.

I glanced over at Mémé, who sipped her glass of wine. It was incredible how much food, kir, and wine she could consume. Granted, she was always hopping up and down between courses to ready the next one, but when she sat down, she applied herself to her plate and glass with impressive industry. I didn't know many eighty-year-olds with such prodigious appetites. My only remaining grandparent—my grandfather—seemed to subsist on poached fish and vegetables, with the occasional indulgence of vanilla ice cream liberally doused in maple syrup.

"Drink up," Franck recommended "Sometimes, once uncorked, these wines don't last long."

My first glass was delicious, but when Jean came by and poured us all a second glass and I took a sip, I almost gagged. It was like drinking balsamic vinegar straight from the bottle. Franck patted my back as I spluttered.

"Sorry." The last thing I wanted to do was insult Jean.

"It's not you," Franck said. "The wine has oxidized. All the tannins that were holding its structure collapsed."

"But it was so delicious."

"It was, but as soon as the oxygen hit it, it couldn't take it."

"That's so weird," I said. "Yet fascinating..."

"Winemaking is an art and a science." Franck was still rubbing my back, and his fingers became more clever as they moved up to my neck.

Just then Jean-Marie tasted his wine and spat it back into his glass. "Stop drinking the Aloxe!" he shouted, even in his haste, pronouncing "Aloxe" the proper Burgundian way with the "x" sounding like an "s." "It's over."

There was a muted chorus of "*zuts*" and "*merde alors*."

Panic surged through my chest. Were Franck and I going to be like that bottle of Aloxe? Briefly sublime and then forever ruined in an instant when I left for Canada? Was what I had with him right then only meant to last a brief moment in time?

"Are you feeling all right, Laura?" Franck leaned over. "You look pale."

Melancholy at the image of a horrendous future rendered me mute.

Luckily, Franck's aunt Renée stood up right then, a sign that she was going to make a toast or a speech. She held up her glass of now-oxidized Aloxe. "It is a metaphor." She made a sweeping arm gesture. This woman could certainly command a room. "Life is like this wine, to be savored in the moment."

Everyone cheered, and then Renée broke off into a gusty French song. Mémé and a few of the older folk around the table joined in. A woman playing an accordion popped out from nowhere. Several more songs were sung. By the end, most people had tears in their eyes.

"Those are all songs popular during the war," Franck whispered to me.

"Do they sing often?" I asked.

"With that generation, the more they drink and eat, the more they sing," Olivier said, repressively. "They're all like that. Makes the meals interminable."

By then, I'd lost track of how long we'd been at the table...six or maybe seven hours? "Don't you love the long meals here in Burgundy?" I asked Olivier, shocked. I knew *I* did.

He groaned. "*Non!* I just want to eat and be done with it."

"I must differ with you there," Franck said. "I've always loved them. When I was little, and the other kids would go off to play between courses, I would sit at the table and watch the adults eat and drink and chat."

Mémé crept up behind us just then. "Drink and chat?" She kissed Franck on the top of his head. "What are you talking about? It sounds most interesting."

Franck smiled up at her. "I was saying nothing makes me happier than a big table and lots of family seated around it."

"Ah! Just like me," Mémé said. "That's what is most important, you know, *la famille*. Are you *très famille*, Laura?"

I raised a brow at Franck. I hadn't heard this expression before, but I sensed the right answer was *oui*. "*Oui*," I said.

Mémé rewarded me with a vigorous shoulder rub. "I knew it! I just knew you were." She jutted her chin out in Franck's direction. "That last girlfriend of yours—she wasn't very *famille*. None of us liked her very much, you know."

"I know," Franck said. "But I'm with Laura now."

My heart felt as though it was going to burst with joy.

"A good thing," Mémé said, "as long as you don't follow her to Canada and get eaten by a bear."

"I would never let him get eaten by a bear." I patted Franck's arm.

"Are you tired yet, Mémé?" Franck said, redirecting the flow of conversation. Even though we had hardly talked about the possibility between ourselves yet, both of us knew his family would not support the idea of Franck moving to Canada. In Burgundy, families stayed close to one another.

Mémé did another one of her funny little jigs. "La Mémé? Tired? Never! I promised I'd be the last one to bed tonight, and I mean to keep my promise."

"We might give you a bit of competition," Franck warned.

Mémé swatted this idea away with her hand. "Phsssssst. You young ones have no stamina. I'm not worried."

The rest of the evening proceeded at the same leisurely pace. Mémé had prepared a buffet of desserts that was truly astounding. There were at least ten different types of cake, as well as chocolate mousse and homemade tuile biscuits, and even some homemade chocolates.

After the dessert, our gang sneaked off to Olivier's car, where we took out our sleeping bags and carried them up the four flights of the rounded staircase, all the way up to the attic. The few standing lamps plugged into the walls allowed me to see that the space was massive, with huge oak beams every few meters. One beam, roughly in the middle of the room, had a thick rope swing tied to it.

We all had a turn on the swing after we placed our sleeping bags on the numerous foam mattresses that had been laid out on the floor. It looked to me as though there would be at least twenty people sleeping with us in the attic—maybe closer to thirty, actually.

After the *café*, most of us reverted back to wine. Olivier, Franck, and Roland, and a few of the other men, moved on to calvados, Pear Williams, and other hard, home-distilled alcohols. They called these *l'eau de vie,* which I found highly amusing as it translates as "life water."

As we sat at the table arguing about philosophy with Roger and Franck, I rested my head against Franck's shoulder. He rubbed my shoulders as he talked. My eyelids began to droop.

I woke sometime later to Franck shaking me gently. "I'll take you upstairs to bed."

I yawned. "Did Mémé make it?" I heard her laugh and opened my eyes to see her across from Roger, sipping a glass of what looked like Cognac.

"The night's not over yet!" she declared.

"What time is it?" I stood up slowly.

"I don't know, maybe five o'clock?" Franck said. Indeed, the night was already beginning to pale into morning. When Franck tucked me into my sleeping bag, he leaned over and gave me a thorough kiss. "I should go back downstairs and finish the party with Mémé. It means a lot to her."

"Of course," I said, yawning. In mere seconds, I fell into a deep, dreamless sleep, still wearing my clothes. Franck had luckily had the forethought to unclip my silver barrette and lay it beside my pillow so it wouldn't poke the back of my head as I slept.

chapter thirty-three

There were sleeping bodies all around me, some short and some long. Olivier was snoring softly nearby, and Sandrine seemed to be sharing her sleeping bag with the Parisian boy she had been flirting with all night. Stéphanie mumbled something in her sleep. I turned my head. There was Franck, sleeping soundly beside me, his handsome profile as still as a statue and his hand intertwined in mine.

The sound of "weeeeeeeeeee" made me sit up. Three impish children—surely cousins of Franck's in some manner or another—were swinging from the huge oak branch on the rope swing.

I had sat up too fast. "Ahhhhhhh," I clutched my head. It felt as though it was going to roll off my neck.

Franck started and woke up. "Laura?" He reached for me with his other hand.

"My head!"

"Do you have sore hairs from last night?"

"Sore hairs?"

"That's what we call it in Burgundy, sore hairs."

I appreciated the euphemism, but what I had was a gigantic hangover. I knew I shouldn't have been talked into that glass of Poire Williams the night before...or the glass of calvados for that matter, on top of the wine I'd already had.

"Did Mémé win?" I asked. "Was she the last to bed?"

"She was." Franck rolled over to face me and groaned slightly. "I was the second-to-last, and she climbed all the way up here specifically to watch me lay down so she could be sure she'd win. Roland is most likely still asleep at the table in the cellar."

I chuckled then sniffed the air. "I have no appetite, but something smells good."

Franck's nostrils twitched. "Waffles. Mémé's waffles."

"There is no way Mémé could be up making waffles if she only went to bed like, two hours ago."

"Do you want to go see?" Franck lifted an eyebrow.

Well…I was already dressed…

We made our way down the stairs to the kitchen, stopping to compare headaches with everybody we passed on the four flights of stairs.

In the kitchen, Mémé was pouring batter into the four waffle makers that were lined up on the stovetop and shouting instructions in regard to where to find plates. There were about fifteen people milling around the kitchen, and of course we had to kiss everyone good morning, which took several minutes.

Mémé caught sight of us just as we were finishing up. "Ah! *Les amoureux*! So, what do you have to say of your Mémé now? I was the last one to bed, and, you see? I am also the first one awake and making breakfast. Here!" She grabbed two plates from the hands of a man who made the mistake of lingering around waiting for a waffle. "You must try my waffles. The toppings are in the dining room."

Dazed by such energy that early in the morning, I didn't even consider refusing Mémé's waffle. Franck and I meekly accepted our waffles and shuffled into the dining room to choose between about ten different toppings—a variety of homemade jams, jellies, and preserves, Nutella, and sugar.

I chose apricot jam and was not disappointed. The waffles were air light and crunchy at the edges, with a soft, almost creamy interior. It was true what Franck had been saying to me in regards to food and…well…other things. "*L'appétit vient en mangeant.*" Appetite grows with eating.

I had been seriously considering wandering back into the kitchen to get a second waffle, until Franck made an offhand comment about lunch. "Lunch?" I asked, incredulous. "What time is it now?"

"I have no idea." Franck shrugged.

Jean was lingering nearby, directing traffic to the waffle toppings, and overheard me. "Twenty-three minutes after ten in the morning," he said. "Precisely."

I got the impression that there was little that Franck's uncle Jean did not do precisely. "*Merci*," I said.

"Lunch will be around noon," he added. "I tried to get them to pin down the time more precisely, but they would not have it. They said it depended on what time everyone woke up and other such irrelevant factors."

"Oh," I said. "Well, in any case, the attic we slept in last night is beautiful. We don't have old houses like this in Canada...this is special for me, so thank you."

Jean flushed pink. "Would you like a tour?"

"I would love that," I said.

So, the next hour and a half were taken up touring the immense house and gardens, and I soaked up every one of Jean's stories of the Occupation and beforehand. We toured the barns and the pig house and the cellars—all made with dry, stacked stones—as well as the attics and the study with its collections of ancient books and dusty stuffed animals with beady eyes. The books probably would have been under lock and key in Canada—and in archival rooms at libraries and stored under humidity control and dim light. Jean let me open a few, but the pages were so fine and delicate that I shut them and put them back quickly. I loved books—especially old books—far too much to risk damaging them.

We ended up back near the kitchen again. I thought the tour was over and started to thank Jean when he said, with the closest thing I thought he could come to excitement, "But it's not over! I haven't shown you the secret cellar."

"The secret cellar?" I didn't bother to conceal my fascination. "The one where you hid some of your wine from the Nazis during the Occupation?"

"*Oui*!" said Jean. "Stay right here. Don't move. I must fetch the ladder."

"Ladder?" I asked Franck after Jean disappeared again in the direction of the front hall. "Aren't cellars underground?"

"Not this one," Franck said. "Which is why the Germans never found it. I would help him with the ladder of course, but I know Jean wouldn't like that. He likes to do things his own way."

Five minutes later, just when I was beginning to wonder if Jean had not, in fact, forgotten about us, he reappeared carrying an old wooden ladder.

"*Voilà*!" he said, and set it up in the hallway where we stood. I peered up. The ceilings were so high that it was difficult to see, but it looked as though the part of the wall above the ladder had a panel inserted into it.

"This is underneath the stairs," Jean explained as he set up the ladder. "Do you see?"

"Yes."

"I know better than to offer to climb up there and open it for you," Franck said to his uncle.

"Yes. I should certainly hope you think better of offering that, when I am perfectly capable of doing it myself," Jean riposted.

He methodically checked the ladder and then began to climb up. He was about two and a half meters off the ground when his wife, Franck's aunt Jacqueline, came around the corner with a dishtowel in her hand.

"Jean!" she shouted up at him. "What in heaven's name are you doing up there? You're going to fall down and kill yourself."

"I'm just getting something," Jean said, unruffled.

"Get down," she ordered. She had been a nurse, Franck had told me, and she had a gift for making people do what she knew was best for them. Everybody, it seemed, except her husband.

"No," he said, calmly. "I will not."

Jacqueline had no choice but to wait beside us for Jean to come back down. Her arms were crossed, and her features wore an expression of exasperation. Still, her lips were twitching with a repressed smile. It seemed with Jean, Jacqueline had met her match.

"Do you have any idea what he is getting out of there?" she asked Franck.

"We're not privy to that information...yet." Franck's lips curved into a smile.

Mémé came rushing around the corner calling Jacqueline's name. She narrowly missed the ladder that Jean was using. He was at the very top now. From my vantage point, it looked as though he was struggling to open a very old lock of some kind.

"What is Jean up to now?" Mémé asked, rolling her eyes.

"Getting something out of the secret cellar," said Jacqueline.

"Ah!" Mémé looked considerably placated. "Bring down something worth our while, Jean!" she called up. "It's not every year I turn eighty after all!"

With a grunt of effort, Jean managed to get the secret door open. A puff of dust showered down on us, and a musty smell permeated the air.

"Be careful!" Jacqueline ordered him, but it was quite clear that Jean had his own agenda, and it did not include paying heed to his wife's instructions. "I just hope he doesn't fall through the floorboards," Jacqueline muttered. "Though it would serve him right... Stubborn as a mule."

Quite some time later, Jean emerged out of the small hole out onto the ladder again. He was covered in dust and cobwebs and what appeared to be stray strings of mold, but this didn't appear to impair his good humor in the slightest. In his hand he held a bottle that didn't even look as though it was made of glass.

"Ohhhhhh...good choice," Mémé said. She clearly recognized the bottle.

"What is it?" I whispered to Franck, my curiosity getting the better of me.

He shook his head, but his eyes sparkled with mischief. "Surprise," he said.

It took quite some time for Jean to get to the bottom of the ladder, but when he did, he looked exceedingly pleased with himself. He turned the bottle he was holding around. It was a pockmarked terra-cotta and looked as though it had just been excavated from an archeological dig. He turned it to show me the hand-written label that was stuck to the side.

Cognac, it read. 1867.

"That's not the date is it?" I pointed at the swirling cursive. "Like, the real date?"

Jean nodded. "Oh yes. It was my great grandfather's bottle, I believe. Would you like to taste some after lunch?"

"Yes!" I nearly shouted, as I didn't want there to be any confusion on the matter. I hadn't had much experience with Cognac, but I did know that I wanted to partake in this historical artifact. "Would you mind if I took a picture?" I asked.

"Of course not," Jean said.

"My camera is just upstairs," I said. I pointed in that direction.

"I'll wait," Jean answered.

I ran up the four flights of stairs and was breathing hard by the time I got to the top. The smaller children were no longer playing on the rope, but Sandrine, Stéphanie, Olivier, and a few of Franck's other cousins were having a heck of a time seeing how high they could swing.

"*Ça va*?" Sandrine asked.

The polite thing of course would have been to go over and kiss everyone hello, but I was worried that such an old bottle would simply vanish into the ether if I dallied. I waved at them. "I'll come say a proper hello later." I grabbed my camera and ran back downstairs.

Jean, true to his word, hadn't moved a hair. He was still holding the bottle in the exact same tilted position. Weren't his arms getting tired?

I snapped about a dozen photos. "My father isn't going to believe this."

"What? You don't have bottles this old back in Canada?" Jean said with a mischievous smile.

"Definitely not. 1867 was the year that Canada was born as a confederation. I think the Canadians were all too preoccupied to be making Cognac." Then again, the French had kept making wine and spirits throughout two world wars and countless other upheavals. Their tenacity was extraordinary.

"Well...I'll tuck this away for right now," he said when I was finished. "There's not enough for everyone, you know. You'll see it again after lunch."

Throughout the lazy morning, quite a few people—those who had far to drive before work on Monday—left. People had come from all over France—Paris, Marseille, Normandy—even though all of Franck's closest family still lived in a small circle in Burgundy.

We played another game of *pétanque* and, this time, Franck's team won, much to my chagrin. Roland was on my team and firmly placed the blame for our loss on my shoulders. I hadn't, he chastised me, been drinking my kir fast enough. Mémé happened to be outside for a few seconds at the moment of Franck's victory, and she agreed with Roland's assessment.

"Kir is not merely a drink," she said in that definite way of hers. "I consider it medicine. How do you think I can outlast all you young things?" She gave me an affectionate swat with the dishtowel she always seemed to have in her hand. "Kir! That's the answer!"

When the sun was high in the sky, people began to gravitate back to the basement, where the tables from the night before were all cleaned and set with fresh paper tablecloths in a sunny yellow and blue combination.

Franck nodded toward them. "Those are Mémé's favorite colors. No beige for her."

Huge bouquets of flowers adorned the table, many of which had been brought for the birthday girl by guests the night before.

Again, the meal began with kir and *gougères*, which miraculously whetted what I had previously believed was my non-existent appetite. How did Burgundians do it? Apart from Roland, there were very few overweight people, and yet everyone could tuck away more food than I ever believed possible.

Mémé threw open the doors again to show all of the dishes from the previous day and a few new ones as well. Franck's uncle from Provence had assured that bottles of red and white wine were placed between every four guests or so.

The atmosphere was slightly more subdued than the night before, surely due to lack of sleep and the fact that we were all still digesting, but it was a warm, cozy kind of subdued. Franck glanced over at me between forkfuls of *tabouleh* salad, and his eyes glowed with pleasure. I wasn't sure I could live without this now. I wasn't sure I could live without *him*. Yet, somehow, I would have to in less than three months.

Jean came in with the bottle of Cognac after the desserts and served Franck and me a glass each.

The cork was black with age and incredibly aromatic. The liquid was a rusty shade. I wondered for a brief moment if it was possible to get botulism or something nasty from very aged alcohol. I decided I didn't care. It would be worth it to taste Cognac from 1867. This Cognac was made before the two world wars, just after the US Civil War had ended with the assassination of Lincoln, and before cars and electricity and airplanes and computers... I wondered about the person who had painstakingly made it and bottled it. *What had they been going through? What sort of pain or pleasure had been surging forth in their lives? Were they in love? Were they in pain? Were they worried or were they happy?*

Jean nodded that it was time to taste. I took a sip. I had been bracing myself for the fire of hard alcohol, but the remarkably mellow liquid was soft and almost sweet. It was delicious. Franck and Jean, both quite the connoisseurs of strong alcohols, sighed in profound satisfaction.

"That is incredible," I said. "I can't believe I'm drinking something this old."

"It's sublime," Franck said, taking another sip and savoring every bit.

Jean smacked his lips. "Still as good."

"Thank you so much," I said to Jean, earnestly. "Thank you so much for sharing this with me."

Jean turned a little pink. "*De rien.*"

That was the attitude of Franck's whole family regarding their incredible warmth and hospitality. *De rien.* It's nothing. *De rien.* It's normal. It's the Burgundian way of doing things.

After lunch, most of the other people left, and, in the corner of the garden, Franck and I found a secluded stone bench that was hidden by a huge cherry tree.

We kissed lazily and contentedly. At one point I sighed deeply.

"What was that for?" Franck laughed.

"I'm just happy." I dropped my head so that it fit in the crook of his shoulder. My breathing slowed down to match his. "Happy, contented...and full."

Franck wrapped his arm around me and pulled me closer. "That's the way you should be." He kissed my forehead and the bridge of my nose, and suddenly I felt tears falling from my eyes. I tried to wipe them away without him noticing, but he put his hands on my shoulders and held me away from him so he could inspect my face.

"Why are you crying?"

"I don't know where the tears are coming from." I wiped them away, but they kept falling. "I just—" I shook my head, the words suddenly blocked in my throat behind a tangle of feelings. "I don't want to leave all of this. It feels like it's just getting started."

Franck picked up my hand and kissed my palm. "It *is* just getting started."

"But I have to go back to Canada." We had both avoided this reality up until that moment and had never broached it straight on.

"So you have to go away for a while." Franck shrugged. "Maybe I can come join you in Canada when my military service is finished in September."

"But for you...leaving your family...work...immigration—"

Franck stopped my doubts with a kiss on my lips. "We will find a way," he said, finally. The certainty in his words anchored me. "Maybe our next chapter is supposed to happen in Canada."

"Do you think so?"

Franck nodded. "Why not?"

I let out a watery laugh. "I'm warning you—the cheese selection isn't nearly as good."

"That *is* a serious problem." Franck's mouth twitched. "But if you are there, I can perhaps manage to bear that hardship."

I couldn't seem to get a word out, so I just squeezed his hand harder.

"You going back to Canada doesn't have to be the end," Franck said. "Me, you, my family, your family, our lives together… If you want, it can be just starting."

I was about to try to tell him just how much I wanted that, when his aunt Jacqueline appeared, armed with her beautiful camera. "*Coucou, les amoreux*!" she said. There was always an unmistakable energy behind her voice. "I realized I don't have a good photo of you two!" she said and peered through the viewfinder at us. I wiped my face surreptitiously and smiled brightly. "Ah! You're perfect just like that," she said. "Don't look up at me. Look up at the sky.

She snapped the shutter several times. "You can show this to your children and grandchildren," she laughed, then rushed off to take more photos.

chapter thirty-four

"You mean you don't know how to drive a stick shift?" Franck asked, appalled. We were driving to Beaune in his father's car but taking a roundabout way—a *very* roundabout way from the looks of it, as we neared a patch of forest that I didn't recognize but that I was fairly certain was nowhere near Beaune.

"No. I learned on an automatic and took my driving test on an automatic."

"And they gave you your license?"

"In Canada, you can pretty much get away your whole life without driving a standard."

"But an automatic isn't *driving*."

"Sure it is. It gets me from Point A to Point B in a car. That's driving."

Franck stopped the car. We were just outside the forest. We'd passed the last village—another one I didn't recognize—about five minutes previously.

He turned to me. "That's it! I have a moral obligation to teach you to drive standard. It's an essential life skill like swimming or learning to ride a bike or wine tasting."

"Wine tasting is an essential life skill?"

"Bien sûr."

"I have to be back in Beaune in two hours to give a speech at the Ursus meeting," I reminded him. I was the keynote speaker at some sort of regional Ursus Club gathering that evening. I was already dressed for it in a summery white skirt and a white silk sweater.

"I remember." Franck leaned over, unclipped my seat belt, and pulled me roughly over the gearshift and into his lap. "How could I forget, with you sitting beside me looking so lovely and pristine? I just want to—"

"What?" I laughed at him between kisses.

"Mess you up a little bit."

The idea of being messed up by Franck was immensely appealing, but I couldn't miss the speech. Over two hundred Ursus members were waiting to hear me. I swatted his hands away. "After my speech. Promise."

"It's your fault for being irresistible," he muttered, but gently deposited me back onto my seat and got out of the car. "If we can't do...anything else, I can at least teach you how to drive standard. It will only take you a few minutes to learn," he said, ushering me into the driver's seat and then walking around to the passenger's side.

I placed my hands on the steering wheel. It felt strange, after not driving for ten months. I briefly thought of the "No Driving" rule, but this was a road in the middle of nowhere, and I was with Franck—what could possibly happen?

"I should tell you now that I almost failed my driver's test in Canada," I admitted. "I got the maximum amount of demerit points that one can get and still pass. I've never been gifted at manual things."

"You've never had a teacher like *moi*," Franck insisted, and slid the keys into the ignition for me.

He instructed me to feel the pedals at my feet. My first instinct was that, compared to an automatic, there was one too many. I wasn't at all sure where my feet should go. He explained patiently, but at the same time I could tell that he did not fully realize how counter-intuitive driving standard felt for someone who had never done it before. Or maybe it was just me.

He took my hand and placed it over the gearshift and rested his hand over top of mine. He switched the gears, sliding from one notch to another. "This is neutral. This is first, second, third, fourth, fifth...reverse. Do you get it?" I nodded. I did, but that didn't mean I could do it by myself.

Franck showed me the pedal again and demonstrated how to ease off the clutch while pressing on the accelerator. He placed a lot of gentle little kisses on my neck and hands as he was demonstrating, which made me think there were many other things I would rather be doing with Franck than learning how to drive a stick shift.

"Here we go." He turned the key in the accelerator. The car lurched forward and then stalled. "Did you have your foot on the clutch?" he asked.

"No. Should I?"

"Yes. That is rather important. Push your foot down on the clutch the whole way."

This time the car lurched about five meters before shuddering to a halt. I glanced over at Franck. "I told you this wasn't going to be easy."

Franck got a determined look that I had begun to recognize. "You just need to practice a few more times."

The farthest I managed in numerous attempts was about ten meters, just a few meters past the entrance to the woods. Even though it felt as though I was doing everything Franck was telling me to do, the car's wheels just spun and we didn't go anywhere—not even a lurch forward.

"*Merde.*" Franck gestured at me to turn off the car. He went outside and inspected the tires. I rolled down my window.

"What's wrong?" I asked as he came around to my side. "Was it my driving?"

"Not really," he said, gallantly. "The road is far muddier here in the shade. I think we're a bit stuck." He kicked the front tire. "My dad is going to kill me."

I grimaced. Maybe his mild-mannered father wouldn't kill him, but his parents wouldn't be happy, that was for sure. This was the only family car, and André needed it to get back and forth for work every day. I checked my watch. The "lessons" had taken up quite some time. We had to head to Beaune within the hour if I was to be on time for my speech. Thank God I was already wearing my good clothes, although when I climbed out of the car and studied the deep well of mud under the front tires, I decided maybe white had not been the wisest sartorial choice.

"What can I do?" I asked.

Franck looked up at me, his eyes wide.

"Why do you look so surprised?" I said.

"It's just...I thought you would be angry at me for getting stuck."

"Technically, I got the car stuck, not you." I watched him a little while longer. I didn't want to bring up his ex-girlfriend but I was too curious to resist. "Would Juliette have been angry?"

Franck hesitated a moment before answering. "Furious. She never would have offered to help either... I like how you're different...how *we're* different—"

"We help each other," I supplied. "We're a team."

"*Exactement*!" Franck looked relieved. "A team." He examined me a bit further, and then looked at his hands, which were already covered in mud. "I want to kiss you very badly right now but I know I can't get you dirty."

"Let's get the car unstuck first."

Franck nodded. "Could you try to find a piece of wood—you know, like a big stick or something? I could try to put it under the wheel to get a bit of traction."

I walked toward the trees, cursing my choice of summer sandals. Finally, I found what I was looking for and emerged just in time to see Franck make another attempt at revving the engine. A huge geyser of wet mud flew up from the front wheel, and I stepped back just in time to avoid getting splattered.

Franck saw me at the last moment. He leapt out of the car. "Did any of that get on you?"

I looked down—but no—my skirt and sweater were still a pristine white. "Nope. We're good."

"Thank God." Franck came over and took the branches from my hands. "These are perfect. Cross your fingers they work."

I watched as Franck wedged the wood under the front tires. It was tough, dirty work, and he was both sweating and filthy by the end of it.

He eyed his handiwork. "You'd better back up," he warned me. "This could get dirty."

I backed away into the shelter of the trees. Franck revved the car again and again. A couple of times I thought it was working, as the wheels seemed to gain traction on the branches, but at the last second the car slipped back down into the muddy troughs.

Franck got out of the car, slamming the door behind him. He let loose a stream of swear words. I ventured closer, not sure what to say. We had to figure out a way to get to my meeting, even if it meant walking. I wasn't supposed to be dating in the first place, so how was I supposed to explain being stranded with my twenty-three-year-old French boyfriend? Too late. I started to reconsider the validity of the Ursus "No Driving" rule.

Franck stood at the front of the car, one hand with clenched fingers on the hood, while he looked down at the mud-mired tires. His entire body was rigid with frustration. Without thinking, I moved closer to console him.

Without warning, Franck shouted an explosive "*merde alors*!" and smacked the large splodge of mud on the car's roof. I tried to dodge the mud but it was too late—it splattered across my shirt and skirt and began to drip down in clumps to the ground. He couldn't have aimed better if he tried. I made an incoherent sound of dismay that made Franck look up and finally see me. His eyes went wide.

"Your clothes..." His voice faded away.

I tried to brush the mud off but only succeeded in smearing it deeper into my now far-from-pristine speech outfit.

"Shit!" I shouted in English. "Shit. Shit. Shit." I looked at my hands, which were now covered in mud too. Trying to clean myself off with muddy hands was ridiculous. Franck's horrified expression made laughter bubble up in my throat. I laughed and laughed until I had to bend over to catch my breath. At last, Franck began to laugh too.

I walked toward him, and he picked up another, smaller glob of mud from the hood of the car and smeared it down the front of his T-shirt.

"Here, let me help you," I said, and picked a clod of mud off my shirt and wiped it across his jaw.

He took his hands and marked a stripe of mud down my face as well.

"Oh my God." I chuckled. "What a disaster."

We looked at each other and started laughing again.

After a while, Franck became still. "I love you," he said.

In that moment, I could hear everything. The coo of the birds above us in the trees, the rustle of leaves, the squish of the fresh spring mud...

His eyes searched mine. "*Je t'aime*," he said again. "I should have told you before now, but I always think I can't possibly love you more, and then we get stuck in the mud and then...I do."

I realized that even though I had no idea how we were ever going to get the car unstuck, let alone get me to Beaune in time, there was nowhere I would rather have been than where I was at that moment. I wasn't supposed to drive, and I wasn't supposed to date, and I certainly wasn't supposed to fall in love, but as I looked into his caramel and green-flecked eyes, I knew that it was too late.

"*Je t'aime aussi*," I said. We couldn't close the distance between us fast enough.

Some time later, a rattling cough interrupted us. I spun around to see a wizened man in moth-eaten, woolen overalls and a threadbare sweater standing at the mouth of the woods, leaning on a twisted walking cane. He looked as though he belonged in a fairy tale.

"*Bonjour*," Franck said. "Perhaps you could help us."

The man's eyes roved over the scene in front of him, as if missing nothing. "I have my doubts," he concluded.

Franck ignored this. "I'm not exactly sure where we are. Could you tell me where the nearest village is?"

The man jerked a thumb over his left shoulder. "Fontaine is over there. Two kilometers."

"Our car is stuck." Franck slapped his hand on the roof. "I was teaching my girlfriend how to drive a standard—"

"That wasn't what you were doing."

"Well…that's what we were doing before we got stuck," Franck clarified.

The man raised one bushy eyebrow.

"I don't think we'll be able to get the car out," Franck said. "I've tried everything I can think of."

The man wandered casually over to the front of the car and studied the front wheels. "You should never let women drive," he said, at last. "Dangerous."

I bristled. "I can drive just fine. I'm just not used to driving a standard." The man looked at me again, again cocking a brow skeptically.

Franck placed a placating hand at the small of my back, and I crossed my arms over my chest and made a sound of displeasure. "We'll just have to walk to the village and see if we can get a drive," I said to Franck. "Or at least use a phone. We have to hurry though—"

"It's a small village," the man said. "Not certain you would find somebody home."

"We've tried everything." Franck gestured helplessly at the mud-mired tires.

The man tugged at the neck of his sweater. "What about stones?"

"Stones?" Franck said. "I hadn't thought of that, but wouldn't they puncture the wheels?"

"Not if they're flat and positioned correctly," the man said, poking at the front tire with his cane.

Franck and I both scanned the woods around us. The only stones I could see were the two enormous boulders placed to mark where the road entered the wood. I was quite certain that several men couldn't lift them.

"I don't see any stones," Franck spoke for both of us.

"Ah!" The man shook his finger at us. "That's because you young people have no idea where to look."

The silence stretched out for a weirdly long time, and the elfin French man seemed to be relishing every second of it.

"*Alors?*" Franck finally prompted.

"Come." The man plunged into the woods, using his cane to whack away errant branches obstructing his path. "*Suivez-moi.*"

Franck followed him, and seeing as I was still holding his hand, I did too. "What if he's crazy and he's taking us in the forest to kill us?" I hissed to Franck, as the trees became denser and began to obscure the afternoon light.

Franck paused, looked pointedly at the crooked figure disappearing in front of us, then back at me. "Laura...please."

He had a point. "Sorry. No insult intended."

"None taken." The twitch of his mouth confirmed this.

We followed the man deeper and deeper into the woods, until the brightness of the spring day disappeared entirely under a tunnel of bushes and trees.

"I always seem to get into strange situations like this with you," I observed.

"I attract them. Ask any of my friends."

The man finally stopped and beckoned us over to where he was standing. "*Voici!*" he declared. "I bet you never would have found this by yourselves." He pulled aside a chunk of bushes with his cane to reveal a mossy wall that seemed to continue on the other side of the bush.

"Why is there a wall here in the middle of the forest?" I asked.

The man fixed his scornful eyes on me and shrugged. "Gallo-Roman of course. Been here long before these trees were planted." He nodded to a cluster of trunks nearby.

Franck inspected the smooth, flat stones wedged between the layers of bright green moss on the wall. "These might work."

The man nodded. "Take a few each and carry them back to the car. You'll see. They'll work."

I stared at the wall and then back at the man who was waiting, tapping an impatient forefinger on the gnarled top of his cane. "But if the wall is really Gallo-Roman—"

"Do you think I'm lying?" the man demanded, cutting me off.

"No. I'm just not used to stumbling on Gallo-Roman walls in the woods where I live."

"Where do you live?" The man was clearly incensed at the sacrilegious idea of woods which did not contain Gallo-Roman walls.

I glanced at my watch, which confirmed my suspicion that we didn't have time to get into the whole Canada conversation if Franck and I had any hope of getting me to Beaune, muddy or not. I waved my hand toward the sky above the treetops. "Not near here."

The man narrowed his eyes at me, clearly regretting his offer to help a non-Burgundian. "What are you waiting for?" He poked Franck's shoe with his cane. "I don't have all day."

"We can't dismantle a Gallo-Roman wall!" I burst out. To even *think* of taking apart a wall that had been built in the third century was a travesty.

Our wizened leader snorted. "It's hardly like this is the only one in these woods. They're everywhere." He waved his cane around. "Besides, the Romans probably made this wall out of stones they stole from a Neolithic wall. A thieving people, those Romans."

Roman thievery notwithstanding, I would *not* remove a stone from the wall, nor would I allow Franck to do it, Ursus speech be damned. This wall would have been in a museum back in Canada. I would take no part in destroying such a piece of history.

Luckily, Franck solved the impasse by crouching down and finding several flat, smooth stones that had fallen off the wall and landed on the forest floor. "I think these will do the trick," he said. "Are you OK with taking these, Laura?"

"I guess," I said. They were already on the ground, after all.

"No difference," the old man grumbled, but ultimately approved Franck's selections of stones.

We headed back to the car, each with several stones in our arms. When we reached it, our unlikely helper brusquely instructed us in the correct placement of the stones under the wheels and gestured at me to stand far away from the car while he signaled to Franck when to rev the engine. I thought this was less from fear that I would get even dirtier and more from the suspicion that the proximity of a woman would throw a pox on the whole delicate operation.

Franck revved the motor, and within seconds the car came out of its mud trap and flew up onto the rocks. He drove it several meters further until it was well out of the muddy forest. The man gave a grunt of satisfaction.

"Thank you for showing us the rocks," I said, eating a large slice of humble pie.

"You young people aren't very clever," he noted. "It makes me worry about the future."

I tried to ignore this bit of rudeness. "Well, I think we learned something today."

He harrumphed. "*Tant mieux.*" He lifted his cane in a perfunctory good-bye and limped into the woods once again.

Franck walked back into the forest to meet me.

"I thanked him," I said when he'd reached me. "He said that our generation isn't very clever and that it worries him."

Franck took my arm and shouted "*merci*" and "*au revoir*" to the man's receding back. The man didn't even bother to turn around.

"Maybe he's deaf," I said.

"More likely he's run out of patience with us imbeciles."

"I think you're probably right... Are we that stupid?"

Franck leaned down and kissed me. "Maybe love makes us stupid," he said. "If that's the case, I'm at peace with being an idiot. Now come on, we have a meeting to get you to."

After a hair-raising drive back to the Forestiers', which I thought Franck had enjoyed immensely, I got changed in record time, tried to wipe off the majority of the mud from my face with a facecloth, put on fresh clothes, then hopped back in the car again.

Ten minutes later, Franck was screeching up the circular driveway of the hotel where the Ursus meeting was being held. I checked my watch. *Half an hour late.* I wouldn't have exchanged that time in the woods for anything, but my heart sank when I saw Monsieur and Madame Beaupre pacing around the entrance to the hotel, clearly distressed. They hadn't met Franck yet, and this was far from ideal circumstances.

I leapt out of the car, apologies already pouring out of my mouth. "I'm so sorry. The car had mechanical problems. We got here as fast as we could."

Madame Beaupre gave me *les bises* and breathed a deep sigh of relief. "We were worried, Laura."

Monsieur Beaupre gave me *les bises* as well, but his eyes were focused on Franck, who, still covered in mud, was getting out of the driver's seat.

Franck came around our side of the car and stuck out his hand. "I'm so sorry," he said. "It was my fault, not Laura's. I'm Franck Germain. One of Laura's...friends. Nice to meet you."

I could feel Monsieur Beaupre go rigid beside me. I wanted to take time to explain, give Franck some time to work his charm as he had on Monsieur Lacanche. Monsieur Beaupre only shook his hand as quickly and perfunctorily as possible.

"Yes. Well." Monsieur Beaupre put his hands on my shoulders and steered me inside. "We need to get Laura behind her podium."

With a nod, we left Franck. I managed to send him an apologetic look over my shoulder. He waved me on with a wry smile that told me not to worry.

"Who is that?" Madame Beaupre whispered in my ear. "He's not a boy; he's a man. You're not dating him, are you? You know that's against the rules."

I opened my mouth but couldn't find the right answer. My relationship with Franck had been unequivocal right from the start, unlike the months of ambiguity with Thibaut. I wasn't merely dating Franck. I had fallen in love with him.

Monsieur Beaupre hadn't lost any of his rigidity. "We'll talk of this later," he said.

I felt caught between two irreconcilable forces. There had to be a way to make the Beaupres happy and to stay with Franck. I just needed to find it.

chapter thirty-five

I was spending every weekend at Franck's family's house, and luckily the Forestiers seemed more than pleased with this schedule. Since the meeting, I'd never had time to talk with the Beaupres and try to explain. My speech went well, but Monsieur Forestier was eager to leave and whisked me and his wife out to his BMW before anyone else had even gotten up from their table.

I was well aware that Franck's family had extended me incredible hospitality. The fact that the Forestiers were never home meant that whenever Franck was in Villers-la-Faye, I was too. For Burgundians, and for the Germains in particular, cooking and baking was a way of showing love. I owed them something.

I had not cooked at all during my time in France. I didn't exactly feel that it was my place to invade the kitchens of my host families. Also, cooking and recipes are different there—everything is weighed using the metric system instead of the Imperial cups and tablespoons method I had grown up with. Besides, I found cooking in France was more than a tad intimidating. The food I'd tasted since arriving there was not only exquisite, but also delicious. I wasn't tempted to throw my hat into that ring.

So, when Franck's family repeatedly begged me to cook something "Canadian" for them, I wasn't seduced by the idea. What was a truly Canadian dish anyway, besides pancakes and maple syrup, neither of which I could find in France? Still, they kept asking, and I felt compelled to make *something*. It occurred to me that I still had two boxes of Jell-O at the bottom of my suitcase.

My mom had bought them for me to bring to France, as she had heard from a friend that the French loved Jell-O. It would be easy and almost foolproof, and it would also introduce them to something they had almost certainly never tried before. Still, the boxes had been at the bottom of my suitcase for almost a year. Would they still be good? Surely powder in a bag didn't go bad...

"I'll make dessert for lunch today," I announced the next morning. We were finishing off a lazy breakfast under the wisteria at the back of the courtyard.

Mémé was staying over for a week while Jean and Jacqueline were on the Côte d'Azur. She clapped her hands. "Lovely! Do you need anything from the store?"

"No," I said. "I have everything I need."

"What are you going to make?" Franck asked.

"A surprise."

Franck's forehead creased. "Do you need help?"

"Nope. I just need about ten minutes by myself in the kitchen this morning."

Franck looked more dubious. Stéphanie, who was procrastinating before going to study for her French *bac* exams the next week, laughed at his expression.

"Relax," I said. "I'm not going to poison you. At least not intentionally."

His brow still didn't relax. Mémé gave him a slap on his shoulder. "Stop being so naughty, Franck. Of course Laura is not going to poison us!" She turned to me. "I can't wait to taste your dessert, Laura."

"*Merci*, Mémé," I said, trying to retain my dignity but suddenly assailed with doubts. Jell-O was certainly original, but it was hardly the stuff of gourmet cooking. Come to think of it, I had never loved it—it was just another one of those things that I sucked down when I was a child without really thinking about it, like bologna and Velveeta cheese. My taste buds had changed that past year though. Evolved was how I liked to think about it. Would I find Jell-O disgusting now?

Later that morning, I shooed everyone out of the kitchen, including Franck's mother, Michèle, who I thought was a little concerned about what I was going to do in her house. I went upstairs and retrieved my boxes of Jell-O from the depth of my suitcase. They were squashed, but the sachets inside remained intact.

I thought back to the Ursus meeting a couple of weeks earlier and the Beaupres' concern about Franck. If they only knew how wonderful he was to me...if I could only make them understand. Of all of my host parents, the Beaupres still felt like my de facto French parents. The fact that they disapproved of Franck was a problem I needed to resolve.

I took the Jell-O boxes downstairs, still ruminating over this conundrum. Luckily, preparing Jell-O according to the instructions on the back of the box did not require much brainpower. I couldn't remember the precise amount of a cup of boiling water but made my best attempt at estimating using a kitchen glass. I doubled the "recipe" and put in two sachets of Jell-O, then covered the bowl with a tight layer of saran wrap and then a layer of aluminum foil. I shoved one of the boxes in the back pocket of my shorts before going back outside.

Franck's parents were pruning the plants and flowers that had sprung up in a wild fashion around the courtyard, and Mémé was sitting at the table coloring with Emmanuel-Marie.

Stéphanie had grudgingly opened up her books, but I didn't blame her for not being motivated to study chemistry, which was her first exam. The sunshine and blue sky did not invite hours of memorizing the periodic table. A year earlier, I had been exactly where she was, cramming for my Grade 12 provincial exams. The French *bac* was far worse though. The marks counted for one hundred percent of Stéph's grade, so those ten days of *bac* exams would decide whether she graduated or not. I had been so right to tell the head nun at Saint Coeur that I was not going to be taking the *baccalauréat.*

Franck and I were giddy with freedom. Franck whispered in

my ear when I joined him on a lawn lounge. "*Qu'il est doux de ne rien faire quand tout s'agite autour de nous.*" How agreeable it is to do nothing when everyone is working around you.

"Do you need something that you can't find? Michèle asked, coming over to me with her *sécateurs*, her face perplexed.

"No," I said, "it's done."

Everyone stopped what they were doing and stared at me.

"But you haven't even been in there five minutes," Franck said. "What could you possibly make in five minutes?"

"You'll see." I tried to maintain an exterior of cool confidence, but inside I started to entertain grave doubts. Meals in Burgundy usually take more than an hour to prepare, often more, and pretty much everything is prepared lovingly from scratch. I had never made the connection, but that was probably why almost everything I put in my mouth there was so sublime. Throwing a few glasses of boiling water over two packages of powder, it struck me only then, couldn't even be considered cooking according to Burgundian standards.

I now started to truly regret the Jell-O, but I was in too far for retreat.

Mémé checked her watch. "I'd better go start lunch." She patted my head on her way by. "I'm sure it will be delicious, *ma Laura.*"

Franck rescued me from my mental torment by suggesting we go over and visit Olivier at his new house. Just two weeks before, Olivier had shocked everyone in the village by purchasing the house right on the street corner beside the *boulangerie* and by moving out of his family home. This meant, though, that he now lived across the street from Franck's house. Franck was thrilled.

"What did you make?" he whispered to me, once we were safely outside his parents' gate.

"You'll see, but I'm having second thoughts."

Franck opened his mouth to say something else, but Olivier had spotted us and was already hailing us from the top of his stairs. "*Venez! Venez!*" he called. "I was just coming over to get you. Franck, I need your advice on something."

Franck took my hand and crossed the street. He smiled up at his longtime friend. "*Alors*, how are you keeping, neighbor?"

"Neighbor, until you move to Canada, that is," Olivier corrected Franck.

"I *am* going to move to Canada," Franck said. "If Laura will have me."

I was thrilled, of course, but a little worried about how Franck's family would take this news when he told them. "I'll have you."

We let ourselves in Olivier's gate and made our way up his stone steps. As we got closer, I made out a skeptical look that crinkled Olivier's sharp brown eyes.

Franck must have seen it too. "It's not some crazy plan," Franck said to his friend, sitting down on the steps in the sunshine to light a cigarette and chat for a bit before we went inside. Olivier sat down beside him, and Franck patted his knee. I settled in Franck's lap. "There's no reason I couldn't go to Canada."

"So you say." Olivier flicked his lighter and lit Franck's cigarette.

"You don't believe me." Humor and exasperation warred in Franck's voice.

"Canada is far away," Olivier said. "Neither you nor I have ever even been on an *airplane* let alone traveled halfway across the world. You know me, Franck, I'm the type of person who believes things when I see them."

"Neither of you has ever been on an airplane?" I asked, dumbfounded.

Both men shook their heads.

"That's incredible."

"Why?" Olivier asked. "It's not that unusual around here. How many times have you been on an airplane?"

I tried to think of all the times I had been back and forth to Hawaii and California, and then back east to Montreal and Toronto, and all the times I had taken the little puddle jumper over to Vancouver... "I don't even know. Too many to count. I can't remember *not* taking airplanes."

Olivier's eyes opened wide. "How strange," he said. I was struck by the gulf between what was considered normal in Canada and what was considered normal in rural Burgundy. How were Franck and I ever going to close the gap between them?

"Don't get me wrong," Olivier said, reaching out and patting my shoulder. "I see how you and Franck are when you're together. It's just that Canada...well...that is something us Villers-la-Faye boys read about in Jack London books. To actually go from here to there..." He shrugged. "I just can't help being a realist."

"Pessimist." Franck corrected him.

"Maybe," Olivier admitted. "Or maybe not." He stubbed out his cigarette on the porch and beckoned us inside. "Now, will you give me your honest opinion of this ruin I have bought?"

"No, I won't," Franck said. "Because I am an optimist. I will see what it could be, not what it is."

Olivier patted Franck on the back. "That's precisely why I need your help."

We spent the next hour touring the strange little house that Olivier had bought. It had been owned for decades before by a recalcitrant village bachelor, a devoted customer of Jacky's Bistro, renowned in Villers-la-Faye for his dubious hygiene. We quickly discovered the reason for that—the house didn't contain a bathtub or a shower. There was only a Turkish-style toilet in a room off the front porch. And one actually had to go outside in order to use this primitive squat hole. The room didn't appear to have any heat source either. It certainly wasn't a place that encouraged lengthy ablutions of any kind during the frigid Burgundian winters.

We debated the mystery of how the previous owner had washed himself. Franck was of the opinion that he never had and had just relied on being caught in a downpour from time to time on his way to or from Jacky's. Olivier, despite being a realist, gave him the benefit of the doubt and decided that he must have used a facecloth every once in a while. I was so stunned by the rustic conditions that still existed in this century that I wasn't at all sure what to think.

The house stank of tobacco and several other questionable and unpleasant odors that slunk around and seemed to jump out at me from dark corners. Franck went over to the windows, wrenched open the shutters, and flung them aside. Sweet summer air flooded the room.

"That's a start," he said, rubbing his hands together. "I doubt that has been done for decades. I don't recall ever seeing the windows of this house open. Do you?"

Olivier shook his head. "Now that I think about it, no."

The room was not only sweeter smelling now, but brighter. Unfortunately, this allowed us all to get a good look at the wallpaper, which was a horrific floral brown that had been darkened over the decades with layers of smoke and grime.

"You have work ahead of you." Franck inspected the wallpaper with his lips curled into an involuntary grimace. "I hope you have good friends."

"I'm counting on that," Olivier said, giving Franck a pointed look. "Come look at this though.

Olivier instructed us to climb up a ladder and through a small hole in the rocks that was about a meter and a half above the floor level. "There's a barn in there," Olivier said, holding my hand to steady me as I went up the ladder. Franck had already hopped down on the other side, and I heard his voice call out. "I can catch you, Laura. There's nothing to be afraid of."

I climbed through the hole and saw that there was a rickety ladder on the other side as well. There seemed to be a lot of old hay everywhere, and I coughed after breathing in a few bits.

"Best to keep your mouth closed in old attics," Franck advised as I made my way down the second ladder.

I looked down at the floor at the bottom of the ladder, which in the dim light seemed to consist of rotting wooden boards with large gaps in random spots. "Is that safe to step on?"

"Not really," Franck said. "But I'll make sure you stay on

the rafters. They're nice and wide, but if you step off them you might go right through."

"Oh," I answered faintly.

"I won't let that happen, though," he assured me, as Olivier popped through the window and hopped down, as sprightly as a monkey.

Franck trapped me in his arms, even though I was in no immediate danger.

"Maybe I'll just stay here near the wall." I moved to let Olivier pass and peered up above me. A few of the terra-cotta tiles had slid out of their places on the roof far above, giving enough light to make out the cavernous space and its stunning structure of crisscrossed oak beams that rivaled those in the attic of Jean and Jacqueline's country house.

"It's beautiful," I said.

"It's huge," Franck said, more to Olivier than me.

"I know." Olivier nodded. "This is why I bought the house. I'm thinking of putting the kitchen in the room we were just in, then opening up the wall here and making this the main living area with a TV room, a few bedrooms, and a full bathroom.

"It's going to be a massive job," Franck said. "We're going to need to pour the floor first." He gnawed his lip. I was fairly certain he was already planning out the work in his mind.

I could make out the flash of Olivier's teeth as he grinned.

As we hurried back across the road to Franck's gate, we could smell wafts of the delicious lunch Mémé had prepared. She had made a *blanquette de veau*, which she had begun marinating the day before. I thought of my three-minute Jell-O recipe, and was tempted to turn back to seek refuge in Olivier's grungy new home.

Franck's family had taken me in and treated me like one of their own. I realized only now what an insult it was for me to have spent so little time cooking for them, especially since staying at Franck's house, I'd enjoyed meal after lovingly prepared meal.

Mémé hurried us over to the table under the wisteria, admonishing us for being late and ruining her main course. It wasn't true, of course. She served the veal along with silken new potatoes and a side of *frisée* salad, with a feisty vinaigrette with a strong dose of both shallots and Dijon mustard. Of course, on the table stood the family ceramic mustard pot with the wooden spoon, filled with Dijon mustard. I took too big a dollop with my first bite of veal and found my eyes watering. Burgundians love their mustard and they love it strong.

"Here." Michèle handed me a slice of fresh baguette. "Breathe this in."

I followed her instructions, as strange as they sounded. The smell of warm yeast and flour actually did stop the smarting in my eyes and nose. "How does that work?" I asked. "It's miraculous."

"It's an old Burgundian trick. Something to do with the yeast in the bread. When you live this close to Dijon, it comes in handy."

I stored this away, knowing that it would come in handy for the rest of my life, as I had developed an unshakable addiction to Dijon mustard.

After the veal, came a smelly Munster cheese from Alsace and a fresh twelve-month-old Comté, as well as a glass jar of cancoillotte—a garlicky runny cheese from the Jura that had to be scooped onto a bit of baguette with a spoon.

This was all washed down with some strong red wine from Provence left over from Mémé's *fête* and made by Jean-Marie from the vines Franck helped plant. I was enjoying the midday deliciousness so much that I had all but forgotten about my "dessert." The sweet smell of the wisteria above us, the heat of the midday sun, and the cool of the shade drew out the perfection of the meal.

Over the cheese course, we got to discussing Olivier's new house.

"It used to be the *maison close* of Villers-la-Faye," Mémé said.

"What's a *maison close*?" I asked. "I haven't heard that expression before."

"Where the prostitutes worked," André said. "You know. *Un bordel.*"

A whorehouse? Franck's family home for as far back as anyone could remember was across the street from the village whorehouse?

"It was extremely well managed," Mémé continued. "The girls were clean and well looked after. The *madame* in charge was an efficient sort of woman. She managed everything perfectly. I always got along with her."

"They were your neighbors when you owned the bakery?" Franck leaned back in his chair.

"Oh yes. They used to come over after working all night to get fresh croissants straight out of the oven. Some of them ended up getting married to village men; others managed to save up a tidy little sum for themselves and retired. There used to be a red-light outside, hanging off Olivier's front porch. It was lit when they were open for business."

"They're illegal now, right?" I asked. "*Les bordels*?"

"Unfortunately, yes," Mémé said. "It's a terrible shame. If I had a political bone in my body, which I don't, I would campaign for them to be re-opened. I'm convinced those girls were better off then than they are now, alone on the streets or bullied by some horrible gigolo."

"You don't think it's wrong for men to go to prostitutes in the first place?" I asked.

Mémé swatted away this notion like an errant fly. "Men have always had needs and acted on them. We're all better off recognizing we cannot change human nature and coming up with a well-organized way to manage it rather than sticking our heads in the sand. *Les maisons closes* were a vital part of village life before those stupid men enacted their silly laws. Honestly, such a shame..."

"Does Olivier know?" Stéphanie asked us. "That his house

was a *bordel*?"

"I'm not sure," Franck said. "I don't think so. I'm sure he wouldn't mind though."

"Why would he?" Mémé shrugged.

I was still sitting, digesting this conversation, when Stéphanie nudged me. "When are we going to try your dessert, Laura?"

My heart sank. I would far rather continue listening to Mémé reminisce about the village whorehouses, but the moment of truth had arrived.

"Can you come help me?" I asked Franck, my eyes pleading. He got up, and we took some dishes back into the kitchen with us.

Franck was busy tidying them up when I removed my bowl of Jell-O from the fridge. I peeled back the Saran Wrap and aluminum foil from the top and peered inside. I jiggled the bowl. It seemed very firm. I jiggled it again. *Too firm.* I guess I hadn't remembered exactly what a cup of water looked like.

Franck had come over and was looking over my shoulder. "What is it?" he asked, his voice a mix of horror and fascination.

"Jell-O."

"What is Jell-O?"

"It's flavored gelatin. It's a popular dessert in North America. I always used to have it at birthday parties and—"

"Gelatin, like on a slice of pâté?"

I'd never made the connection before. "Sort of, but instead of being savory, it's sweet."

"Sweet gelatin?" He couldn't keep the look of horror off his face.

"Yes," I said, getting a bit defensive now. "This one is grape flavored." I pulled the squashed box out of my jeans' pocket and showed him. He read it carefully.

"*Raisins de Bourgogne*?" he read, his voice incredulous.

Oh God. I hadn't noticed. I grabbed the box back and read it again. The flavor was called Burgundy Grape. That pretty much sealed my shame. I tried to shove it back into my pocket but Franck was too quick. He stuffed it into his. His lower lip was trembling as he tried to hold back his laughter.

"Mémé came into the kitchen then, otherwise I would have asked Franck to help me dispose of the Jell-O and collaborate in the story that it had accidentally fallen on the floor.

"Oh!" Mémé declared. "Is this what you made?" She peered into the bowl, and for the first time ever I saw her looking cowed. "It looks very *intéressant*!" she said, at last. "I'll take it outside. Come with me, Laura, so you can do the presentation. You get some bowls and spoons, Franck."

I had no choice but to follow her, so I tried to muster all the self-confidence I could about my Jell-O. No way out but through.

"Here it is." Mémé set down the bowl in the center of the table, and the Jell-O jiggled as Jell-O has a habit of doing. Its lurid purple color glowed through the clear glass in the sunlight. How was I going to explain this?

"This is a dessert that is traditionally North American," I began. "It's what we all ate growing up. It's called Jell-O."

Franck's whole family stared at the bowl, locked in stunned silence.

"What is it exactly?" Stéphanie finally asked.

"It's flavored gelatin," Franck supplied.

"Like the gelatin on pâté?" Stéphanie echoed her brother's question, sounding equally as incredulous.

"That's it."

"But sweet?"

Oh God. Why didn't I foresee this?

"Yes. Grape flavored."

Mémé clapped her hands. "Wonderful! Who wants some?"

It was clear from their round eyes that nobody did, but luckily Franck's family had excellent manners.

Franck's father, André, said politely, "*S'il vous plaît, Mémé*," and held out his empty bowl. Mémé handed the big serving spoon to me, and I served a couple of wobbling spoonfuls. André took the bowl back and stared dubiously at it while I served the others.

"*Bon appétit*!" Mémé dug into her bowl. She seemed to keep

her first spoonful in her mouth for a long time before swallowing. "Interesting," she said. "You North Americans are certainly...innovative."

Stéphanie took a spoonful, swallowed it, then pushed away her bowl. "I'm sorry, Laura. I just can't. It's not that it tastes bad exactly, it's just that, for us, the idea of gelatin as a dessert... It's always a savory thing and never eaten by itself. It's just too strange."

Michèle and André managed to take a few more spoonfuls than Stéph but couldn't finish their bowls either. Franck just sat back and looked at us all, amusement making his lips twitch.

Emmanuel-Marie dumped it out on the tray of his high chair and said, "*C'est dégueulasse*!" before beginning to smoosh it between his fingers.

Mémé was the only one who finished her bowl. "It was strange," she admitted. "And it wasn't very good, but it was *intéressant*."

I covered my face with my hands. "Oh my God," I groaned. "I can't believe I thought making Jell-O for you was a good idea. I'm so, so sorry."

"Not just Jell-O!" Franck leaned over and kissed me, then gave way to the unholy mirth that had been consuming him ever since he'd left the kitchen. He whipped the flattened box out of his jeans' pocket. "You haven't learned the best part yet. Do you know what the flavor for this particular Jell-O is?"

"No!" I tried to grab the box from his hands, but he held it too high above his head.

"*Raisins de Bourgogne*!" Franck announced with delight, lobbing the box over my head to Stéph. She caught it and read with disbelief.

"Unbelievable," she said. She passed the box to André and Michèle. Everyone burst into laughter—everyone except me. I dropped my head down onto the table and hid there.

I felt the warmth of Franck's breath near my ear. "It's funny, Laura, not disastrous. It makes us love you even more. To be perfectly honest, I'm relieved to discover there is something you *can't* do. You can be scarily over-achieving, you know."

I banged my head softly on the tabletop.

"Come on," he said. "Laugh. They all love you."

He kissed the whorl of my ear, and I lifted my head.

Mémé patted my back. "Cooking and baking isn't everything," she said, comfortingly. "You have many other good qualities."

If only the Beaupres could see how kind Franck and his family were, I knew they would be reconciled to me contravening the "No Dating" rule. Besides, I was learning that there were many more unwritten rules that were even more important than the four official Ursus rules—three of which I had already broken. One of them was "Do not make Jell-O for French people under any circumstances."

chapter thirty-six

Madame Forestier drove me to school on my last day. The French students, of course, would be cracking the books to prepare for their *baccalauréat* exams in ten days, but for me it meant I would be saying good-bye to my school friends, apart from Sandrine and Stéphanie, whom I saw every weekend in Villers.

It was such a contrast to the first day I was driven to school by Madame Beaupre. I had felt so lost and so unsure. Now school had served its purpose—springboarded me into a social life and also helped me learn French. But—as I was spending more and more time in Beaune's cafés anyway as the classes became increasingly devoted to review and studying—it seemed natural to make the final break.

I felt I hardly knew the Forestiers. They were a rarity in Burgundy—a couple where both Monsieur and Madame held down full-time and all-consuming jobs. They were gone by the time I left for school most mornings and came home most nights well after I had gone to bed. In their house, I felt as though I was living in a self-service hotel. They were kind the rare times when I saw them, but invariably harried and distracted. If they had been my first host family instead of my fourth, my year would have been completely different. At least by this point, I was so well ensconced in my gang in Villers-la-Faye that the Forestiers' hands-off approach suited me perfectly.

Still, I thought fondly back to my months with the Beaupres. They still felt like my true French family. I tried not to think back to those difficult winter months trapped in Noiron with the Girard offspring, then my months beside the bell tower with the formal but not unpleasant Lacanche brood. I met Franck during my time with the Lacanches, but I never did manage to feel at ease with Monsieur Lacanche, who still struck me as someone who had the authoritarian soul of a despot, even with his family.

At school that day, I said a series of *au revoirs* to my friends, and a bunch of us went out to a café called Le Sporting for lunch. Unlike my usual haunt, Le Square, this spot was not favored by the students from Stéphanie's school.

We played a game of pool and drank a celebratory round of kir, then one by one my school friends left to study.

Thibaut was the last one to leave. He stayed behind to help me arrange the pool cues that everyone had left in a haphazard French way all over the room.

"Good luck on your *bac*," I said as we gave *les bises* goodbye. It was strange—although I had spent quite a lot of time in the past year with Thibaut's tongue in my mouth, the idea now seemed completely unnatural. Already, I couldn't imagine kissing anyone except Franck.

"If you give me your address, I'll write you," Thibaut said as we walked out of the café onto the sunny sidewalk.

I looked sideways at him, amused. "No, you won't."

"You're right; I won't," he admitted as we crossed the ring road to go to the school. "How about this? If I don't pass my *bac* and have to go back to Saint Coeur next year, I'll be sure to torment le Dragon for you."

I laughed. "Now *that*'s friendship."

The next week, I was invited to attend a huge celebratory meal at the Clos de Vougeot, which Monsieur Beaupre and I had cycled around in September. These dinners are legendary in

Burgundy and put on by a renowned group called les Chevaliers du Tastevin, which roughly translates as the "Knights of the Wine-Tasting Cup."

I didn't realize what a big deal it was until I mentioned it at Franck's over lunch that weekend.

"You're going to a Chevaliers du Tastevin dinner at Clos de Vougeot?" I had never seen Franck's father's pale blue eyes so wide.

"The Ursus Club organized my invitation. I haven't been given much information, but it sounds like fun."

"Fun?" Michèle said. "Many people dream of going to one of those evenings their whole lives! They are a sacred ritual in Burgundy. Usually you have to be wealthy or famous, or both, to be invited."

They all stared at me, as though suspecting I had been hiding a secret identity all this time.

"I have no idea how my name got on the guest list, to be honest."

Franck squeezed my knee. "Can you bring a guest?" His eyes sparkled with mischief.

"That wasn't mentioned. Sorry."

"I'm joking," he said. "Invitations to Clos de Vougeot are highly coveted. They don't throw them around like confetti."

I was told by the Forestiers that I needed to dress up for the evening, so I went out with Stéphanie and Sandrine to Beaune and found a black dress with a tight bodice and a flared skirt that stopped just below the knee. When I put it on that evening at Franck's house—I was spending the weekend with the Germains again, and Franck was dropping me off for the *soirée*—I felt a little awkward. Was it the right level of dressy for Burgundy?

As I slid on my high heels, I heard Franck's now familiar footstep on the stairs. The sail curtain to his room parted, and he came in. I was sitting on the edge of the bed. "Do you think this will do?"

Franck had gone completely still, his eyes fixated on the bodice area of my dress. "You look beautiful," he said, finally.

"I'm not sure it's safe letting you go among the Knights of the Wine-Tasting Cup looking like that."

"I'll be fine." I got up and pressed a kiss against his jaw. "I'll be safeguarded by all those Ursus members. And when it's over, I'll be coming back to Villers to you."

"I can't wait." Franck's fingers played across the bare skin on my back between my crisscrossed shoulder straps. "Can I mess you up a bit now though?"

An hour and a half later, Franck dropped me off in front of the massive stone entrance to the Château de Clos Vougeot. The whole place was strategically lit to highlight the twelfth- to sixteenth-century stonework. It was still light out, but I had no doubt it would be spectacular once night fell.

First, we were treated to an *apéritif* of kir in the courtyard, where I chatted with several Ursus members and kept an eye out for the Beaupres. I smiled to myself. Monsieur Beaupre was surely running late, as usual, and driving Madame Beaupre crazy.

The Chevaliers mingling in the crowd looked impressive with their red-and-yellow-striped robes and neck sashes and huge, silver wine-tasting cups hanging around their necks.

The sound of trumpets silenced the crowd, then a parade of men in full Chevaliers de Tastevin regalia including the robes and square, red-and-yellow hats, strutted around, led by men blowing on coiled hunting trumpets.

We were escorted into the main dining hall, which was spectacular and lavishly set for what looked like over three hundred people.

I sat down at my designated spot between two Ursus members I had met only briefly before. I tried to count the number of different-shaped glasses in front of my place setting but lost count before more hunting trumpets heralded the arrival of the food on gargantuan platters, which were carried aloft by the waiters.

The first course was placed in front of me—a thick wedge of what looked like duck terrine, artfully displayed on salad leaves and paired with a dollop of jelly. A white wine was simultaneously poured into the glass on my far left.

The leisurely pace of Burgundian meals that I had grown accustomed to was absent here. Everything was run with such clockwork precision that we guests settled down to the business of consuming the courses as they were served, so as not to disrupt the schedule. After the terrine, there was the fish course—steaming monkfish medallions in a sauce redolent of saffron, served from oval copper dishes shined to a golden glow. Just as I mopped up the last bit of my sauce with a piece of fresh baguette, my plate was replaced with another containing two piping-hot poached eggs in red wine sauce (a local specialty known as *oeufs en meurette*, which was served with mushrooms and thin, crisp slices of garlicky baguette).

I barely had time to contemplate the mystery of how all of this was being served hot and without a single mistake, when a thick slice of veal topped with morels in a creamy mustard sauce appeared in front of me. The accompanying wine was a delectable Hospices de Beaune from 1985, which was both powerful and perfectly balanced.

I took a deep breath after this course. I barely had time to talk to my table mates, who all seemed as focused on their delicious food and wine as I was, like elite athletes during a prestigious sporting event.

"I wonder what's next?" I asked the man to my right.

Just then tiny glasses of sorbet swimming in marc de Bourgogne appeared, answering my question. This was a *trou bourguignon*, meant to refresh the palate and help digestion before the cheese course.

"Most meals in Burgundy are a marathon," my neighbor commented. "This one is a sprint."

I laughed and just then caught the eye of Madame Beaupre who was seated three tables further along. I waved at her and she waved back, but with some reserve. Were they still upset about Franck, or was it something else entirely? I wanted to talk to them, but just then a plate of cheese materialized in front of me, along with my favorite l'Ami du Chambertin (which Madame Beaupre had introduced me to) and a creamy Brillat Savarin and a sharp Comté. I had lost track of which wine I was drinking, but this red looked as though it merited the wide-bowled glass into which it had been reverently poured. I took a sip. Perfection. The best wine was always served with the cheese course, and this one had to be a Grand Cru.

I wondered if I could get up to go over and say hello to the Beaupres after my cheese course, but everyone stayed seated at their designated places. Nobody even dared take a bathroom break, from what I could tell. I could hardly blame them—some crucial delicacy would be missed, and going to the bathroom wasn't in keeping with the synchronized nature of the proceedings. Mother Nature be damned.

Giant *escargots* made of white chocolate, accompanied by prune liqueur, were wheeled in on trolleys, only to be ceremoniously splintered and transformed into shards of chocolate-coated, crunchy almond toffee.

Would I even be sober enough to be able to convince the Beaupres that Franck was a good thing for me? Or maybe, I reasoned optimistically, the alcohol would ease the discussion. It still mattered to me very much what the Beaupres thought of me and that they approved of Franck.

I was still pondering this when a group of red-and-yellow-outfitted men went up to the elevated stage at the front, picked up their instruments, and led all of us in a rousing rendition of "*Le Ban Bourguignon.*" I could now clap and twirl my hands and sing "la la la" with the best of them.

Just as I was about to get up and sneak over to the Beaupres under the cover of all the raucous singing, I heard my name called out repeatedly. One of my neighbours pointed to me, and the singers beckoned me up on stage. I walked none too steadily, concentrating hard on putting one foot in front of the other.

Once on the stage, I turned and smiled at the crowd, but I

couldn't make out any individual faces under the bright lights.

"What is your name again?" the lead singer asked me, and then pushed the microphone under my mouth.

"Laura," I answered.

"And how old are you?" he asked.

"Eighteen."

"Ahhhhhh...*une belle jeune Laura, mais dis donc, qui l'aura*?" It was a play on my name—a beautiful young Laura, but the question is, who will get her?

And then he was off, making suggestive but playful jokes with my name while I blushed. He also made several comparisons between me and fine wine, and women in general and fine wine, and at long last made me sign my name in an enormous ledger, then placed my very own wine-tasting cup around my neck. The trumpets started up again, and the singers led everyone in another raucous *Ban Bourguignon* as I was ushered back to my seat.

I was unsure exactly what had just happened, but I was certain that it was a once-in-a-lifetime experience. A few other people were beckoned to the stage and gently roasted as I had been. I didn't dare get up, as anyone who did became the butt of the singer's ribald jokes.

More hard liquors were served, and I opted for a marc this time, and then, many speeches and songs later, coffee and petits fours appeared.

At long last, things wound down, and people began making their way toward the doors. I teetered a bit, unused to the combination of high heels and six or seven glasses of wine. I hurried, though, to catch the Beaupres before I missed them.

I gave them both *les bises* and noticed that they seemed tired. "That was quite an experience," I said with a smile.

"Did you enjoy it, Laura?" Madame Beaupre reached out with her finger and brushed my cheek with affection.

"Very much. Franck's family told me what an honour it is to attend one of these events."

I cursed myself. That hadn't been at all the way I had been planning to bring up the whole Franck thing. It also made me sound as if I was spending all my time there, which, although it was the case, was not the impression I wanted to give the Beaupres while we were still on such uncertain ground.

Their faces instantly became troubled. "You two seem to be becoming very serious," Monsieur Beaupre observed. "Too serious," he added, bluntly. "You are still our responsibility all this year, Laura. We are worried about you. I would not want Sophie dating an older American man."

The heels of my shoes were sinking into the mud in the courtyard. Franck was going to come and pick me up. I hoped he wouldn't appear before I had time to try to explain…

"Franck is…different." I understood their concern, but I couldn't seem to find the right words to reassure them. "His family is extremely kind. It's—"

"It is against the 'No Dating' rule, Laura," Madame Beaupre said gently. "You know that. We have thought a lot about this and wondered how we would feel if it were Sophie. We would be extremely uncomfortable if she became seriously involved with an older man so far away from home."

"I understand that," I began. "But—"

Just then someone started honking a car horn imperiously. Madame Beaupre peered over toward the commotion and looked accusingly at her husband. "You parked behind those two cars, so now they can't get out."

"*Eh merde*," Monsieur Beaupre murmured.

"Just…think about it, Laura," Madame Beaupre said as they rushed toward their car. "Act prudently."

They sped off, and only then did I start scanning the cars for Franck. I caught sight of him at last, leaning against the door of his father's car across the vineyards from the main gates to the château. His eyes were fixed on me and flashed in the dim light of the illuminated buildings and car headlights. I felt suddenly electrified. I began to make my way over to him.

Prudent.

He held out his arm as I neared and then encircled my waist, pulling me against his solid chest. "You are so beautiful," he murmured into the whorl of my ear. "I could never tire of watching you."

How could I be prudent in the face of how Franck made me feel? He held nothing back, so neither could I.

chapter thirty-seven

It was three weeks before my plane was due to leave for Canada, ostensibly with me on it. So much had happened. A few days before this, Franck had finished the last day of his required military service and moved back from Dijon to Villers-la-Faye. I wasn't being at all prudent, relatively speaking. I was, of course, spending every possible moment with him in Villers-la-Faye.

One day, I stood waiting for Franck to come and pick me up once again, when Monsieur Forestier paused as he rushed out to his car for a meeting in Beaune. "Why don't you just move to Villers-la-Faye?" he said suddenly.

At first, I was sure it was a reproach. "I'm sorry I've been spending so much time there—"

"No. I didn't mean that." He shook his head, impatient as ever. "I mean seriously. You only have three weeks left. You're eighteen years old. I know my wife and I are barely ever here…we would understand."

All of a sudden, the sublime possibility burst upon me. *Three uninterrupted weeks with Franck.* "Really?"

"Really," he said. "I am not so ancient that I forget what it is like to be eighteen and madly in love."

I lost no time. I went right back into the house and called my parents and managed to extract their permission, although I did have to bend the truth a bit by emphasizing I was staying at Stéphanie's house.

That evening, I was moved out of the Forestiers' and into Franck's bedroom.

After six idyllic days in Villers-la-Faye, I received a phone call from Monsieur Lacanche, my autocrat of a third host father, who also happened to have just assumed the reigns as the President of the Beaune Ursus Club. I had no idea how he had found out about my move, but he was livid and informed me that I was going to be called to account for my behavior the next night at my final Ursus meeting. I tried to explain, but he didn't give me the chance and hung up after delivering that ominous summons.

Franck knew my dread and came up to his bedroom with me the next night to keep me company as I got changed for the meeting.

I put on a nice pair of linen pants and my coral silk shirt. Finally, from the bottom of my suitcase, I extracted my Ursus blazer. I hadn't worn it in several months. As I looked at the profusion of pins on it, I felt repelled, as though the jacket and I were opposing magnets. Monsieur Lacanche had made it clear that, as far as he was concerned, I had betrayed the entire Ursus Club and all my host families.

I had acted like a certain type of person to get to France—an extrovert, a rule follower, somebody who put a high priority on pleasing others. The line between that person and my true self had always been unclear. However, I was beginning to think that maybe I was none of the things the Ursus wanted me to be. Not anymore. I could continue pretending, but somewhere along the way I had lost that ability. For that, I was going to have to pay the price.

If a middle ground existed—a way to make everyone happy—I couldn't see it. My choice was clear: either follow the rules and miss out on spending these last two weeks with Franck (something my soul told me was vital) or break the rules and spend the rest of my life wondering.

Franck took the blazer from my hands. "You don't have to put this on until I drop you off. Are you sure you don't want me to come in with you?"

I shook my head. "That would just complicate things. I need to do this alone."

Franck bit his lip. "I'll feel like I'm letting you go into a cage of hungry lions."

"It won't be that bad," I assured him, trying to convince myself that maybe I could still concoct a plan that would make everyone happy. "They are probably just worried about me. It'll be good to get everything out in the open."

The restaurant for my final Ursus meeting was on the far side of Beaune. Franck and I didn't say much during the drive. He just held my hand as much as the changing of the gears allowed. As for me, I just tried to absorb as much of his love and support as I could hold. Instinct told me I would need it.

I didn't know what I would say or do if they were to forbid me from returning to Franck's house that night. I wasn't even sure they could stop me—I was eighteen. The not knowing drove me crazy, almost as much as the idea that, for the first time in my life, I was perceived as a bad girl.

When Franck dropped me off, I could already see the Ursus members and their wives milling around the entrance to the restaurant. I took a deep breath. Franck leaned over and gave me a kiss, a quick one on the cheek in deference to our audience. He squeezed my hand.

"I'll go home right now and wait by the phone. As soon as you need me to come pick you up, I'll get here as fast as I can possibly drive."

I squeezed back, not trusting my own voice, and then got out of the car.

I stood for a few seconds on the circular driveway, pulling on my navy blue Ursus blazer over my shirt. It was a warm June evening and the jacket felt oppressive, just like the role I was going to have to play. I took a deep breath, plastered a smile on my face, and walked toward the crowd. Clearly most of them had not heard what had happened, or, if they had, didn't care. I spotted the Forestiers in a corner and went over to them.

"I'm so sorry," I said. "Monsieur Lacanche told me how angry the Ursus members are that I moved out of your house and moved to Villers-la-Faye.

"What are you talking about?" Madame Forestier asked me in her usual efficient way. "We gave you permission to do it. My husband told me he even suggested it!"

"Don't you remember what I said to you?" said Monsieur Forestier. "You're eighteen, for God's sakes. You need to live your life."

"But Monsieur Lacanche said—"

"Monsieur Lacanche *est un vieux*—"

Madame Forestier halted her husband's words with a strategic elbow to the ribs.

Hope sparked in me. Maybe this evening wasn't going to be as terrible as I had imagined. "I really thought you were angry with me," I said. "I worried I had somehow misunderstood... I felt terrible after talking to him."

"Don't feel terrible on account of us," Monsieur Forestier said.

Just then someone tapped me on the shoulder. I whipped around to look into the face of Monsieur Beaupre. He gave me the *bises*, but with none of his trademark congeniality. My memory leapt back to him miming how to use the *escargot* tongs at La Maison des Hautes-Côtes. He looked like a completely different man now without his trademark smile. Part of me longed for how simple things had been back at the beginning of the year. I didn't have to make anybody angry. I didn't have to make any difficult choices.

"Please follow me, Laura," he said, his tone grave.

I did, casting back a helpless look to the Forestiers. Monsieur Forestier gave me thumbs up and a wink that heartened me a smidgeon. Maybe the rest of them weren't angry, just worried, as Monsieur Beaupre was...

Monsieur Beaupre led me into a little room off the main dining room and shut the door behind him. Waiting for me in there were my two other host fathers.

My eyes moved from one to the other. "*Bonjour*," I said. My voice shook. I had no practice with that flinty insouciance that Stéph sometimes showed to her parents, and even to her brother. Besides, I couldn't just blow off these men. They had done a lot for me, especially Monsieur Beaupre.

Monsieur Lacanche came over and gave me a mechanical *bises,* but with no warmth. Instead, the air around him vibrated with barely constrained rage. There are *bises* and there are *bises*, I realized. The usual *bises* are all about acceptance, but there is another kind—the kind Monsieur Lacanche had just given me—that is a frigid reproach.

Monsieur Girard came and kissed me too. He didn't radiate fury, but he wouldn't meet my eyes either.

My brain frantically searched for a diplomatic way out of the situation. There had to be a way to be with Franck and to not have these men hate me for it. How could I make them understand the emotional importance of what was developing between Franck and me without sounding like a maudlin teenager?

"We are extremely angry with you, Laura," Monsieur Lacanche began. His skin had gone even paler than usual, and his eyes were narrowed and implacable. "Do you know what we were seriously contemplating two days ago?"

"No," I whispered.

"We were this close..." He took a few steps closer to me and held his fingers slightly apart just centimetres from my face. I could feel that part of him wanted to hit me. "We were *this close* to coming to Villers-la-Faye and taking you forcibly to put you on the next plane back to Canada."

"I'm sorry," I said, thanking God or the Virgin Mary or whoever was responsible for this horrendous event not coming to pass. "I didn't mean to worry you. The Forestiers knew where I was. It was actually Monsieur Forestier's idea. My parents know where I am and they approve. I thought it was—"

"Have you forgotten about the "No Dating" rule?" Monsieur Lacanche shook his finger in my face. "You have flagrantly broken that. You have let us all down. You are a disgrace. I have never met a more ungrateful—"

Monsieur Beaupre stood up and put a hand on Monsieur Lacanche's arm. "I think it is almost time for the meeting to begin. Laura still has to do her speech."

Tears of shock pricked at my eyes, and I had to clench my hands together to keep them from shaking. Still, I was not going to give Monsieur Lacanche the satisfaction of seeing me try to back out of the speech, even though I had no idea how to go back out there in front of one hundred Ursus members and act as if I wasn't devastated. I sensed that deep down he wanted to see me break.

"You must still do the speech." Monsieur Beaupre touched my arm.

"Of course I am going to do the speech. Is the slide projector set up?" I asked, amazed that my voice sounded relatively solid.

"Yes," said Monsieur Girard said. He had said nothing, but his gentle soul was clearly distressed by the whole scene.

"We will continue this discussion after the meeting," said Monsieur Lacanche. He stalked out of the room.

I just nodded, then went to the head table and talked mechanically to the people around me. At first, I felt as though I had betrayed all of them, but it became clear that most were not aware of my recent fall from grace.

The multi-course meal was as delicious as usual and accompanied by perfectly matched wines, but to me it all tasted like dust. I still had to get through my speech, and then the recriminations afterward. Would they still try to rip me away from Franck? If so, what would I do?

I found myself wondering, not for the first time, if they would have reacted differently if I had started dating one of the Ursus members' sons instead of Franck. Franck's family and friends in Villers-la-Faye were so far removed from the social world of the Beaune Ursus Club that they might as well have lived on a different planet. Franck was neither a known nor an approved entity, and I was sure this made my situation more unpalatable for my host families. As far as my own parents were concerned, they believed and trusted me when I told them that

Franck was great. They couldn't know about the complex social dynamics that played a big part of life in this little corner of Burgundy.

Finally, Monsieur Lacanche got up and, adopting a jovial attitude that was in complete contrast to that which he had shown in the anteroom, he introduced me to the crowd and explained that I was going to share a slideshow about my year in France.

I stood up. My mouth was dry. Monsieur Lacanche handed me the slide clicker with a public smile, followed by a private glare. The lights were dimmed.

I began explaining the first few slides—my arrival in Nuits-Saint-Georges to live with the Beaupres and my thanks to the men who had taught me to wine taste during that first Ursus meeting (an essential skill, I said, that got me through the year). Appreciative laughter rippled through the crowd.

There was the trip to Paris with the Beaupres, skiing in the Alps with the Lacanches... Guilt made it hard to speak. They had done so much for me. I owed them all, but did I owe them so much that it was worth throwing away what was possibly the greatest love of my life?

I couldn't know where Franck and I would end up. Neither of us had a crystal ball. We were full of determination, but we were up against some formidable foes—Franck's family, immigration laws, lack of money, and my parents, to name a few. Still, if I didn't live this love affair out until the very last second, I would always wonder: How would it have ended, if I had been bolder?

I had been the model Ursus student for the majority of the year. Hadn't I given enough of myself? As I went through the slides, I tried to locate that line between doing what my soul needed and being what other people wanted me to be.

I got to the final slides and finished off with a sincere word of thanks. I felt an enormous wash of gratitude for the Ursus Club and all the new marvels they had introduced to me that year. They had completely changed my life. They had completely changed me.

The round of applause I received at the end was warm. I had done it. My eyes met Monsieur Lacanche's steely gaze. It wasn't over. At least, not as far as he was concerned.

The people slowly drained out of the room, most of them coming over to me for a last *bises* and a good-bye. We promised to stay in touch, and I promised to be back in Burgundy to visit them. I had no idea when or how that was actually going to happen, but it was easier that way. I saw Madame Beaupre on the opposite side of the room. I tried to make my way over to her, but by the time I was halfway there, she had disappeared. She had left without saying good-bye. That hurt more than any of Monsieur Lacanche's words. I didn't just *like* Madame Beaupre, I *loved* her. The fact that she left meant that as far as she was concerned, my choice to stay with Franck was a betrayal.

Finally, the Forestiers came over to say good-bye.

Monsieur Forestier leaned down and whispered in my ear, "It's your life. Live it. Don't let them bully you into thinking that it is theirs. You have given us enough."

He gave my shoulder a squeeze. Tears filled my eyes. I wanted him to stay, but that wasn't Monsieur Forestier's style. He was an odd, non-conforming member of the Ursus Club, who seemed to despise most of his fellow members. He was in a rush to leave, as usual. Besides, I got the feeling that he was the type of person who left others to fight their own battles, for better or for worse. Still, a part of me couldn't help but feel that he was leaving me to the lions.

Lastly, it was just me and my three remaining host fathers left in the room.

I took a deep breath. "As I said before," I said, "I apologize for my actions and I have apologized to the Forestiers. However, I will be leaving in two weeks, and I plan to spend them in Villers-la-Faye."

"But you are our responsibility!" Monsieur Beaupre protested. I knew he was thinking of how horrified he would be if Sophie moved in with some American man she had just met. I searched again for the words to reassure him. Franck wasn't like other men. What we had together was truly unique. Yet, before I said them out loud, I realized how cliché they would sound to Monsieur Beaupre's ears. Unconvincing. Immature. Like the words of an eighteen-year-old girl caught up in her first love affair.

"I know that. I know how worrisome this must be for you, and I'm sorry for any trouble my move caused. However, my parents know where I am, and they approve."

Monsieur Lacanche's mouth twisted. He didn't like being thwarted. "I cannot believe the gall of you!" he exclaimed. "Did you even bother to look around the room tonight? Did you see all the people who have worked so hard to host you over this past year? How does it feel to throw it all back in their faces?"

His words felt like a physical blow. I knew from how he acted with his own family that Monsieur Lacanche was not used to having his authority subverted or questioned, but it was still a shock to see this turned on me.

"Most of them don't even know," I said, at last. "Even if they did, I'm not sure that they would agree. I was exactly what you wanted me to be for the majority of this year. I am grateful, but I'm eighteen now. I have grown up."

"Eighteen! True love! Pah!" Monsieur Lacanche scoffed. "You are a huge disappointment, Laura. What if word of this gets out? I highly doubt other parents will allow their children to be part of an exchange program that would let such a thing happen under their noses. The rules are there for a reason, Laura, and you have flagrantly ignored them."

Monsieur Girard studied a spot on the carpet, but Monsieur Beaupre finally moved closer to me, as if to protect me from Monsieur Lacanche, and indicated him to stop.

Monsieur Beaupre turned to me. "Can't you just go back to being our Laura? That's all we want...just for you to go back to the Laura that you were at the beginning of the year when you stayed with us."

I looked into his warm brown eyes. There was as much kindness and generosity there as there ever was. I thought of our bike ride through the vineyards and sneaking grapes from the

Romanée-Conti enclosure, then our wine tasting with the purple-stained Henri. He wasn't furious with me, as Monsieur Lacanche was. He was confused by my behavior and distressed at my obstinacy. I longed to give him what he wanted—to make him and Madame Beaupre happy. Part of me yearned to go back to being "their" Laura. But...after searching for it for the past two hours, there it was, as clear as daylight—that line I could no longer cross. Making them happy would mean sacrificing my precious time with Franck.

"I can't," I said.

"Why?" He squeezed my shoulder and peered into my eyes, as if searching for my answer there.

"That Laura doesn't exist anymore," I said softly. "She's gone. I'm sorry."

His hand dropped away. "Then I suppose there is no more to say."

The weight of disappointing him settled like lead in my stomach.

Monsieur Lacanche opened his mouth. From his bristling energy it was clear he, for one, had *much* more to say, but Monsieur Beaupre gestured at him that it was over.

"Then I suppose this is *bon voyage*," Monsieur Beaupre said to me.

I nodded dumbly.

"*Au revoir, Laura.*" He kissed me quickly on each cheek, his lips compressed tight. Monsieur Lacanche stalked out of the room, not deigning to give me *les bises* or make any kind of peace with me.

Monsieur Girard shuffled over and gave me a kiss and an apologetic shrug. "*Bon retour au Canada, Laura,*" he said. "I'm sorry it had to end this way. Write us to let us know you got home safely."

He shut the door behind him, and I waited until I could no longer hear their voices. I crumpled onto one of the many vacant chairs and traced a long thin wine stain on the white tablecloth with my finger. When I lifted up my hand, it was shaking.

I don't know exactly how long I sat there. Five minutes,

perhaps? Fifteen? This newness of disappointing people was terrifying. Part of me wanted to run after the men and repair the damage, but if I did that, I would have to give up my last two weeks with Franck. I had experienced many once-in-a-lifetime things during my year, and I knew without a doubt that these last moments with Franck counted among them.

Franck. I was starving for him, for the home of his arms. I rushed out into the now-deserted hotel lobby and asked to use the phone. The woman behind the desk gave me a sour look. Still, she did end up surrendering it in the end. I dialed Franck's number with shaking fingers.

"*Allô*?" he picked up before the first ring had finished. "Laura?"

"*C'est moi*," I said, my voice already shaking. "Can you come now?"

"Of course. How did it go?"

I burst into tears. The woman behind the desk stared at me.

"Hang up," Franck said. "Go outside. I'm leaving now and I'll drive fast."

All I could do was nod, which was not particularly useful in a phone conversation. I placed the phone back down on the base, mumbled an incoherent "*merci*," and ran outside. It was already past ten o'clock, and dusk was slowly settling on the vineyards that encircled the hotel parking lot.

I walked as far as the stone pillars that marked the entrance to the hotel drive and crumpled to the side of one, my back against the stone wall. The stones were still radiating heat from the summer day. Their warmth melted something inside of me. Fat tears ran down my cheeks in waves. My chest heaved. I cried for the girl that I used to be and that I would never be again. I cried for the simplicity of my life before, where in pleasing others I had somehow, at least most of the time, pleased myself too.

Soon, Franck's car screeched to a stop in front of me. How he'd spotted me, I didn't know, for the sky had already turned indigo and I was curled over against the stone wall. He leapt out of the car, leaving the engine still running.

He grasped me under the arms and lifted me up. "What did they do to you?" he demanded.

I shook my head and tried to curb my tears. "No. It wasn't like that...they were angry and it was awful. I had to hurt them...there was nothing I could do."

Franck gently helped me into the passenger seat of the car. He got in and turned to me. "If you have to go back to them, I understand. I don't want you to be sad."

"I don't want to go back to them. I won't." I collapsed against his chest. Words were still hard to get out.

"Thank God." He breathed in my hair. "But...I'm sorry you had to make that choice." He smelled of his familiar scent of warm apples. Franck lifted my chin so that he could better search my eyes. "Regrets?"

"*Moi, je ne regrette rien.*" I quoted Edith Piaf.

I could feel Franck smile. "Still, it doesn't make it easy."

A post-sob shudder ran through me. "No."

"Maybe life isn't meant to be easy."

"Is that what you learned after spending months in your room gorging on philosophy?" My voice was still watery with the tears I had shed.

"Pretty much."

I laughed softly, and a bit sadly, as Franck kissed me in the twilight, the string chorus of crickets playing all around us.

chapter thirty-eight

After dinner on my second to last night in Villers-la-Faye, just before finishing off one of Mémé's bowls of chocolate mousse for dessert, Franck asked if I wanted to go for a walk in the vineyards.

The evening air was sultry and heavy with that Burgundian oven-baked heat that doesn't exist on the West Coast of Canada. The weight of the air reflected my mood. Since the Ursus meeting, everything seemed infused with more apprehension. My life had become so complex—my time in France rapidly running out, the moments with Franck, uncertainty about the future, my longing for things to happen a certain way…

"I think there's going to be thunder," Michèle warned.

"We won't go far," Franck said, already reaching for my hand.

When Michèle left to take some dishes into the kitchen, I nudged Franck, "Your mom doesn't need to worry. Thunderstorms are no big deal. At home, we get out the deck chairs to watch them."

Franck arched a brow. "Not the thunderstorms around here. They can be violent and extremely dangerous."

"I want to come! I want to come! *Moi aussi*!" shouted Emmanuel-Marie.

"But *petit frère*, I want to go on a walk with my *amoureuse*." Franck ruffled his hair.

"Laura is my *amoureuse* too!" Emmanuel-Marie said. "And

I want to walk with her!"

Franck was no match for Emmanuel-Marie's insistence or charm. "All right. You can come with us. But can you run back fast with us if it starts to rain?"

Emmanuel-Marie nodded. "*Oui.* I run very fast."

"Get your shoes on then."

Michèle helped Emmanuel-Marie lace up his sandals, and we all walked out of the courtyard, Franck and I each holding one of his small hands. The vineyards were just down a short lane, past Félix's house and beside a ramshackle little cottage that Franck told me had been used by generations of winemakers. It had a massive, gnarled grape vine growing up the corner of the house and across the side wall.

"There used to be chickens running around inside that place," Franck said. "The people who lived there when I was growing up were real country people of the old sort. Rustic, to say the least."

I paused for a moment and gave the cottage a closer look, wondering if Franck meant the cottage or its inhabitants. Probably both. It was unkempt but boasted undeniable charm. "It could be adorable."

"We'll need a *pied-à-terre* in Burgundy and a cabin in the woods in Canada," Franck said. We both talked like this, planning our future together as if it were a reality rather than still a dream.

"I hate to disappoint you, but I didn't grow up in a cabin in the woods. Most Canadians don't, you know."

"An igloo?" Franck knelt down to re-tie Emmanuel-Marie's shoe lace that had come loose.

"That's it. I grew up in an igloo. Anyway, you'll see for yourself soon. You'd better pack your toque and your mukluks."

Franck stood up again, and we continued walking on either side of his little brother. "I think I may need to buy a team of huskies too," he said. "You know, for my dogsled."

"Of course. That's just sensible, dogsleds being our only mode of transportation in Canada."

Franck used his free hand to blow me a kiss over his brother's blond head.

We were on the vineyard paths now, the ochre dust billowing behind our footsteps. I couldn't remember the last time it had rained. The air felt as though it was pressing down on us. A trickle of sweat ran down my spine.

"Do you think you can figure out a way?" I said. It was Franck who needed to find a way to come and join me in Canada. I would do everything I could from my end, but I knew the effort required would be unequally distributed between us. I had briefly toyed with the idea of coming to university in France, but I knew my French, while fluent, was hardly good enough to be accepted at university. Besides, I needed a French *baccalauréat* as well as a high school diploma to qualify.

"I'm tenacious when motivated," Franck said. "I've never been this motivated before in my life."

Emmanuel-Marie let go of our hands and began to run along the path ahead of us.

It would take a lot of luck and a massive amount of effort, not to mention patience and fidelity, but I had never wanted anything more in my life. Part of me felt scared to want it so very much. I still felt guilty about the Beaupres and believed somehow that if I let the Universe know how badly I wanted Franck and me to be together, our plans would be thwarted as karmic punishment. Still, although there were no guarantees it would work, or that it *could* work, at least we agreed that we would try—that in itself was something of a miracle. I knew it was unusual for people to meet their soul mate at eighteen and stay together, but something about Franck and me felt...unique, and right.

"*Moi aussi*," I said. Franck gathered me against him, and we kissed until Emmanuel-Marie hollered at us to hurry up.

Franck put his arm around me and drew me closer, and we started walking again. Time seemed suspended—the soft music of crickets, the strange orangey-red light, the bright green of the vineyards, and the heavy air and dusty path all locking it into place.

"Our children," Franck said. "They'll be half French and half Canadian. Can you imagine what an amazing childhood that would be? To move back and forth between countries?"

We had wandered farther than we'd intended, weaving fantasies of our future together. A crack of lightning over the neighboring village of Chaux snapped me out of my reverie.

I looked behind us. Villers-la-Faye was encapsulated in a golden haze, nestled in the valley between Mont Saint-Victor and Les Chaumes like some sort of medieval village plucked out of an ancient fairy tale. It was just as it was when I first saw it on our way up to la Maison des Hautes Côtes, except now it was cloaked in the most unearthly light. A rumble of thunder reverberated in my backbone. Villers also looked far away from this vantage point.

"*Merde*. We went too far." Franck was looking up at the sky. "That storm is coming fast." He ran forward and grabbed Emmanuel-Marie's hand—the one he wasn't using to hold on tightly to the bouquet of cornflowers and poppies he'd been collecting from the edges of the vineyards. "Come on, Manu. We need to head home."

"*Mais non*!" his brother protested. "I haven't finished my bouquet for Laura yet."

The hairs on the back of my neck prickled. Lightning flashed behind us. There was only a few seconds respite, then a low, baritone rumble made the ground shake beneath our feet. Emmanuel-Marie looked up at Franck with eyes so wide I could see a full circle of white.

"We'll get home quickly, don't worry," Franck said to him. He scooped up his little brother and threw him up on his shoulders. "Hang on."

A fat raindrop plopped on my head, and then another, and another. Within seconds the rain was coming down so hard that the path beneath our feet had turned into a river of mud.

We ran. My sandals slurped and stuck to the mud underfoot. We slipped and slid as the curtain of rain brought our visibility down to almost nothing. The lightning was behind us, but not far enough behind, given the sizzle of the flashes and the thunder that filled every particle of air around us.

We were almost to the end of the vineyard path when a blinding white flash struck an apple tree just in front of us. Franck yanked me against him and Emmanuel-Marie. A scorched, black branch crashed down across the path in front of us.

I was sure my heart was going to leap out of my chest. I had never seen, let alone been in the middle of a storm like this. If this was a *coup de foudre*, I had never realized that—sublime and amazing though it was—it was also perilous.

"Come on!" Franck yelled through the rain, and, clinging together, we leapt across the branch and ducked into the lane that led past the old winemaker's cottage. A few seconds later, Franck pushed open the gate to his house and almost fell into the courtyard. Franck's father was standing on the other side of the gate with his car keys in his hand, his face white.

"Thank God!" he said. "I was just about to come and find you. We were terrified."

André drew us all inside, and Franck set Emmanuel-Marie down in a puddle on the kitchen floor. "*Ça va, Manu?*" he asked, leaning down to feel Emmanuel-Marie's wet head and face and making sure that there were no injuries.

"I was scared," Emmanuel-Marie exclaimed. I noticed now that Franck's hands were shaking.

"It was my fault." Franck straightened up again.

Just then a flash of lightning struck the courtyard just outside the kitchen window. We all jumped back. The entire house shook. I fought the urge to drop to the ground, roll under a table, and brace my neck, as I had learned in earthquake drills in elementary school.

"Thank heavens you made it back in time," Michèle said. She had already gotten three large, fluffy towels from the linen cabinet and was wrapping them around us. My eyes met with Franck's. No need to mention the tree right away. We were all jittery from adrenaline—better to wait a bit.

Michèle stripped Emmanuel-Marie's clothes off. "You two should do the same," she said, "or you're going to catch your death."

"We can't have a shower," Franck explained to me. "The electricity can run through the water and electrocute us."

"OK," I said. My teeth were beginning to chatter.

"Come on." Franck took my dripping arm and led me up through the kitchen door to the staircase.

We got up to his bedroom, and Franck drew the curtain over the small door. I stood under the skylight where the rain was pounding down in biblical proportions. My soaking clothes created a puddle on the pine floorboards.

Franck pushed my towel away and began to unbutton my soaked cotton shirt. It stuck to my skin.

"So that's a *coup de foudre*?" I asked.

Franck's fingers paused. "Yes. It can be scary, can't it?"

"Terrifying." I took an edge of Franck's towel and dried the drips trickling down his neck from his hair. "Amazing too."

"Yes." Franck divested me of my shirt.

"What are you doing?"

"I need to check if you are injured," Franck said. "It would be negligent not too."

I shivered.

"Are you cold?" Franck asked.

"No." I pulled off his soaked T-shirt. "That wasn't from the cold."

The sky above us flashed white with lightning, and the whole room glowed, then shook.

"We're leaving tomorrow for Paris," Franck said. "Then you for Canada, then me trying to figure out every possible way to get to you. In the meantime, though, we have this afternoon."

"We do." How was it that when I had been longing to find my soul mate, I'd never considered how hard it would be to find him, fall in love, and then have to leave?

Another *coup de foudre* crashed over us, and we fell onto Franck's bed.

chapter thirty-nine

André drove us to the train station. His little car was packed to the gunnels with my suitcases and bags. I had given away everything I could—clothing, books, hair brushes—to Stéphanie, Sandrine, and Michèle. And in their place, I'd filled my bags with gifts for family and friends and memorabilia of my year in France, especially things that reminded me of the past few months with Franck—a little ochre stone from the vineyards of Villers-la-Faye, the gargoyle that matched the one I had bought him in Dijon, a wrapper from a chocolate that I had eaten that first day we had gone for a café in Savigny. They were all talismans to help me hang on to the miracle of the past year.

Franck and I were silent as André's car wound out of Villers-la-Faye through the vineyards. I peered out the rear window, looking at the village that had changed my life. It was nestled, seemingly unchanging, in that perfect little crook between hills. I wished, not for the first time, that I could know the future.

Franck squeezed my hand, and we exchanged charged looks. I could tell by the tense line of his eyebrows that he was worried too. We both wanted a future together, but nobody was handing out guarantees.

Please God, let me come back to this place. I sent up a little prayer, even though I had never been religious.

We wound down the hill to Nuits-Saint-Georges, past the church and my old bedroom beside the bell tower at the Lacanches' house. They undoubtedly thought I was the most ungrateful chit of a girl. This pained me, but I knew that I would make the same choice again. That must be one of those painful parts of growing up—realizing that sometimes what was right for me and what others believed was right for me could not be reconciled.

André pulled up to the train station, and between Franck and him, they barely let me lift a single bag. I was going to miss this gallantry at home. Once he had assured himself I was settled with Franck on the right train platform, André bid me a solemn *au revoir*. I thanked him for his hospitality and his help and gave him a warm kiss. He said he hoped to see me again soon, but as this probably required the departure of his eldest son as well, I was not surprised to see a conflicted look in his ice-blue eyes.

Finally, it was just the two of us, Franck and me, on the platform. I had to say good-bye to Burgundy, but thanked God I didn't have to say good-bye to him…yet.

Franck, with some difficulty, leaned over the pile of bags and lifted my chin up with his thumb. "How are you doing? Overwhelmed?"

"I can't believe I'm going back to Canada. It seems like another life. This is my real life now. Here. With you."

"We'll make a new life together," Franck said. "Just for the two of us. Montreal will be perfect, a place between your old life and my old life."

"It's freezing in the winter," I quipped to keep away the tears that were lingering constantly at the edge of my eyelashes.

Franck's eyes gleamed. "I hope so. We can keep each other warm."

The metal train tracks began to reverberate. I looked up and saw the TGV coming in the distance. There it was…my future…please God, *our* future. I just needed to get on.

In Paris, we stayed at the apartment of another one of Franck's ubiquitous second cousins who seemed to populate Burgundy and the rest of France. The cousin in question had gone to Marseille on a training course, so we had his apartment to ourselves. It was only three streets away from the gare de Lyon, where our train had pulled in.

When Franck opened the door, I marveled at the apartment's postage stamp size. The kitchen was basically a cupboard, and the shower was a shower nozzle that was hung over a bathroom that, instead of a toilet, housed a rather a Turkish-style affair with a hole in the ground. I had a difficult time imagining this second cousin—whom I'd met briefly at Mémé's party, and who had dazzled me with his impeccable elegance and Parisian *je ne sais quoi*—living in this place. The bed was a single mattress of dubious age, pushed up against the main room, which also contained a tiny table and chairs. Once my bags were piled up against the far wall, there was barely enough room for us.

"All apartments in Paris are like this," Franck explained. "You get used to the lack of space. It never bothered me, because in Paris, you only come back home to sleep anyway. There's too much to do outside."

I threw my backpack down on the bed. "What should we do first?"

"Do you want me to show you *my* Paris?" Franck said. "My favorite places?"

I wrapped my arms around his torso and felt the smooth planes of his muscles against my chest. I couldn't conceive of not being able to do this. "Yes," I said.

"Are you ready?"

"To have you show me around Paris? I think I've been waiting for that my entire life."

"Then let's go make the most of the next twenty-four hours."

It was getting near lunchtime, so Franck led me to the Latin Quarter to buy us something he called a shawarma.

He took us down into the Metro, which he, like Madame Beaupre, knew by heart. It was stifling and there was no sitting room, so Franck held on to a strap and I wrapped my arms around his waist, our bodies moving in sync with the rocking motion of the Metro car. I buried my face into the soft cotton of his T-shirt and breathed in the familiar scent of him. In twenty-four hours, I would have to fly away from this. It was unthinkable.

Franck led me up the stairs underneath a beautiful art-deco sign for the Saint-Michel Metro station. I snapped a few photos, and then he plunged us into noisy narrow streets with swarthy men standing on the doorways of Greek restaurants whose windows were full of displays of distinctly unappetizing plastic food. They exhorted us in Greek-accented French to come in.

"Will we be eating in one of these places?" I asked Franck.

"Those are just for the tourists. Most of the shawarma shops are for tourists too, but there are a few which are still the real deal."

We turned and followed streets that got narrower and twistier. How could he possibly remember where he was going?

Finally, we ducked into a shop that was well away from the main thoroughfares and filled with hearty customers eating large bundles of bread and meat wrapped in wax paper. They were talking in a language that definitely wasn't French or English. There wasn't a tourist in sight.

They turned to us and stared, but Franck just smiled and placed our order with such aplomb and obvious knowledge of the place and its offerings that the men went back to their conversations. I watched the man behind the counter shave off paper-thin slices off the huge rotating slab of meat and put it into a pita along with a dizzying array of sauces and cut up vegetables that Franck chose for us.

"Do you think you can handle the spicy sauce?" Franck asked. "They don't even think of offering it to tourists."

That sounded ominous, but I didn't think of myself as a tourist, so... "*Bien sûr.*"

The man behind the counter worked fast and in no time was handing each of us our wax paper bundle.

I took a bite. Warm and spicy and flavorful and completely,

wonderfully foreign. "This is delicious."

Franck took my hand and led me out of the shop and through more crooked little passageways until we pulled up in front of a blue-and-white-painted shop with what looked like Greek pastries in the window. I cocked a brow.

"Our dessert," he explained. "Should I just get us an assortment?"

None of the pastries looked familiar to me, so I nodded, my mouth full of delectable shawarma.

The large woman behind the counter greeted Franck like an old friend and lovingly packed up a neat little box of pastries. She tied a blue ribbon around it, fashioned it into a makeshift handle, and passed it to him.

Franck led me through the maze of streets and across place Saint-Michel into a little garden just off the Seine. He closed the gate behind us, and I was suddenly surrounded by a sense of peace and, apart from the background noise of car engines and the occasional honk, an almost rural quiet. *Here, amazingly, right in the center of Paris.* He found a spot to eat behind a rock under a tree and spread out his jacket for us to sit on. I sat half reclined on his lap, trying not to drip spicy shawarma sauce on his jeans.

"This is perfect," I murmured. "Did you come here often?"

Franck nodded. "The Sorbonne is just up the street. I'll take you there after."

We chewed contentedly in silence for a while.

"I don't want to leave tomorrow," I said, blinking back tears yet again. I wanted to hold on to this moment, draw it out for eternity.

Franck smoothed the hair off my forehead. "I'll move Heaven and Earth so that we can be together again soon. Do you trust me on that?"

I nodded. Of course I did. It was just that...he felt like my home. I couldn't imagine being away from him for even three hours, let alone months...or longer.

"Besides..."—Franck's finger dropped from my forehead and began to trace the whorl of my ear—"it's not tomorrow yet.

It's still today."

"I am starting to realize I live in the future most of the time," I said ruefully, wiping a drip of sauce from my chin. That was another reason why we worked so well together. Franck possessed an innate capacity to live in the present, and he managed to drag me there too. I kissed him—a spicy kiss thanks to the shawarma.

After we finished off every last crumb, Franck untied the blue-and-white box and had me pick my first choice of pastry. Honey oozed from all of them. I picked one that looked particularly tempting and took a bite. It was the perfect chaser to the savory mix of tastes in the shawarma.

"This is delicious," I said. "Greek?"

"North African, actually," Franck said. "Tunisian and Moroccan."

I had enjoyed countless memorable meals during my year in France, but this lunch with my *amoureux* in Paris was the most memorable of them all.

After we finished eating, we lazed in the dappled shade until the pull of the city outside the gates became irresistible.

"I know!" Franck said, as he gathered our wrappers into the now-empty pastry box. "I can't believe I didn't think of it before."

"What?"

"There is a place right near here where we must go," he said. "It's the perfect place for you."

My curiosity was piqued, and I followed as Franck led me across la place Saint-Michel, dodging oncoming traffic with the aplomb of a Parisian, and then walked over a few more streets. He pulled up in front of the most delicious-looking bookstore I had ever seen. Shakespeare and Company was written in old black letters on a yellow background.

"I know how much you love books," Franck said. "Hemingway used to hang out here. I wonder if it's not in fact your spiritual home."

We wandered in and lost track of time as we explored the winding stacks of books and all the incredible nooks and crannies where writers still gathered, wrote, and sometimes even slept. I found a secondhand copy of *A Moveable Feast*. It was one of my favorite books by Hemingway, and I had read it before coming to France.

I bought the book, and they added the most beautiful bookstore stamp on the front cover.

"That," I said as we strolled out arm in arm, "was perfection. I want to move into that place for a while."

"Maybe we'll figure out a way to come back to Paris and live here for a period of time," Franck said. This idea sparked a thousand other seductive images in my mind.

"*Café*?" Franck asked and I nodded.

We walked back through the streets of Saint-Michel and then up to the Sorbonne. It was a magnificent building with a majestic dome and a pillared stone entrance fit for royalty. Beside it was an excavation site where a team was industriously digging up Roman ruins.

"*This* is where you went to school?" I said, marvelling at the beauty of the building and the square in front of it.

"Yes."

"I'm so sorry I didn't believe you went to the Sorbonne that day in Savigny after we first met."

Franck tugged my ponytail. "You didn't, did you? I had forgotten about that. *Femme de peu de foi*." Woman of little faith.

"I was so suspicious. It's just that every day at school, the other students' favorite game was tricking me." I thought of Thibaut. I still couldn't believe that I'd tried to convince myself that he might be the one for me. The fact that things with him were always unsettled and difficult should have been a clue.

"I loved going to school here." Franck looked up, admiring the Sorbonne's exquisite lines against the cerulean July sky.

I sighed. "That would be so amazing." I'd always had a soft spot for grand old buildings that celebrated academia. *The Sorbonne. To actually take a class in one of its amphitheaters...*

Franck grabbed my hand and led me through the front door.

"Are we...?" I decided it was better not to ask if we were

allowed inside or not. Even if we weren't, I was willing to try.

We passed three guards who were armed with black assault rifles. Luckily, Franck assumed a nonchalant expression and didn't hesitate, as he knew where we were going. In our shirts and summer shorts, we easily passed for students.

He cracked open a door and drew me into the most beautiful amphitheater I had ever seen. Rounded domes were everywhere on the ceiling; it looked more like a cathedral than a schoolroom. Franck indicated a worn wooden bench beside us. The floor was lined with them—row after row.

"Sit down," he said. "Look up." Huge swaths of the walls and ceilings were covered with exquisite frescoes. "Even though the teacher wasn't very good, I would never miss a lecture here. I spent most of the time staring up at the ceiling."

We had been sitting like that for about ten minutes when the door opened and one of the armed guards walked in. "What are you doing in here?" he shouted. "Get out!"

We scurried out of the building and into the square, laughing.

"That was totally worth it," I gasped.

"Oh yes," Franck agreed.

"What about that coffee you promised?"

Franck led me to one of the cafés on the square.

We ordered and spent several minutes soaking up the intellectual vibe. Could I dare dream that Paris, too, was part of my future...*our* future?

"We have to decide what we're going to do with the rest of our afternoon and evening until the balls begin." Franck unwrapped his sugar cubes and stirred one into his espresso.

I had forgotten about the firemen's balls. Franck had told me late in bed one night how every fire station in Paris hosted a ball for Parisians to celebrate Bastille Day on the night of July 13. We could go from one neighborhood of Paris to another and dance.

"We'll be going late tonight."

"Very late?" I asked.

"Maybe all night." Franck grinned.

"Will we sleep?" I asked, although truth be told, I wasn't really thinking about sleep.

"There will be time tomorrow," Franck said. "Trust me."

The rest of the afternoon was filled with wonders: mint tea in the tiled courtyard of the Grande Mosque, ice cream from the Berthillon ice cream shop on the Île Saint-Louis in the middle of the Seine, then a walk along its banks and another café.

Because it was July with its long days, Franck even had time to show me Notre-Dame, and lastly, the pont des Arts, before dusk fell. We stood on the wooden bridge looking out over the railing toward the Eiffel Tower and watched the blue sky turn indigo. Franck stood behind me, with his arms enveloping me with his chin resting on my head.

"I want to live here with you," I said.

"On the pont des Arts? I think the *gendarmes* might have something to say about that."

"Well, if not on the pont des Arts, then somewhere else in Paris."

"There is so much more I have to show you," Franck said. "We could go for *cafés sur le zinc* in the morning, take in a little bit of the Louvre in the afternoon, go to a *brasserie* for a glass of wine in the evening...you could study at the Sorbonne..."

"What would you do?"

He shrugged. "How can I know what the Universe is going to bring me? I knew I wanted to travel after my military service, but I didn't know that the Universe was going to bring you to me. I never could have imagined this. I love that. The not knowing."

"Do you really?" The not knowing drove me crazy. The uncertainty of life was something I'd always struggled with. I could never even fully enjoy a book—no matter what type of book—unless I read the ending first. Then I could relax into it and enjoy the story. Unfortunately for me, life wasn't like that.

Yet, I thought of Franck as a child, sitting up on the wall at his grandmother's house, eating baguettes that Mémé had lovingly slathered with butter and jam for him—while I was building driftwood forts on the beach. The Universe had patiently waited for us that night in Nuits-Saint-Georges—for me and my red-ribboned tap shoes and Franck with his sore back after moving stones all day. Wasn't *that* proof the Universe knew what it was doing? Maybe I just needed to let go and trust it with my future, and Franck's future, and—dare I believe it—*our* future.

Franck kissed the crown of my head. "I think we're lucky that we have to fight for each other."

"Really?"

"Yes. That way we will never take what we have for granted."

"It *is* sort of a miracle," I said, leaning back into him.

"Not 'sort of.'" He kissed the back of my neck, and just then the lights of the Eiffel Tower to the west lit up, bathing us in their glow.

chapter forty

A few hours later, Franck and I were nestled in a *brasserie* in the 6th arrondissement. We'd just finished a dinner of a goat cheese salad, steak frites, and *fromage blanc*. This had all been washed down with a strong house red, which made me teeter between joy and sadness every few seconds.

He reached over and checked my watch. "The balls will be starting."

We paid up and stepped out into the Paris evening. Every cell in my body rejoiced at how I was actually living the moment—diminutive French cars whipping by and honking at each other, the warmth of Franck's arm around my shoulder, the muggy air of Paris in the early summer, the whistle of firecrackers being set off by kids in adjacent streets, the jingle of a few francs in my pocket...

Better yet, I understood everything that was happening around me—every expletive yelled by the pedestrian who had just been cut off by a Mobylette roaring around the corner, the chatter of lovers chatting at a café table we passed, the waiter taking an order... It was an entirely new life I was living, and it hadn't, in the grand scheme of things, taken that long to create.

Franck led us along several dimly lit back streets.

"How do you always know where you're going?" I asked. "You never even look at a map."

"I walked a lot when I lived here," he said. "Kilometers and kilometers every day. There was always a new adventure waiting."

We could hear the noise of the fire hall for several blocks before we arrived. The street echoed with the sounds of laughter and loud accordion music. People were spilling out of the courtyard of a large stone building. Strung across the courtyard in a haphazard fashion were strings of multi-colored lights. A wine stand was set up at the rear of the courtyard. Its menu was simple: a glass of red or white for the price of ten francs.

People were already dancing, young and old, chic and bohemian. Franck ordered us each a glass of wine, which was served in plastic goblets. We sipped as we watched the festivities erupting around us. The night was warm, and tiny stars began to light up the sky like sparks. I put my empty glass back on the table, and Franck followed suit. He swept me into the middle of the dancers, and we lost ourselves in the accordion music. He spun me around and around until the revelers surrounding us became a blur, and I felt like a small part of a much greater whole. Nobody in the crowd hung back on the sidelines. If they had no one to dance with, they danced anyway and were soon swept up into the frenzy of celebration.

We humans need this, I thought. We need to let go of the routine of our everyday lives and just celebrate the mere fact of being alive. The French are awfully gifted at that.

Soon Franck took my hand and led me out of the mass of writhing dancers. We walked for about ten minutes, laughing and enjoying the sight of the fellow revelers out in the streets before we ducked into the next fire station for another glass of wine, then into the whirlpool of another celebration.

The night's festivities stretched out from fire station to fire station, from neighborhood to neighborhood.

At about five o'clock in the morning, the sky began to pale to welcome a new day. The day I'd dreaded since I'd met Franck. The day I had to leave him.

"I know a *brasserie* not too far from here that is open all night," Franck said. "Should we go and rest our feet?" Mine were throbbing from all the dancing, so I agreed.

In the *brasserie*, we huddled together on the leather seat. I inspected my blisters, which were impressive, we both agreed, and we snuggled as we waited for our order of two large *cafés au lait* with croissants and jam.

The chime of a church bell rang six times.

"That was the bell at Notre-Dame," Franck said.

Normally I would have loved that fact, but it only drove home that my time left with Franck was no longer measured in days, but in hours and minutes.

"You've gone quiet," Franck observed.

I tore up my sugar wrapper into tiny, then tinier pieces. "I hope you can get to Canada quickly," I said, finally, the other hundred things I wanted to say creating a dam for the tears in my throat.

"We'll be together soon," Franck said, reaching over to still my hands. "I know it."

"How do you know it?"

"This is too good for it just to stop."

I didn't want to waste any of my last few hours with Franck by sleeping, but by the time we got back to his cousin's apartment, we were both dead on our feet. We took a shower and then collapsed on the mattress on the floor. Our hands roamed over each other—memorizing.

Franck found a Francis Cabrel tape among his cousin's extensive music collection that was stored in one of the cupboards in the kitchen. He played it, and we listened to the words.

Tu viendras longtemps marcher dans mes rêves
Tu viendras toujours du côté
Où le soleil se lève...

"We have to leave for the airport in about two hours," Franck said. "Let's make this count."

The longing I knew I would feel once we were apart was

already palpable. I couldn't hold back my tears.

We must have slept afterward, because I woke to the sound of the alarm.

He reached over me and pushed the button down, then rolled back and gathered me in his arms. "There is no easy way to do this," he admitted. "It is going to be *difficile*. I'm just realizing now how much." His hand smoothed my hair.

I nodded against his chest. There were no words, in any language, to say good-bye to Franck. How was I supposed to say goodbye to what I had discovered with him over these past few months? When I had yearned for my soul mate, I had somehow never considered that loving deeply could mean hurting just as acutely.

He kissed me once more. "We have to go."

We left the apartment and made our way down the steps to the Metro. Franck insisted on carrying the huge majority of my luggage—no small feat. Getting it through the turnstiles and over the barriers between the Metro and the train station kept us distracted. When we did manage to get on a train, Franck guarded the luggage and pulled me tightly against him, guarding me too.

Finally, we got to the airport and checked me in as well as my bags. I looked at my watch. We had half an hour until I had to go through the boarding gates. I thought of all the half hours I had wasted in my life with sleep and watching TV and waiting at the dentist's office. Now every single minute of this half hour was like the most precious gift.

We found a grubby café near the boarding gate, but it did serve, like most cafés in France, a decent espresso. We sipped ours slowly, holding tight to each other with our free hands.

"We have to start working on getting you to Canada right away," I said, caressing his thumb with mine.

"That's exactly what I'm planning on doing once I leave here," Franck said. "As soon as your plane takes off, I'm going to make an appointment at the Canadian embassy. Even though you won't be here, physically beside me anymore, I won't rest until I figure out a way for me to come to Montreal and for us to be together."

"It sounds almost too good to be true."

"It's too good *not* to be true."

I stared at him, frantic to imprint every detail of his face on my heart. "You're right."

Franck led me to the foot of one of the space-age tubes that would carry me up to the boarding gate. I remembered coming down on a similar one eleven months earlier, sweaty under my Ursus blazer and, after the aborted landing, disoriented, not understanding anything.

A crackly voice came over the loudspeaker. I couldn't make out much, but I did hear my flight number.

"Do we really have to say good-bye?" I said, rooted to the spot. I wanted to stay with him longer, just a few seconds longer. Leaving him felt physically impossible.

Franck shook his head. "*Au revoi*r means 'until I see you again.' But we can use something else. *À bientôt.*"

"Until soon."

Franck nodded and swallowed hard. I touched his lips with mine. "*Je t'aime.* Always know that. No matter what happens...even if we never see each other again." That thought made despair clutch at my heart.

Franck kissed me back. "You can remind me yourself in a few months when I arrive in Montreal." He steered me to the entrance of the tube. He gave me one last kiss and pushed me through it. "I won't stop watching until I can't see you anymore," he said. "Never doubt that I love you."

The flat escalator moved underneath my feet, dragging me away from him. There he stood, straight and tall, with his eyes watery, but also with that twitch to his lips. I knew he was trying to convince me not to be so sad, that we would be together again soon.

I'm not sure exactly how I found my departure gate. Tears streamed down my face, unchecked.

I was the last one to board the flight from Paris to London. My seat was beside an English-looking businessman in a tailored suit, who stared at my tear-stained face with terrified eyes. I didn't care. I listened to the Francis Cabrel tape Franck had bought me for my Walkman, and sobbed.

The plane began to back away from the gate almost immediately. I stared out the window at the receding circular terminal of the Charles de Gaulle airport. Franck was inside there somewhere. In a matter of minutes, I would no longer be in the same country as my soul mate.

Francis Cabrel began to sing "L'Encre de tes yeux," the same song we'd listened to after getting back to the apartment that morning. "Je n'avais pas vu que tu portais de chaînes. A trop vouloir te regarder j'en oubliais les miennes."

The engines roared, then my plane hurtled down the runway. The wheels left France and I was in the sky once again, untethered, flying toward an unknowable future.

I pressed my forehead against the cool plexiglass of the oval window. I felt as though if I just looked hard enough, I would see Franck on the rapidly shrinking ground beneath me. My tape ended, and I could only hear the noise of the airplane as it climbed higher in the sky.

So much had happened in the space of one year. I was a completely different person than that eager-to-please seventeen-year-old who'd stumbled off the plane in Paris. I had sampled everything from snails to pig's feet, I now spoke French fluently, and I'd found true love. I had also learned that an unavoidable consequence of listening to my soul was making some people unhappy. Maybe one day I would make up with the Beaupres, but for the moment I had to accept that the person I now was and the person they needed me to be were irreconcilable. Life was infinitely more complex than it had been eleven months earlier, but it was also infinitely richer.

The pilot's voice crackled through the speaker. "If you look to the left side of the aircraft, you'll enjoy a stunning view of the Eiffel Tower."

There it was, piercing the summer sky with all its symbolic glory. To an imaginary soundtrack of accordions that only I could hear, I daydreamed about Franck and me living together in Paris—walking along the Seine, drinking stiff espressos served on zinc counters, taking classes at the Sorbonne... Hope rushed through me. Franck was right. This thing we had was too good for it to just end. We would have to continue fighting for it, for *us*, but wasn't that a privilege?

He held part of my heart with him in France, and I would safeguard part of his until we saw each other again.

La Fin

Sneak peek of Chapter One *My Grape Québec*

chapter **one**

I stopped crying somewhere over Greenland. My mind reeled at the idea that soon I was going to be a continent and an ocean away from my life in France and, most importantly, from Franck.

I knew how skeptical our friends and his family were that the two of us would manage to stay together. I had to admit that facts were stacked against us.

First of all, there was the sheer geographical distance between France and the extreme West Coast of Canada. At least that would be lessened a bit when I flew to Montréal at the end of the summer to start studying at McGill University.

Starting University would take me half a continent closer to him, and I was already eager for the small amount of progress.

The other barriers weighed heavy on my heart. Money was a big problem. Neither Franck nor I had any. He'd just finished his year of indentured military service required by the French government. It wasn't a year when anyone was able to save – his living expenses had been covered but that was about it.

Getting Franck to Canada required a plane ticket and those were a significant sum, at least by our broke standards.

The most daunting obstacle of all was immigration. Canada was known to be scrupulously fair in its immigration laws, which wasn't necessarily a good thing for us. While Frank had the equivalent of an undergraduate degree from the Sorbonne, he would practically have to have a PhD in some specialized subject in order to make him qualified to be an eligible immigrant.

It was possible to "buy" one's way into Canada with a significant investment in the local economy, but obviously that was out of the question. Another thing that Canada looked for in its immigrants was the ability to speak both of its official languages, French and English. Obviously French wasn't a problem for Franck, but he spoke virtually no English besides the scattering of words that I had taught him. As most of these were mostly swearwords, I couldn't think that they would be much help in his immigration application.

I glanced at the map on the screen in front of me on the back of the seat. Our route had us going down over Greenland and then skirting the northern tip of Québec before flying down over Winnipeg and Calgary, then into Vancouver.

There was a part of me that was excited to see my friends and family that I hadn't seen for an entire year. At the same time an odd apprehension scratched at me from inside.

Who was I now? My year in France had changed me completely. I was scared that the person I'd been – the person I'd become – would cease to exist outside of France. I liked the person I'd become there – deeply in love with Frank and determined to forge my own unconventional future. I much preferred her to that good girl I'd been before I left for France, full of good intentions to follow the rules and make everybody happy.

Maybe it wasn't back home on my island in the Pacific that I could live my French self fully. Maybe that would have to wait until my plane landed in the province my plane was flying over right now. I pressed my forehead against the window to see if I could catch a glimpse of Québec, my future home, and hopefully my future home with Franck, below me. All I could see was a blanket of clouds beneath me – as impenetrable as my future.

A few days later, I began weeping in the grocery store parking lot. It felt like my grief had come out of nowhere. One second, I was happily going on a shopping trip with my Mom, with that cozy feeling of doing familiar things with people I loved, and the next, I was struck with the reality that my life-changing year in Burgundy had somehow managed to bring me back here, exactly where I had started. All of a sudden, I was bent over with grief that, in fact, perhaps nothing had changed at all.

My Mom rubbed my back and tried to understand what was wrong. I couldn't stop the tears long enough to explain, and my breath came in short, ragged jags.

"How about you stay in the car while I get the groceries," she suggested. "I'll be extra quick."

I nodded and she passed me the keys.

I slid into her Subaru that smelled the same it had always smelled – of warm plastic and mint chewing gum – and tried to collect myself.

Franck and I had talked on the phone that morning, and he told me that he'd visited all the Canadian embassies, consulates, and immigration offices in Paris before returning to Burgundy. His determination hadn't wavered one iota, but the news was not good. He did not at all fit the profile of an eligible immigrant to Canada and no-one he'd talked to had given him even the slightest sliver of hope.

It had been reassuring and comfortable to see my family again, and to catch up with friends, but at the same time, I felt more and more each day like me and Franck, and me and France, were receding bit by bit, and that they would soon be out of my grasp. That thought made by blood fill with ice. I tried to reason myself out of this panic that tightened around my chest like a rope, but I could only think of one thing: I couldn't get to Montréal fast enough.

merci

It seems that the more books I write, the more people I have to thank. First of all, *gros bisous* to Franck, who still tolerates that I write about him and our life together (but I'm relieved that he has no interest in actually *reading* my 'Grape' books).

A massive *merci* to all my wonderful readers who have embraced my memoirs, transformed them into bestsellers, and are an unflagging source of encouragement on my good and bad writing days.

Thank you to Eileen Cook for an insightful content edit, *comme d'habitude*, and to Karen Dyer (author of the smash hit *Finding Fraser*) and Lisa Kosleski for their fantastic beta-reads. A huge hug and fist-bump to Pamela Patchet for being my ideal reader and a constant source of brilliant and shrewd input. I couldn't write or put together any of these books without knowing that she is there, cheering me on.

Mary Ellen Reid did the most thorough copy-edit I have ever been privileged to witness (although truth be told I almost keeled over when I realized I needed to make close to 10,000 changes). The polish of *My Grape Year* is largely due to her eagle eye and meticulous attention to detail.

Thank you to my family and all my friends in Victoria, France, and elsewhere around the globe who always have my back and are a constant source of inspiration for me.

As always, I owe a huge debt of gratitude to the PSC community at PSC Partners Seeking a Cure who help me get through the bad days with this rare auto-immune liver/bile duct disease and cheer me on during the good times. As always, I keep the memory of Sandi Pearlman and Phillip Burke close to my heart, and I try to follow their example of making every one of my days a source of good. To that end, 10 percent of all after-tax royalties of everything I write are donated to PSC Partners Seeking a Cure for much-needed research.

www.pscpartners.org.

I urge everyone to sign up to be an organ donor and to support an opt-out system in their country. The current organ donation system in Canada and the United States is broken. People die every day waiting for potentially life-saving organ transplants. Also, all PSCers out there need to sign up for our patient registry and help speed up much-needed research to find a cure for this currently incurable disease. Here is the link:

pscpartners.patientcrossroads.org.

Last of all, thank you to my Bevy—Charlotte, Camille, and Clémentine—for just being their wonderful selves. Every day I can be around to parent them is a lucky day. I know all three of my daughters will be heroes in their own fairy tales, and I can't wait to watch them unfold.

a conversation with **Laura Bradbury**

To many, leaving to a foreign country by yourself for a year at the young age of seventeen like you did in *My Grape Year* sounds like a bold leap. Did it feel that way to you at the time?

Yes and no. I was absolutely determined to leave home after graduating and see a bit of the world. I had grown up on the West Coast of Canada and had only traveled to Hawaii and California. I wanted to see *more*, and an exchange year abroad seemed like the perfect way to do that. Being what I term a "Bold Planner" personality, I had Plan A, Plan B, Plan C, and Plan D to live abroad for a year. The Ursus exchange (there isn't actually an Ursus Club—I changed the name for privacy purposes) was my Plan A, although the exchange spots were coveted and the process of getting selected was competitive.

It did feel daring to be going away for a year, but bold action was what felt right at the time. Going directly from high school to university without traveling was not an option I even considered. Although, being a planner, I had already been accepted to my university of choice (McGill in Montreal) and been granted a deferral. This kind of organized audacity became a pattern in my life (and in subsequent books in my Grape Series). If any of my daughters need to decide between playing it safe or taking a leap, I always find myself recommending the leap. I remind them they are here because I took one!

It is amazing how a twist of fate, such as you being sent to France instead of Belgium by the Ursus Club, can change a person's life trajectory, like it did for you in this story. Do you still marvel at that?

Definitely. That continues to be a source of wonder and fear for me. I look at my life now, with Franck and the journey we have had together and our three girls, and I wonder how my life would have been if I had been sent to Belgium as originally planned, or if I hadn't been chosen for the Ursus exchange at all and went to the UK on a different exchange program (my Plan B). My life would be completely different.

I often contemplate how so much can hinge on such a tiny moment or a random decision made by you or someone else. In a split second, a person's world can shift on its axis, and everything changes. That is the wonderful thing about the human journey, but it is also scary when you realize how easily things could be different. Of course, this leads me to debate whether these twists of fate are predestined and part of an overall greater plan for us or whether they are indeed completely random. So far, I haven't been able to decide.

You are very open about your struggles with an auto-immune liver disease (PSC). Did dealing with serious health issues while you wrote *My Grape Year* impact your writing process or what you chose to highlight in the book?

My diagnosis with PSC just before I turned forty flipped my world on its head and completely transformed every facet of my writing life. In the decade before I was diagnosed, I had written several fiction books to about 50–75 percent completion. I couldn't seem to finish anything. In retrospect the reason for that is simple—when you finish something and share it, you can be judged. My writing was so important to me that the idea of being found lacking in that department was paralyzing. The day after I was diagnosed, I sat down in front of my computer and began writing *My Grape Escape*. I didn't stop until I finished and published it. My fear of being judged had evaporated, seemingly overnight. Instead, I feared dying with all my words still trapped inside me.

I believe I chose writing a memoir because I was suddenly, horribly conscious of the fact that I may not be around to tell my daughters the story of where they came from and the things I had learned so far in my life. There was too much to fit in a letter, so I wrote a book. And then another one...and then another...I had a lot more to tell them than I initially realized!

When I was writing *My Grape Year,* I was getting sicker but was still not deemed sick enough to be eligible for a life-saving transplant (which I had on March 22, 2017—yay!). I was constantly in and out of the hospital for dangerous infections that took up permanent residence in my liver and bile ducts. I was existing in a space of vast uncertainty. Sometimes it felt like all that was keeping me tethered to life was love and writing. The theme of choosing love, even if it makes other people unhappy, is central to *My Grape Year*, and I believe what I was living while writing *My Grape Year* drew out that theme in the story.

It seems as though in *My Grape Year* you are able to discover your inner rebel, and the fact that you are in France makes this easier.

It did! It's funny, going to high school I didn't even know I had an inner rebel. I was always the easygoing one who did not cause trouble. I always saw it as my responsibility to make everyone happy and comfortable. This trait was encouraged by my school and the society I was brought up in and was so deeply ingrained in me it became second nature. I believed that was my true personality.

When I arrived in France, I was fascinated to discover that French people value anarchy and independent thought. Rebelliousness is a coveted trait (which partially explains their abiding passion for protests of any kind). It is cultivated within families and among friends. I found myself deeply drawn to this defiant French attitude, although I tried to keep everyone happy until I was confronted with the reality in *My Grape Year* that, sometimes, keeping everyone happy is impossible. The act of choosing Franck over Ursus was terrifying, but it freed my inner rebel, which has been running amok in my life ever since. That is a great thing.

How does your family feel about being characters in your memoirs?

They try to pretend it is not happening. In fact, none of them have read my books. My Grape Series is very much my story and my memories. Their memories belong to them, and I respect that. However, I do like the idea that the books are there for my girls if they ever want to read them down the road. After all, I was facing possible death, and that was one of my main motivations for writing them in the first place. Franck has absolutely no desire to be a public figure of any kind and begs me on a regular basis to start writing fiction. I have started my first novel, but I still have several Grape books in mind. I just don't talk a lot about that in front of Franck and the girls! They were equal parts horrified and happy when my books unexpectedly took off. I think for the next while I will alternate between fiction and nonfiction.

One thing that struck me while reading *My Grape Year* was your lively sense of humor. You don't always find that in memoirs.

I don't think I could eliminate humor from my writing, even if I wanted to. I am entertained daily by the quirky, bizarre, and hilarious aspects of this human journey. I adore books that make me laugh, and I challenge myself to write certain scenes with that goal in mind. I don't know how I would have gotten through the transplant process without a huge dose of black humor. Franck and I joked about the most inappropriate things, as did my incredible liver donor and I. Also, the PSC and transplant communities are lively places. It is freeing to recognize that parts of our journey (like the "preparation" required before a colonoscopy) are just absurd and to laugh at them collectively. I found in France there are so many quirky characters. People follow their odd passions with such devotion and sincerity. They also have an alarming tendency to say exactly what they think. I am endlessly fascinated and amused by this, and I try to share that with my readers.

What is next for you?

The latest book in my Grape Series, *My Grape Paris*, is now published, so I am working on my first fiction—a culture-clash romance featuring a British lord intent on reclaiming his family's place in high society and a dogsled racer who was brought up in the Northern wilderness and has no respect for etiquette or protocol. She also has a wolf for a pet. I'm realizing that all my fiction projects have a culture clash romance at their heart. I'm also working on a recipe book at the request of my readers, who wanted my favorite recipes from France. (I post many of these recipes in my newsletter. Sign up at www.bit.ly/LauraBradburyNewsletter.)

I have the next Grape book, *My Grape Québéc*, percolating in the background, as well as a memoir of my PSC/transplant journey entitled *Survival Tips for the Flawed and Fearful*. I want to make every moment with my new liver count, as I consider every single day "bonus" time I have been gifted by Nyssa, my liver donor. This means spending time with my girls, Franck, and our wonderful family and friends. It also means traveling and reading and writing and beachcombing and advocating for changes to organ donation legislation in Canada, as well as raising funds for PSC research. When my life changed again on its axis when I was diagnosed with PSC, things got very, very simple. That is a huge gift.

discussion guide

1. In *My Grape Year* young Laura takes a bold leap, leaving everything she knows behind and traveling to France for a year. Have you ever taken such a leap? If so, what was the result? Have you ever had to decide between taking a leap and not taking one and opted not to? In retrospect, are you happy about your decision, or do you regret it?
2. Laura defines herself as a "Bold Planner." Do you identify with this approach to life? What two words would you use to describe your overall approach to decision making and life planning?
3. Have you ever had, like Laura does in this story, a twist of fate that has completely changed the trajectory of your life? If so, can you imagine what your life would be without that? Do you believe such events are predestined or completely random?
4. Is there a creative endeavor you would love to explore but are too fearful or busy to make time for? What is it? Can you think of a way to bring this into your life? Reflect whether you would look at things differently if you were diagnosed with a serious illness.
5. If you were facing health challenges, is there anything you would like to make sure is transmitted to your children?
6. How rebellious would you say you are? How much of a people-pleaser? Do you feel these tendencies are innate or can be learned and change because of life experiences? Have you had life experiences that have made you more one or the other? It's safe to say that certain cultures encourage or suppress rebelliousness. In that light, how would you judge where you live?

7. Is there any part of your life you would like to write about? If it would involve writing about loved ones, how do you think they would react? Are there some people you just could not write about? Why?
8. Almost everyone has a passion about a certain eccentric or quirky thing. What is yours? Do you believe your social surroundings encourage you to follow and respect this passion? How do you feel about that?
9. Humor can help you cope with stressful situations. Can you remember some books that have made you laugh? Do you have friends or a partner who share your unique sense of humor? Is a shared sense of humor something you find appealing in a romantic sense? How important is it?
10. Which of Laura's future books are you looking forward to the most?

about Laura

Bestselling author Laura Bradbury published her first book—a heartfelt memoir about her leap away from a prestigious legal career in London to live in a tiny French village with her Burgundian husband in *My Grape Escape*—after being diagnosed with PSC, a rare autoimmune bile duct/liver disease. Since then, Laura has received a lifesaving living donor liver transplant from her friend Nyssa, published many more Grape Series books and the long-anticipated cookbook to accompany her memoirs, entitled *Bisous & Brioche*. She has also written *The Winemakers Trilogy*, romantic novels set in the Burgundy vineyards, and with renewed health, writes with even more passion than ever.

Now living and writing on the West Coast of Canada with a new liver and three Franco-Canuck daughters (collectively known as "the Bevy"), Laura runs three charming vacation rentals in Burgundy with her husband, has an enviable collection of beach glass, and does all she can to support PSC and organ donation awareness and research.

find **Laura** online

The Grapevine Newsletter
bit.ly/LauraBradburyNewsletter

Facebook
facebook.com/AuthorLauraBradbury

Twitter
twitter.com/Author_LB

Instagram
instagram.com/laurabradburywriter

Pinterest
pinterest.ca/bradburywriter

BookBub
bookbub.com/authors/laura-bradbury

Books by Laura Bradbury

Grape Series
My Grape Year
My Grape Québec
My Grape Paris
My Grape Wedding
My Grape Escape
My Grape Village
My Grape Cellar

The cookbook based on the Grape Series memoirs that readers have been asking for!

Bisous & Brioche: Classic French Recipes and Family Favorites from a Life in France
by Laura Bradbury and Rebecca Wellman
Bisous & Brioche

The Winemaker's Trilogy
A Vineyard for Two
Love in the Vineyards

Made in the USA
Coppell, TX
08 October 2020